CORRECTIONS AND COLLECTIONS

CORRECTIONS & COLLECTIONS

ARCHITECTURES FOR ART AND CRIME

JOE DAY

FIRST PUBLISHED 2013 BY ROUTLEDGE
711 Third Avenue, New York, NY 10017

Simultaneously published in the UK
by Routledge
2 Park Square, Milton Park, Abingdon, OXON
OX14 4RN

Routledge is an imprint of the
Taylor & Francis Group, an informa business

PUBLISHER'S NOTE
This book has been prepared from camera-ready
copy provided by the author.

ACQUISITION EDITOR Wendy Fuller
EDITORIAL ASSISTANT Laura Williamson
PRODUCTION EDITOR Siobhán Greaney

LIBRARY OF CONGRESS
CATALOGING IN PUBLICATION DATA
Day, Joe, 1967–
Corrections and collections : architectures for
art and crime / Joe Day.
pages cm
Includes index.
1. Art museum architecture—United States.
2. Prisons—Design and construction—United
States. 3. Architecture and society—United
States. I. Title.
NA6696.U6D39 2013
725'.60973—dc23
2012048824

ISBN 978-0-415-53481-9 (hbk)
ISBN 978-0-415-53482-6 (pbk)
ISBN 978-0-203-78603-1 (ebk)

Printed and bound in Great Britain by
TJ International Ltd, Padstow, Cornwall

CONTENTS

FOREWORD

BY MIKE DAVIS

MILLIONS OF TOURISTS, guidebooks in hand, have trooped through Venice's Palazzo Ducale, admiring Titian, the Tintorettos, Palladio and Veronese, but not realizing the ruthless power incarnated in the building until they have crossed over the Bridge of Sighs and explored the ghastly dungeons. For half a millennium, as the Palazzo was continuously built and rebuilt, the rulers of the Republic of St Mark insatiably collected both high art and prisoners within its walls.

In 1923, shortly after Mussolini's Squadristi marched on Rome, the derelict Palazzo was formally transformed into a museum. Rather miraculously a century or more of graffiti was left on some of the cell walls, comprising a collection perhaps unique in Europe. A defiant 'Viva Malatesta!' dates one of the last of Palazzo's prisoners — an anarchist arrested around the turn of the century.

Prison within a museum; museum within a prison. The curation of men, the incarceration of art. Fruitful or just clever mirror images? Joe Day takes us farther up-river with such inverted analogies than most of us would have conceived possible.

Indeed, I must warn the reader that this remarkable book — a brilliantly original reconceptualization of (late?) postmodernism that has no need to quote Foucault or Baudrillard — will rattle some of their categories. At least that was my experience. I opened *Corrections and Collections* with the anticipation that I would savor provocative comparisons between the architectural geometries of modern museums and prisons, but I did not expect the distinctions between the two to blur so quickly.

As Day makes overpoweringly clear, this is not a simple confusion arising from the generic characteristics of contemporary institutional architecture. Prisons and museums share profound and troubling characteristics that transcend more superficial affinities with other monolithic design schemes like hospitals, administrative centers, and university architecture. Indeed, what begins as analogy becomes a systematic isomorphism that finally has to be recognized as a strange species of unexpected identity.

The Mobius Strip, to recall its formal definition, is a 'non-orientable surface with only one side' that tricks our eyes into believing that there must be two sides. To the obvious objection that whatever their similarity in design, prisons and museums have completely different 'programs', Day confronts us with their disturbing phenomenological equation. Like the strange topology that August Mobius discovered in 1858, one will search in vain for the authentic boundary or edge between our society's two most favored building projects. Day's thesis, refined to a single sentence, is that the warehousing of surplus people and over-valued objects on an unprecedented scale is the expression of a single social logic.

In Southern California, as he shows in fascinating but sometimes frightening detail, this logic has created an extraordinary landscape. Along the west-east axis of the Santa Monica mountains and at the base of the foothills that link them to the San Gabriel mountains, the great oil, railroad and real-estate dynasties of the region monumentalize themselves in a corridor of in-your-face-Manhattan art mausoleums: the Getty Villa, the Getty Center, the UCLA Hammer, LACMA, MOCA, Norton Simon, and the Huntington.

Their counterpart is a carceral solar system that revolves around Downtown Los Angeles' central jail complex — the largest in the world — with 25,000 inmates a few blocks from MOCA and the latest Broad Museum. In the nearest orbits are more jails, followed by a dozen state and federal prisons in LA's suburban and desert peripheries. As Day points out, this is our most eloquent answer to the urban employment crisis.

The design strategies that emerge from this sinister conflation of collection and punishment correspond to a hybrid of aesthetic minimalism, traffic management, and neo-Benthamism. Thus jaded correctional officers sit in front of monitors watching stored human objects masturbating, screaming or simply vegetating, while self-conscious museum visitors feign sophisticated appreciation of more and more contrived art installations while a voice inside their heads asks, "This piece of shit is worth $15 million dollars?"

Even if it violates the precision of its mathematical definition, the concept of 'nonorientability' seems powerful in understanding Day's analysis of these mirrored and alienated phenomena. The coevolution of prisons and museums corresponds to the radical absence of orienting hopes or emancipations.

00.INTRODUCTION

TO SEDUCE OR SUBDUE?

To find the future, listen for acronyms. Abbreviations are economic bellwethers, and where there is spending, proper names often must pay. Over the last twenty-five years, the California Department of Corrections has redesignated all thirty-three of its state prisons, or CSPs, with two to five letter acronyms, adding to an already impressive list of abbreviations used to run those facilities, such as AD-SEG, SHU, LWOP, 270s, and J-CAT.[1] At a stroke, the storied bastions of San Quentin, Folsom and Pelican

CUBE WITHOUT A CORNER. Sol LeWitt (1988)

Bay became SQ, FOL and PBSP, respectively, mere nodes in a vast punitive archipelago. In the same years, most major museums trademarked cute, populist contractions of their names as brand logos. Long a redoubt of proper names, especially those of artists and connoisseurs, the art press now features a proliferation of MoMAs and MOCAs, Dias and MAKs, ICAs and CACs.

CORRECTIONS & COLLECTIONS explores and connects two massive expansions in our built environment. Prisons and museums led the last great wave of American urban renewal. Before the many new housing, sports, education and transit projects of the last quarter century could take shape, civic space in the United States was first cordoned into zones of cultural and societal transgression, and then reapportioned to lure new inhabitants while containing the old. After two centuries of incremental growth, the number of correctional facilities and museums in the United States tripled in twenty-five years, from roughly 600 prisons and 6,000 museums in 1975 to more than 1,800 prisons and an estimated 18,000 museums by 2000.[2] In both, this multiplication only begins to describe the expansion, taking into account neither the many additions to existing buildings, nor the escalating size of new ones. Neither trend has slowed in the new century.

The United States is not alone in either building boom, but unique in pursuing them simultaneously. Through the post-WWII period, the EU nations and Japan invest a far greater percentage of public funds in museum construction, and, though they now lag us, the largest Asian powers, especially China and Russia, share our enthusiasm for imprisonment. First to cope with and then to capitalize on each summer's wave of international tourism, continental Europe, led by France and Italy, pioneered the curation of historic-urban centers, often funneling 10–15% of national tax revenue into cultural affairs (to our paltry 2% of public funding). China and Russia outstripped our rates of incarceration in the early 20th century, when their factory prisons and gulags set the pace for mass imprisonment.[3] The United States, however, is the only nation to pursue corrections and collections together, and with such a vengeance, since the 1970s. While many countries have favored one sector or the other by government fiat, twin US policies of tax breaks for art patronage and mandatory minimum sentences for drug-related offenses (as well as lucrative government bond issues for prison construction) have yielded an oddly symmetrical landscape of the beautiful and the damned.

Over 740 of every 100,000 Americans are incarcerated — nearly an antipodean 1% of the total US population. As Michelle Alexander points out in *The New Jim Crow: Mass Incarceration in the Age of Colorblindness*, the racial imbalances of those in custody are stark as well: "The US imprisons more of its black population than South Africa did at the height of apartheid."[4] The growth of some state prison systems outstripped those of all but a few nations. California's alone has swollen more than tenfold since 1975, from 16,000 inmates to 173,000 in 2010.[5] In a 1995 survey of fifty-nine nations, only five countries held more inmates than the state of California, and the United States' total of 1.6 million inmates in that year outstripped the other four: China with 1.2 million, Russia with just over a million, and Ukraine and India each near 200,000.[6] US prisons have added an additional 600,000 inmates since 1995, for a current total of 2.2 million prisoners — more than three times the total for all twenty-seven EU countries combined, more than ten times as many per capita as Japan, and, strikingly, almost six times as many per capita as China.[7]

As gargantuan as US prison statistics have become, we incarcerate far fewer people than visit our museums. We host almost exactly as many people *each day* in US museums as we detain annually in US prisons. American museums averaged a collective 2.3 million daily visits in 2005, and, as with our prisons, the numbers are concentrated in a few states and cities.[8] Just one New York museum, the newly renovated Museum of Modern Art, drew 2.6 million visitors in 2005, the year it reopened, and 3.1 million in 2010.[9] The disparity in our collective experience of exhibition and incarceration should not distract from how much

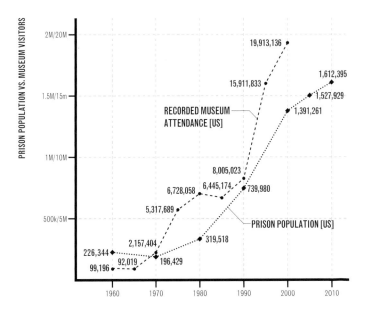

PRISON POPULATION VS. MUSEUM VISITORS

2M/20M

19,913,136

1,612,395

15,911,833

1.5M/15m
1,527,929

RECORDED MUSEUM
ATTENDANCE [US]
1,391,261

1M/10M

8,005,023

6,445,174
6,728,058
739,980

5,317,689

500k/5M
PRISON POPULATION [US]

2,157,404
319,518

226,344
92,019
196,429

99,196

1960   1970   1980   1990   2000   2010

more radically pervasive both have become than ever before, or anywhere else. *Corrections and Collections* takes advantage of the almost universally familiar experience of new museums to cast some light on the generally impenetrable, but profoundly life-altering logic of our many new prisons.

These two trends point to an unlikely reality for contemporary American architecture and urbanism. Much of the most innovative civic architecture of the last twenty-five years has met the demands of two conflicting, but distinctly public, mandates: clear the streets of the threatening poor, and provide easy, alluring access to priceless trophies. Led as much by second cities such as San Diego and Chicago as by New York and Los Angeles, almost all US urban centers have been reorganized to consolidate their cultural assets and corral their disadvantaged inhabitants.[10] In cities large and small, museum districts now back up to correctional corridors, bracketing the experience and, for many, the very idea of American urbanity.

BEYOND R&D

Pace Bataille, the slaughterhouse has attracted little attention from either architects or artists. Late capitalism, with its focus on accumulation, would not, could not, institutionalize death and waste. Museums, on the other hand, have proliferated and expanded, adapting to the growing pressure of visitors and their expectations, as well as the increasing bulk and variety of what artists may be producing.[11]
JOSEPH RYKWERT

THOUGH AT OPPOSITE ENDS of any spectrum of public engagement, class eligibility, and civic pride, museums and prisons share agendas of accumulation and logics of visual hierarchy. They are in many ways complementary architectures, buildings that organize our most problematic citizens and valuable treasures for reconsideration. Both are defined first by how they manage vision: what is seen, by whom, and in what sequence and circumstance. Both grapple with how to simultaneously secure their contents and showcase them. Surprisingly, many of the salient differences between exhibition and incarceration hinge less on the distinctions between holding objects and people — a variable that often boils down to the "thickness" of a building's perimeter and the requisite lumens of light allocated to an inmate or artwork — and more on modulating the size, proximity and role of an audience.

Historically, matters were more nuanced, and this parallel perhaps more far-fetched. From their typological inception in the Enlightenment, prisons and museums evolved not simply to contain criminals and artifacts, but to promote distinct agendas vis-à-vis their holdings and the public. Prisons arbitrate among at least four perennial objectives: Removal, Retribution, Reformation, and Rehabilitation. That is, prisons *remove* those convicted of crimes from society, punish or seek *retribution* from them for their misdeeds, *reform* them in mind or spirit, and, more recently,

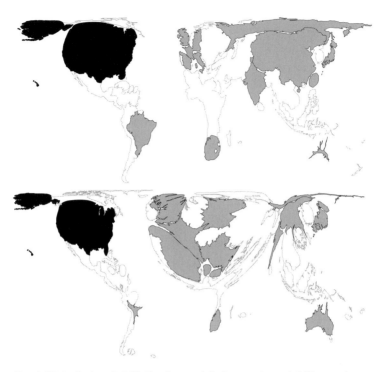

Top: PRISON POPULATION MAP | Bottom: TOURIST ENTRIES PER ANNUM

initiate their *rehabilitation* from addiction and mental illness. In theory, they do any and all of these to protect the law-abiding, to exact contrition from the convict, to transform him or (increasingly) her into a less-problematic citizen, and to deter society at large from criminal behavior by presenting its consequences. Sociologically, if not architecturally, all prisons can be assessed in terms of how they weight these goals, and how they meet them.

Museums could be said to address four parallel concerns — four Ds — Display, Displacement, Didactics, and Diversity. Museums obviously *display* objects; they *displace* both the viewer and viewed out of everyday circumstances in order to make both the rare accessible and the common "foreign"; they operate *didactically*, to open teaching dialogues on the relevance and interrelationship of those objects; and, increasingly, they try to *diversify* both their holdings and their audience. Museums perform these various roles to safeguard what we deem valuable, expose and explicate that value, and expand the terms by which we assign it.

Both the four Rs of incarceration and the four Ds of exhibition continue to shape buildings, but their terms are now weighted very differently than they were twenty-five years ago, to say nothing of 250 years ago at their typological inception. To these four intrinsic purposes for each building type, we must now add at least one extra aim apiece: for prisons, a double-R for rural revival; and for museums, a double-D for density development. As even a cursory look at either building boom will reveal, these projects are judged now now less in terms of how they affect or organize their contents, and far more in terms of their civic performance *in situ*. Apart from the preservation and transformation of their "holdings," prisons and museums now promise their host locales politically quantifiable benefits in terms of jobs, land values, and tax base.

As Douglas Crimp notes in *On the Museum's Ruins*, his call for an "archeology" of the museum akin to Michel Foucault's examination of prisons, both building types "seemed to be equally space(s) of exclusions and confinements."[12] For all the talk of "warehousing" that marks contemporary discussions of both, prisons and museums remain highly specialized institutions, at once vaults and vessels for their respective holdings. The increasingly secretive and embattled attitude of correctional personnel finds its societal antithesis in curatorial expansion and public outreach, but both are highly exclusive cultures, charged with roles that border on secular mysticism. One seeks to transform people — criminals — into mute and manageable objects, the other to make objects — art — into living statements.

PRISONS AND MUSEUMS DEFINE and polarize a complex array of societal and cultural transgressions. It is a central, perhaps defining irony of our time that extreme behavior, once it has been judged licit or illicit, sends either its protagonist or its product to either building. Prisons assimilate the guilt and culpability of

the convicted in much the way art museums presume the value of works they exhibit. Some inmates may eventually be exonerated, and many paintings will not stand the test of time, but within their spatial and temporal confines, the specific freedoms celebrated by museums and revoked by prisons could be said to have out-stripped their respective markets — their contents become quite literally, if not permanently, priceless.

The fact that museums and prisons highlight the activities of individuals at the margins of the labor market seems to have become only more crucial as the US economic balance has tipped sharply from manufacturing to services and retail. Museums and prisons play complementary roles in shaping a postindus-trial workforce, one preoccupied with individual viability rather than collective welfare, obsessed with the trappings of wealth and the exceptional behavior it both requires and rewards, and eager to take high-stakes gambles for personal gain and recog-nition. If *transformation* — of society, matter, knowledge, self —

HOLDING CELL, Nico Bick (2011) | Opposite: **RELIEVED PRODUCTION CYCLE,** Liam Gillick (2007)

was a driving ambition of the 20th century, its angrier, sexier, and less reliable sibling *transgression* has taken an early lead in the 21st.

The emphasis of this study falls on new museums for fine art and new mega-jails that now punctuate broader networks of exhibition and discipline, but these urban projects are hardly isolated phenomena. In the outer rings of exurban and rural expansion many specialized penal institutions have proliferated concurrently: prisons for women, medical rehabilitation, youth authority, and privately owned prisons head a long list. Museums of fine art are but one of a panoply of fast-multiplying genres that also include museums of natural history, celebrity, warfare, calamity, science, trade, technology, archeology and anthropology, not to mention the many new museums of architecture and design. Urban jails and art museums, however, have spurred the most experimentation. Art museums are the "high game" for architects, the nexus of a rivalry between artists and architects over who will challenge and update our cultural assumptions most effectively. Big city jails are the gateway islands of our new gulag archipelago, cities unto themselves that form and define the threshold of societal sanction.

BOOM TIMES

"Why is it," asked Crimp in 1987, "that as we enter the era of post-modernism, we are witnessing the largest growth in museum building since the nineteenth century?"[13] Though the centrality of both museums and prisons in urban planning dates back to the Middle Ages, their current vogue reflects some unlikely reversals at the end of the 20th century. For much of the post-WWII period, each was perceived to be in steep decline toward anachronism, with much speculation anticipating their demise. For Crimp and many art theorists, the irony of this surge in museum construction lay in the oft-proclaimed "death" of painting and sculpture — the arts that museums traditionally feature — at the hands of photography and film media. Just as the aura of original works was thoroughly occluded by mass-produced imagery, however, we witnessed an unexpected, hysterical scurry to preserve and display art objects. One could see the prison boom in a similar light: given the vast critical literature of the 1960s and '70s that decried the failure of rehabilitation through incarceration, few would have predicted then the rise of prisons as a leading political panacea over the following decades.

But both turned out to be fragile ironies. In the case of museums, the more lushly illustrated art publications became, the better they served as publicity for the original works. Rather than replacing the one-off, mass reproduction has cheapened and expanded the allure of the masterpiece, undermining the exclusivity of the museum rather than its worth. Museum stock hasn't gone down; it has instead risen and split many times over. Museums have shed their image as musty containers of stale relics. Endless, anonymous galleries and permanent collections have given way to multimedia spaces, gift stores, and cafes. Curators once intent on revealing a Grand March of Periods opt instead for fast-changing themed exhibitions and blockbuster retrospectives, packing exhibits with the life-traces and biographies of artists alongside their work.

When, on the other hand, the reformative ideals of modern incarceration were judged bankrupt in the 1970s, the recognition of that failure carried with it not an exposé of misguided public policy, but an indictment of the urban poor, now deemed completely incorrigible. Law-and-order politicians found renewable political capital in creating miserable prison conditions through overcrowding and then promising to ameliorate the same through more construction. If prisons transformed inmates into hardened criminals rather than upstanding citizens, the solution for US voters was not to reexamine the institutions, but to keep prisoners inside as long as possible. As one officer on a tour of the federal work camp at Boron, California, put it, "We are not paid to fix these people. We are paid to store them."

The geometric escalation in US prison populations, fueled by "three-strikes" legislation and especially mandatory minimum drug sentencing guidelines, required both gargantuan rural penitentiaries and major new criminal justice "hubs" in big cities. In the late '70s, an invention termed Podular Supervision, based distantly on Jeremy Bentham's infamous Panopticon, led to a wealth of new carceral options in what are collectively known as "New Generation Justice Facilities." The spatial efficiency of new podular housing units allowed a fractal-like escalation of new prison and jail configurations including metropolitan towers, total isolation units, and the fast-evolving "270" block pioneered in California state prisons. Regional and national prison booms have led to a thoroughly mechanized, self-refining building process in which advances in security, surveillance, and cost savings are quickly generalized. In order to pass seamlessly into dense urban fabric near courthouses, new inner-city jails mimic surrounding corporate towers and office parks, allowing inmate warehousing in previously forbidden quarters.

Very different, but parallel, dynamics drove a concurrent museum boom in the second half of the 20th century. Watersheds in Minimalism, Louis Kahn's museums for Yale University (1958 and 1976) and the Kimbell family (1972) inspired an American tulip craze in academic and private art museums, including Renzo Piano's Menil Pavilion, Philip Johnson's home galleries, and later the contentious Wexner Center by Peter Eisenman. At the other extreme of scale, Piano and Richard Rogers' Centre Pompidou and I.M. Pei's East Wing for the National Gallery, both completed in the late 1970s, ushered in the era of state-sponsored modern art vaults. International museum competitions have generated a "design diplomacy" of ever more extroverted proposals. Architecture *in extremis* reigns as minimalist and maximalist schemes vie for the attention of increasingly desensitized jurors. A few prolific architects — among them Richard Meier, Frank Gehry, Tadao Ando, and again Piano — build so many museums that personal typologies have evolved, impervious to differences in climate, locale, and cultural context. Though the art world cognoscenti lament these "signature" structures, they now form a quantifiable, replicable currency of civic identity and marketing. All of these trends converged through the 1980s and 1990s in an unprec-

FOREST OF TOMBS, Tadao Ando, Kumamoto, Japan (1992)
Opposite: COYOTE RIDGE DETENTION CENTER, Rosser (2008)

edented exploration of forms for exhibition space, often unbur-
dened by stellar art to display. As Rosalind Krauss has noted,
the success of these micro-museum "attractors" laid the groundwork for massive cultural projects, as well as inventive philan-
thropic asset leveraging, that defined the urban '90s.

TIMELAPSE

Ever since Minimalism made it inevitable that artists and architects would produce work that was claimed not only to occupy
the same ground but to produce the space of art itself, art and
architecture have engaged in a disciplinary competition about who
should do what for whom and at what cost, which discipline is more
properly part of the service economy, and which is higher in the
cultural hierarchy.[14]
SYLVIA LAVIN

Decade by decade since the 1960s, museums and prisons have
traded a variety of design tropes — innovations that quickly
become habit across both fields. First we witness a tug-of-war
between Late Modernism and Minimalism, resolved often in a
penitential middle ground of sheer facades and repetitive, linear
organizations. Though the 1980s are generally considered the
apex of architectural Postmodernism, with its vying schools

of Historicism and Deconstruction, prisons and museums go through transformations that are more accurately read in terms of post-Minimalism, with its focus on theatricality, body-space relationships, and scopic regimentation. In the 1990s we celebrated the culmination of the 20th century with a rash of commemorative, encyclopedic, and elephantine "total" institutions, sprawling and towering detention centers and memorial museums.

After 2000 and especially after 9/11, prisons and museums took on a darker cast, post-apocalyptic and militarized, both in their subject matter and their staging of international debacles: the looting of the National Museum of Iraq in Baghdad; the failure to settle on a museological program for Ground Zero; the Abu Ghraib atrocities; and the controversies surrounding US prisoner-of-war treatment at Guantanamo. As many notorious prisons in other countries become museums of national memory, a new strain of secret, far-flung, and extrajudicial "black site" prisons plays a disturbingly unbridled role in US foreign policy.

The structure of this study describes four sequential but overlapping temporalities, each with a chapter fleshing out its defining innovations and another tracing its logic of expansion:

14

MINIMAL — Chapters 01 and 02 look at the confluence of prison and museum design in terms of Minimalism, as the disciplinary ideals of asceticism — removal, deprivation, and repetition — became central to art production and exhibition in the 1960s and '70s. Chapter 01, Reduce, looks at how strategies of simplification and abstraction, which had long typified prison architecture, came to dominate museum design in the post-WWII period. Louis Kahn's three major museums are watersheds in this regard, with each introducing a distinct aspect of penitential aesthetics into buildings for art. With a newly simplified architectural vocabulary, institutions of constraint and display multiplied quickly in the 1970s. Chapter 02, Repeat, notes the role of the Rockefeller brothers in these twin institutional expansions, and examines the many economies of scale afforded by repetition of spaces and structural elements in a single building, as well as the massive growth in networks of exhibition and discipline as standardized forms were replicated in many locations.

POST-MINIMAL — Chapters 03 and 04 introduce post-Minimalist strategies of the 1970s and '80s that shifted both the nature and rationale of incarceration and exhibition, fostering an even more accelerated proliferation of both. Chapter 03, Rotate, examines how we have consolidated the tasks of surveillance and exhibition into single, concentric volumes after the models of Jeremy Bentham's Panopticon and Frank Lloyd Wright's Guggenheim. This reassessment led to an array of podular prisons and "centers" for contemporary art that ask to be read as templates for personal and collective transformation rather than mere institutions of containment. Central here are the "easy" spaces and flexible gestures that Frank Gehry pioneered in his trajectory from the repurposed industrial shells of his early Aerospace and Temporary Contemporary museums through the civic convolutions of Bilbao and later proposals.

Chapter 04, Proliferate, explores how these more efficient prototypes multiplied and escalated into far-flung and internodal networks, championed by proselytizers such as Thomas Krens of the Guggenheim Foundation and Donald Novey of the California correctional officers union. Both prisons and museums are now franchised according to tested prototypes and conceived as iterations in a larger skein of strategic planning. Krens and Novey pioneered new management regimes of constant expansion, pooling old and new institutions, both "ready-made" and signature buildings, under the yoke of a single brand. An orchestrated circuitry of viewing and holding spaces, or "infotestines," debrief new arrivals on the lore and future of these networks, and now typify most jails and single-topic museums.

MILLENNIAL — In the decade preceding the new millennium, the thrust of museum and prison design became both more comprehensive and more particular. Chapter 05, Neutralize, explores the many new prisons and museums that sought to diffuse an urban situation, a historical event or even their own presence. Authorless but gargantuan metropolitan jails were disguised as office towers or power stations. Diplomacy through design factors in to both the many cross-border museum commissions to "global" architects and in the banal facades of tower jails built to appease squeamish urban neighbors. Chapter 06,

Privatize, turns to privately-funded "personal" museums and for-profit prisons, both testing grounds for new architects and architectural solutions. Usually smaller and more agilely managed, private facilities of exhibition and detention are hotbeds of innovation, and of eccentricity. Often considered "lite" in their holdings — built for low-risk inmates and questionable art — these institutions enjoy far more latitude in their design and philosophy.

POST-MILLENNIAL — Since 2000, institutions of display and discipline have taken on international, or transnational, dimensions, many of them unanticipated and controversial. Chapter 07, Collide, notes the confluence of art and crime in prisons-turned-museums, museums as crime scenes, and in the work of artists and inmates that no longer observe clear distinctions between curatorial and custodial agendas. These post-Millennial demands were anticipated by Rem Koolhaas in his early schemes for Arnhem Prison, which proposed a panoptic display of failed architectures of reformation, and in his many unbuilt museums: an encyclopedic, and captive, catalog of exhibitionary strategies.

Paradox is more the rule than exception in Chapter 08, Disperse, as new architectures of fixity attempt to reflect and respond to constant change and disaggregation. As the internationalization of incarceration has imperiled many basic standards of correctional conduct, the wholesale displacement of curation to temporary settings has rendered many cultural limitations quaint in other ways. Transient art fairs now surpass museums in ratifying any emergent avant-garde, hosting spectacular installations and promulgating new agendas for future art practices.

DOMESTICALLY, the urban prisons and museums built since the 1970s punctuate the end of the industrial and corporate stewardship of our cities. The public emphasis of these new prisons and museums is not on their internal holdings and workings, but on their ability to shore up depopulated central-core areas. New jails do this by underpinning civil sector expansion. New federal and county detention centers house exponentially more inmates than they could forty years ago, awaiting more trials and appeals in more courtrooms, watched over by more guards, prosecuted and defended by more attorneys, supported and managed by many more civil servants. Museums yield parallel benefits in retail and residential terms, with their high-profile presence (and often exorbitant costs) benchmarking neighboring real estate and "activating" street life. Their twin surges reflect a distinctly suburban reassessment of civic allure, danger, and expendability.

Institutions of discipline and exhibition have thus replaced malls and office towers as the anchor tenants of what we used to call the CBD, or Central Business District. Though some note the rise of "Stealth architecture" and a "Bilbao Effect," little investigation has been made of this twinning in contemporary urban renewal. *Corrections and Collections* explores the spatial dialectics of surveillance and spectacle created by these newly proximate architectures — an intersection in contemporary civic space better grasped in the wasted (but highly curated) digital game terrains of *Grand Theft Auto* than in most current urban theory.

The recent explosion of both building types underscores an unpopular notion that if public architecture occasionally rises to the level of "frozen music," it also, invariably, concretizes politics. We have voted to build prisons at the direct cost of higher education; private philanthropy is increasingly torn between funding larger and more grandiose museums and subsidizing charities and services for the disadvantaged. The legacies of royal authority and privilege, prisons and museums play more complicated roles as democratic institutions. Though long philosophically derided, prisons and museums "fail" in ways that seem only to spawn new proposals, enthusiastically promulgated then categorically dismissed by subsequent critics and reformers.

TURNTABLEISM

Notes on the Paintings:
1.   These are paintings of prisons, cells, and walls.
2.   Here, the idealist square becomes the prison. Geometry
     is revealed as confinement.
3.   The cell is a reminder of the apartment house, the hospital
     bed, the school desk — the isolated endpoints of industrial
     structure.
4.   The paintings are a critique of idealist modernism.
     In the "color field" is placed a jail.[15]

PETER HALLEY, NOTES ON THE PAINTINGS, 1982

THIS STUDY BROKERS among many modes of inquiry and
models of argument. Polemics, surveys, and journalism have
all been brought to bear on prisons and museums, and a much
wider array of discursive forms pertain to the integrally related
topics of art, crime, and urbanism. For histories of each building
type I have relied especially on those by Robin Evans, Norman
Johnston, and Leslie Fairweather for prisons; on Eilean Hooper-
Greenhill, Tony Bennett and Alan Wallach for museums; and on
Anthony Vidler regarding both. I've also consulted many surveys
of state-of-the-art buildings and calls for their reform.[16] The vast
majority of the coverage of recent buildings is by journalists,
reportage in time- and site-specific pieces that render indelible
the human impact and statistical improbability of these buildings,
and these are cited as they relate to the text. Teaching with Mike
Davis at SCI-Arc in the 1990s gave me both a pretext for visiting
many prisons and a tutorial in how to see and portray them in a
broader context.

A few theorists have considered the affinity of museums
and prisons before, almost all in the wake of Michel Foucault.
Foucault's *Discipline and Punish: The Birth of the Prison* (1975)
dominates the field of penology still, and his assorted writings
on art and archives extend his lessons on power, coercion, and

transparency through cultural domains. With Erving Goffman's *Asylums* (1961), *Discipline and Punish* had a resounding impact on a '70s generation of planners who sought to "deinstitutionalize" prisons and jails. I've met guards who have read Foucault and brought up the Panopticon while giving tours of California state prisons. More broadly, his theories of pervasive surveillance and self-policing have been borne out exponentially, in ways Foucault could not have predicted, in electronic surveillance, digital monitoring, and the ubiquitous video coverage of urban space.[17]

David Lyon's *The Electronic Eye* and later writings cover the post-Foucault gamut in this direction, and many have elaborated on various tangents of his theories on incarceration, prominent among them Robin Evans and Thomas Bender. A surprising array of scholars has tried to extend Foucault's analytical method to museums: among them Douglas Crimp, Svetlana Alpers, Tony Bennett, Eilean Hooper-Greenhill, and Thomas Markus.[18] More recently, discussions of art and architecture have broken along partisan lines, with the editorial alumni of *ArtForum* and *October*

ANDREA FRASER, Little Frank and His Carp (2001)
Opposite: PRISON WITH UNDERGROUND CIRCUIT, Peter Halley (1983)

usually enjoying both first and last say. Rosalind Krauss' "The Cultural Logic of the Late Capitalist Museum" and Hal Foster's recent collected essays, *Design and Crime* and *The Art-Architecture Complex,* examine the incursion of the market into the museum, and the declension of high culture into design.[19] The thematic sequencing of this study is in many respects the result of trying to process and respond to these positions.

However, more directly salient for my work has been institutional critique generated by artists. Robert Smithson looms large over this dialogue with "Some Void Thoughts on Museums," as does Brian O'Doherty's *Inside the White Cube.*[20] After both Marcel Duchamp and Broodthaers, many artists have posed their own "counter-museums," as in the cluttered realms of Thomas Hirschhorn and the micro-utopias of Liam Gillick.

Little Frank and His Carp, a 2001 performance by Andrea Fraser based on a recorded docent's tour of the Guggenheim Bilbao, reflects sharply on Frank Gehry's architectural techniques, formal imperatives, and its resuscitation of the Basque economy. In her book *Museum Highlights* (1998), Fraser also parses many of the Foucaldians above by way of Pierre Bourdieu's sociology of institutions, and alludes to Loïc Wacquant's recent excoriations of mass incarceration.[21] The early cutaway models of Langlands & Bell, a British art partnership, presaged the many pairings of prison and museum plans included here. Richard

Ross' photography of both prison and museum interiors, within his larger oeuvre of *Architecture of Authority,* haunt these pages, as do abstractions of those same dynamics by Peter Halley.

Most of all, I have been inspired by a handful of paired essays by novelists: Aldous Huxley's "The Prisons" on Piranesi and "Reflections on Goya" in *Texts and Pretexts*; Joan Didion's pieces on The Getty and Alcatraz in *The White Album* and *Slouching Towards Bethlehem*, respectively; and more recently, Jonathan Franzen writing on the Mercer Museum and the SuperMax prison in Florence, Colorado, in *How to Be Alone*. Read together, each of these pairs achieves in microcosm what I hope this study will deliver in aggregate: a broader, more complex, and engaged discussion of prisons and museums both as manifestations of prevalent, unacknowledged philosophies, and as repositories of our most overwrought desires and least examined fears.

CARCERI D'INVENZIONE NO. XIV
final state, Giovanni Battista Piranesi (1750)

AS PRISONS REIN IN PEOPLE who no longer have clear options or places in our economy, museums host a perpetual trade fair of optional lifestyles for those who can afford them. With the rise of multimedia and installation work, museums of contemporary art showcase a wide array of possible futures: many of them attractive, some of them threatening, none of them as universal or all-embracing as the modern movements they often allude to wistfully. For the bulk of Americans who fall somewhere between destitution and affluence, prisons and museums translate into an endlessly pixilated spectacle of chain gangs and gala balls, prisoner abuse scandals and ostentatiously overpriced exhibition tickets — an aunt in an art fair or a brother in custody — with few degrees of separation either way.

Corrections and Collections limits its scope to the architectural residue of these seismic shifts. The radical changes and advances in design for exhibition and discipline in the last forty years reveal fantasies and pathologies of a society in flux. Prisons and museums have long been held as the nadir and apex, respectively, of city life. The metropolitan ideal that gave rise to this opposition, however, is yielding to both the increasingly cosmopolitan logic of global exchange and cultural experimentation, as well as the counter-urban machinations of suburban wealth and rural political will. *Corrections and Collections* draws a comparison between museums and prisons to set the issues specific to each in higher relief, and to leverage the fast-expanding public awareness of one to illuminate the other. In the effusive public celebrations that mark the completion of new museums — monuments to our collective and individual audacity — we should listen carefully for the low, broad echoes of assent that have underwritten an unprecedented infrastructure of restraint.

MINIMAL

Chapters 01 and 02 look at the confluence of prison and museum design in terms of Minimalism, as the disciplinary ideals of asceticism — removal, deprivation, and repetition — became central to art production and exhibition. Chapter 01 looks at how strategies of simplification and abstraction, which had long typified prison architecture, came to dominate museum design in the post-WWII period. Louis Kahn's three major museums are watersheds in this regard, with each introducing a distinct aspect of penitential aesthetics into buildings for art.

01.REDUCE

KAHN GAMES

Art, which was immediately felt, was the first word, one can say
the first line, but I think the first word, the first utterance.
It could have been, 'Ah,' just that. What a powerful word that is.
It expresses so much with just a few letters.[22]
LOUIS KAHN

PERHAPS THE LESS SAID, the better? In college, I was both
saved and bored by Louis Kahn.

Kahn is a hallowed figure in the field of architecture, perhaps
the last heroic, "form-giving" Modern Master. As his son Nathan-
iel portrayed him in the 2003 documentary *My Architect*, Kahn was
the ultimate "architects' architect" — an exemplary, almost mysti-
cal practitioner of the building arts. But when I first encountered
Kahn's projects as an undergraduate at Yale in the mid-1980s, I
was underwhelmed.

A spate of recent bylines reminded me of my ambivalence
toward Kahn, and toward the city where I first encountered his
work. Kahn's two buildings in New Haven, Connecticut, face one

another one block from the School of Architecture, where Kahn taught in the 1940s and '50s. Completed in 1953, the Yale University Art Gallery (YUAG) was Kahn's first cultural commission and it reopened in the spring of 2007, after a three-year restoration, to national fanfare and renewed universal acclaim. It was in fact the first gallery for modern art built on a US college campus, and a bellwether for many to follow. His second project, the far larger but equally well-regarded Yale Center for British Art (BAC), was completed posthumously in 1976.

Some of my mixed feelings had to do with the subtlety of Kahn's work, some to do with issues of my own. After only a year or two of studying architecture, I had quickly developed a facile skepticism toward my field, especially the recent evidence of it in New Haven. Kahn's two museums were fine, quiet gems, but to me they were just the least catastrophic of the many late-modern failures that capital-A architects had visited on that city. By my reckoning, Louis Kahn, Eero Saarinen, Paul Rudolph, Marcel Breuer, Kevin Roche, and Cesar Pelli had all run aground there, and all due to hubris. All of them inflicted unwelcome and unwelcoming buildings on a downtrodden city. Though perhaps the least guilty, Kahn was — at least until his triple polygamy came to light — also the least compelling.

YALE UNIVERSITY ART GALLERY, CHAPEL STREET ENTRANCE, Louis Kahn, New Haven, Connecticut (1953)

From beauty, Wonder. Wonder has nothing to do with knowledge.[23]
LOUIS KAHN

Please. At that point in my education, architecture wasn't about construction, it was about polemics, and Kahn's rhetoric, which was sacrosanct at Yale, seemed like a lot of banal, faux-Zen sophistry to me. Kahn's collected teachings, reverently transcribed by acolytes in volumes like John Lobell's *Between Silence and Light*, made Frank Lloyd Wright's many efforts at auto-hagiography look sophisticated by comparison. The cult of Kahn was a stultifying force in a school too beholden to its role in promoting him, and then Robert Venturi, as distinctly American masters, concluding Modernism and birthing Postmodernism, respectively. As Manfredo Tafuri argued in a piece called "The Ashes of Jefferson," which I cited reflexively in those years, such simplistic pride in Kahn and Venturi reflected a naive US chauvinism made possible not by Kahn's and Venturi's superior talent or insight, but because they were the first beneficiaries of post-WWII American global dominance.[24]

Like many of my peers in the 1980s, I cared a lot about Theory, and Kahn's voice seemed too simple, almost stunted. My tastes ran to complex ruminations on imaginary architecture: Manfredo Tafuri on G.B. Piranesi, Michel Foucault on Jeremy Bentham, Roland Barthes on Charles Fourier. Deconstructions of the Enlightenment — the more visionary the rhetoric, and the less realized the designs, the better. From the latter 20th century, I favored leftist Eurotopians who eschewed building entirely: radical, not liberal, proposals for hyper-abstract cityscapes by Superstudio, Archigram, and Constant. I was looking for praxis-on-paper, architectural speculation that promised societal and personal liberation. By those lights, Kahn seemed utterly beside the point.

But his buildings rescued me in more prosaic ways. Like many Californians who "go East" for college, I struggled with the climate and culture of New England (and with shame over that struggle, as my family is mostly from Connecticut). New Haven's winter is hardly competitive with points farther north for snow and cold, but it is punishing in its mediocrity: wet, windy, and relentlessly gray. For the first three sunless months of 1986, I felt trapped in a freezing, poorly focused, black-and-white film loop. Though some places proved more salutary than others, I found over time that only Kahn's galleries consistently eased my winter-long depressions. I had lost whatever Yankee resilience I was supposed to have inherited, but could at least count on the Turrell-like inner light of the Center for British Art to answer my homesickness, and the hovering stillness, as well as the Duchamps, in the Art Gallery across the street to restore my perspective. I timed my trips to that side of campus according to museum hours, to at least pass through either building, coming or going. Kahn was a phenomenal builder, as I grasped even then, and I needed both retreats in a visceral, desperate way.

It was probably this unwelcome sense of vulnerability that led me to think about prisons as I hid in Kahn's museums, and eventually to think about each in terms of the other. In their austerity and seriousness, Kahn's galleries make it easy, and even seductive, to see the penitential in the museological. The Art Gallery and Center for British Art share a number of key attributes with prisons: indirect access and fortified circulation; clerestory lighting rather than view windows; an oddly luxurious attention to, and exposure of, poured concrete construction. Spaces vary in terms of, rather than in spite of, their modular realization in Kahn, a rule that holds almost universally in incarceration. A structural bay is to Kahn as the cellblock is to most prisons: carefully, specifically conceived and then multiplied, not modified. In this sense, as I would learn much later, Kahn's museums are a first instance of Minimalist, as opposed to Modernist, renunciation of subjective form-making.

The Minimalism pioneered by Kahn was unremitting in its logic and in its limitations. The Yale Art Gallery meets the street in a sheer wall of brick fascia unmodified save for concrete ledge-

Left: YALE CENTER FOR BRITISH ART, ATRIUM, Louis Kahn, New Haven, CT (1974)
Right: BREST PRISON, ENTRANCE, Antoine Choquet de Lindu, Brest, France (1751)

bands at each of its floor levels. Rather than puncture this facade with a grand, frontal entrance, Kahn recesses the last section of wall from top to bottom into the mass of the building, and tucks the front door into the gap. Inside, the planar emphasis moves from the vertical to the horizontal, with each floor slab hovering over the next in a pyramidal waffle of reinforced concrete, explaining the striations of the exterior wall.[25] In contrast to the austere masonry of both its blank face and heavy floors, the north and east sides of the building are glazed in transparent curtain walls, opening the workings of the building to Yale as emphatically as its sheer front wall closes them to New Haven.

Conceived with wartime rationing of materials and economy of means still in effect, Kahn's design accommodated far more "program," or spatial uses, than is currently the case for that building. Originally, the Yale Art Gallery also housed the nascent schools of art and architecture, with its upper two floors given over to studio space. Many of the building's most groundbreaking features, when read now strictly as a museum, date back to this original cross-programming, especially its combination of closed and open elevations to the front and back. The building's recent renovation finally resolved the problematic exposure of its rear flank with blinds and UV film, but the Art Gallery remains remarkably open to its surroundings.

Kahn's second New Haven project, the Yale Center for British Art, broadened the scope of university art museums considerably. The BAC, as it was known, holds a library, lecture hall, seminar and restoration rooms, as well as roughly 30,000 square feet of transcendent gallery space, in a single, immaculately calibrated concrete space-frame. Like Sol LeWitt's early studies in repetitive cubic geometry, the Center for British Art is both a tightly bounded and infinite project. Its outer form and organization are everywhere evident, utterly without mystery. By contrast, its structural and surface refinements, its modulated cladding in glass and weathered stainless steel, and its sequence of interior spaces are endlessly nuanced. Kahn's last building and his most revolutionary in terms of its urbanism, the Center for British Art is the first museum to integrate a full block of storefronts for rent along its length at street level, thus merging "town" into the "gown" of rarefied art space.[26]

The Yale University Art Gallery and the Center for British Art chart an increasingly inverse relationship between the quality of art to be displayed and the quality — or at least the cost — of the architecture built to showcase that art. Though both buildings arose to house recently donated collections, the much smaller YUAG holds an indisputable array of modern and premodern masterpieces, many of them gifts from the keen-eyed but fiscally limited Katherine Dreier; the Center for British Art is a far more ambitious building for far more specialized genre works, donated by Paul Mellon, for whom the BAC was a minor, personal foray after he led the fundraising for I.M. Pei's East Wing of the National Gallery. Built on a shoestring, the YUAG just barely met the needs of the university and the curatorial standards of the work it was designed for. By the time the BAC was envisioned, the art was understood to be a pretext for ambitious architecture and urban investment. The BAC cost $17 million, more than 10 times the YUAG's initial budget of $1.5 million.[27] (The $40 million spent to renovate and restore the YUAG, and to shore up Kahn's first but late-recognized masterpiece, only underscores this point.)

Kahn was unique in his post-WWII generation for building his best, rather than his worst, projects in New Haven. The YUAG and BAC are the first and final drafts of Kahn's core principles, not the stylistic rehashes so common in academic commissions by major architects. Standing to either side of the city/campus divide of Chapel Street on Yale's western edge, they are perhaps Kahn's only truly integrated civic projects, and they recalibrate both the quality and scale of buildings in that city.

But, for all of the above, I considered Kahn more lucky than good (I had no idea then how unlucky Kahn actually had been, up to and including the heart attack that ended his life in a Penn Station men's room). To my undergraduate eyes, Saarinen, Breuer, and Rudolph had all done better, more exciting projects elsewhere. Architects who had been inspired under other cir-cumstances to create buildings akin to a bird in flight (Saarinen's TWA terminal), a cyclopean mask (Breuer's Whitney), or a totem of stacked fists (Rudolph's Indonesian tower) had in New Haven been reduced to a more impoverished kitsch of turtles (Saarin-en's ungainly hockey rink), tire treads (the embossed facade of Breuer's Pirelli headquarters) and pseudo-*brut* texture (the jack-hammered roughness of Rudolph's School of Art and Architec-ture, to say nothing of the urban war crime he committed in the 1,500-car Temple Street parking structure). So I should come clean: what bothered me most about their buildings in New Haven wasn't their often obtuse insensitivity to their meager surround-ings, but the lack of ideological or even iconographic aspiration these architects had shown elsewhere. They all seemed to short-change New Haven, and, with the circular reasoning of the diur-nally depressed, I concluded maybe the city deserved no better.

CON GAMES

Artists themselves are not confined, but their output is. Museums, like asylums and jails, have wards and cells — in other words, neutral rooms called 'galleries.'... The function of the warden-curator is to separate art from the rest of society.[28]

ROBERT SMITHSON, FROM HIS 1972 ESSAY, "CULTURAL CONFINEMENT"

This is born-dead neo-penitentiary modernism.

NEW YORK TIMES CRITIC ADA LOUISE HUXTABLE REVIEWING THE NEWLY OPENED HIRSHHORN MUSEUM IN 1974

NEW HAVEN WAS HARDLY ALONE in its shortcomings by then. Revisiting the art and architectural writing of the 1970s, one can't miss a strident, paranoid tone of the times. Throughout that decade, the cultural and the societal were often equated in dubious ways. Though Robert Smithson wasn't the first artist to liken museums to prisons, he did so at a precise moment when American architects, to the bewilderment of even their most ardent champions like Ada Louise Huxtable at *The New York Times*, had stopped trying to tell them apart.

Beginning in the 1950s and peaking in the 1970s, institutional architecture of all stripes in this country became ominously homogeneous, with civic, cultural, and educational buildings all rendered as stark, increasingly massive, abstractions. The Kennedy Center, McCormick Place, Boston City Hall, the World Trade Center, Transamerica Tower — all of them landed in their host cities like lost meteoric fragments from *2001: A Space Odyssey* or *Logan's Run*. Both the last heaving efforts of Modernist architecture and a first leviathan embrace of recent Minimalist sculpture, the institutions of these years — whether described then in terms of Rationalism, Metabolism, or Reyner Banham's New Brutalism — haunt us now principally in their brooding silence. This "neo-penitential" public architecture was cast in concrete, and in irony: these were years in which, by and large, those same cities fought off the construction of prisons within their confines.

Though these behemoths took decades to rise, their extinction, at least stylistically, was more abrupt. By 1980, Postmodernists after Robert Venturi and Tom Wolfe had disavowed the immediate past in US architecture in favor of allusion to more distant, bucolic times. The architectural expression of most building types returned to traditional, often classical silhouettes. However, museums (especially museums for fine art) and prisons continued to pose questions of presence and abstraction apart from, and often at odds with, their legibility as specific kinds of building. Architectures of exhibition and discipline evolved more seamlessly out of the austere, simplifying, and monumental ambitions of Minimalism than did other building types.

Though there are masterworks of architectural Minimalism — and I will return to more of them by Louis Kahn and others — it is in lesser works that the sensibility is easiest to read. Ada Louise Huxtable was right about the Hirshhorn Museum: it is a hovering doughnut, hot-dipped in concrete, and a mediocre building by the otherwise gifted Gordon Bunshaft. Though the escalator passage up through the deeply cantilevered O-ring of the galleries is momentarily sublime, the ride, and one's feeling of wonder, passes in seconds. Once inside, the Hirshhorn has all the concentric failings of Wright's Guggenheim, without the latter's spatial dynamism. Externally it manages to be both an overbearing and, at the same time, ill-defined presence on the National Mall. When Huxtable dubbed the Hirshhorn Museum "neo-penitential," she went on to list its shortcomings thus:

> "It offers a rigid resistance to everything around it or part of it that should properly interact with it. Neither a sympathetic background nor an enriching balance of esthetic tensions is created. Its mass is not so much aggressive or overpowering as merely leaden."[29]

Merely present rather than challenging; more massive than composed; neither figure nor ground: it is precisely these failings, by Modernist standards, that make the Hirshhorn thoroughly, if not winningly, Minimalist. The Hirshhorn exemplifies a Minimalist code of limit conditions that values the *blank, bounded,* and *cellular* over more broadly modernist notions of transparency, layering, and interpenetration of spaces. In this light, all of Huxtable's points against the Hirshhorn — its "rigid," closed geometry; its "leaden," blank expression; its refusal of both "sympathetic background" status and "enriching balance of esthetic tensions" — could serve as an indictment of almost every major building for art built in the 1960s and '70s, and a clear indication of how far architects had followed Minimalist artists, unaccompanied by their lingeringly Modernist critics. The designer of the Lever House and many other mid-century landmarks, Bunshaft struggled to work in a new vocabulary to produce, as he put it, "a large piece of functional sculpture," but that struggle went unacknowledged by those who hoped to find in the Hirshhorn a continuation of, rather than a departure from, high Modern architecture.

One can see why those critics balked. The impact of Minimalist architecture on cities was bound to be controversial. Blankness, in particular, proved both an architectural virtue and an urban vice. Tall, unadorned, and unbroken facades, however abstract and well-proportioned, de-scale neighborhoods and provide ample surfaces for graffiti. And to the degree that Minimalist art posed problems of *containment* — containing space as form and containers repeated in space to generate form — its architectural corollary was not exhibition but incarceration. Whether by intention or not, Minimalist art and architecture owe their basic vocabulary, scale, and organization to prisons more than any other building type: spaces tailored in terms of the body, accumulated in serial configurations, and bounded by blank walls. No tendency in recent art and architecture underscores the coincidence of the *aesthetic* and the *ascetic* more than the advent of Minimalism.

SOLITAIRE:
LIMITING SPACE AND EXTENDING TIME

With respect to the Plan of a Prison…I had heard of a benevolent
society in England which has been indulged by the government
in an experiment of the effect of labor in solitary confinement on
some of their criminals, which experiment had succeeded beyond
expectation.… I drew one on a scale less extensive, but susceptible
to additions.[30]

THOMAS JEFFERSON, C.1800

We find in the United States two distinctly separate systems:
the system of Auburn and that of Philadelphia.…
     The two systems opposed to each other on important
points, have, however, a common basis, without which no
penitentiary system is possible; this basis is the isolation of
the prisoners.[31]

ALEXIS DE TOCQUEVILLE AND GUSTAVE DE BEAUMONT, 1833

DESIGNING PRISONS REQUIRES a dystopian mathematics
of refusal. The most critical variables to be mitigated in incarceration are risk, movement, and cost (of either construction
or staffing), with the reduction of stress, institutional legibility,
and even the possibility of escape all of related but subordinate
concern. Most of the tension in modern prison design arises from
the incommensurability of certain reductive agendas vis-à-vis
others: lower cost construction often results in increased repairs,
staffing, or overhead; fewer distractions for prisoners, in the form
of education or exercise, lead to more stress and violence. (As
we will see, in postmodern incarceration, the promise of further
reduction of any of the above variables can serve as justification for further construction in its own right, as is evident from
the ongoing cost/benefit regressions and projections underpinning New Generation Justice Facilities.) It's hardly surprising
that prison design should be framed in mechanistic terms, only

remarkable that such calculations become routinely self-contra-dictory. Prisons prove that few efficiencies come without trade-offs and that in circumstances of total, constant, and unwilling cohabitation, any design shortcoming will be exploited immedi-ately and often with lethal consequences. Though we may all be "Prisoners of Architecture" according to Rem Koolhaas, no one tests buildings quite like actual inmates.

In the United States, those inmates are kept apart more than anywhere else — 80,000 are held in solitary confinement today, rivaling the total prison populations of the UK and Japan. Though some of the design tactics now common in both prisons and museums are simply perennial hallmarks of incarceration — few openings and blank walls, for example — many of those that relate to Minimalism date to 19th and early 20th century penal experiments in *isolation*: isolation of the inmate via solitary confinement, iso-lation of prisoner labor and costs, and isolation of incarceration itself in remote sites.

Before the outward legibility of prisons was minimized, the experiential parameters were. US prisons are distinguished by a cycle of innovation that first resituates inmates in unforeseen ways then capitalizes on that new situation through massive economies of scale. Our most recent SuperMax units are simi-larly distinguished by their radical asceticism in both spatial and temporal terms — inmates are held in seamless white cells mod-ulated only by a sink/toilet and built-in concrete sleeping slabs, alone for twenty-three hours per day, with all twenty-four hours lit by fluorescent bulbs to guarantee a clear video feed to remote guard stations. Isolation is a fetish peculiar to our democracy, and one that California prison historian Shelley Bookspan links to our preoccupations with individualism (which she notes esca-lates westward) and punishment as a "deprivation of liberty."[32]

For those shocked to learn in 2006 that Vice President Dick Cheney had invested heavily in private prisons through the Van-guard Group, it's worth recalling that Thomas Jefferson drew some of the first jails constructed in the United States, and was

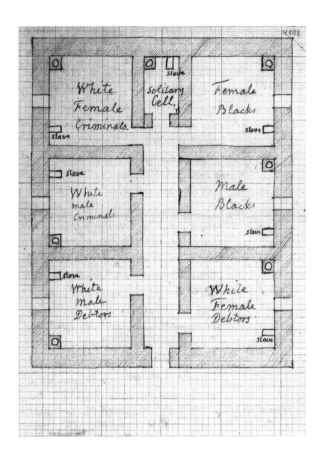

White Female Criminals.

Solitary Cell,

Female Blacks

stove

stove

White male Criminals

Male Blacks

stove

stove

White male Debtors

White Female Debtors

stove

NELSON COUNTY JAIL. Thomas Jefferson. Nelson County, Virginia (construction completed in 1823)

heavily invested, at least intellectually, in the debate over how to detain citizens of a democracy.[33]

MOST HISTORIES OF US PRISONS begin with America's first penitentiaries, based on competing models of the factory and the monastery. However, an earlier colonial example is worth considering first, as it predates our fascination with "a room of one's own." With ambitions both brutal and strangely ersatz, the builders of Newgate Prison in Simsbury, Connecticut, reconfigured a spent copper mine, adding crenellated turrets above and excavating dungeons for thirty to 100 inmates seventy feet below grade. Designed primarily to hold and terrify "Redcoats" during the Revolutionary War, the Connecticut Newgate alludes in its name, and likely in its miseries, to the first and more infamous London Newgate of the 17th century, which actually occupied a medieval city gate.[34] The United States not only incarcerates more people than any other nation, but we hold those we perceive as different from ourselves differently, and less well: before we imagined better machines for transforming Americans, we built a Hobbesian, dystopian theme park for foreigners. By comparison, Jefferson's early sketch for a jail built in Nelson County, Virginia, seems refreshingly egalitarian, with six 12'x12' holding rooms assigned by race, gender, and seriousness of offense (though, of course, these came with no guarantee that they would be filled equally). Jefferson also includes a windowless room the size of a closet for solitary confinement, which was amended by the builders to include a sliver of light.[35]

By the early 19th century, however, a famous rivalry developed between "New York" and "Pennsylvania" theories of prison reform, both, as Tocqueville and Beaumont note, based on solitary confinement, though differing radically on the programming of inmates' time. In the New York bastions of Auburn (1818) and Sing Sing (1825), inmates marched single file and in silence, from cell to work assignment and back. In the Quaker-sponsored Eastern State Penitentiary in Philadelphia, begun in 1821 by John Haviland, convicts were allotted a cell and adjoining yard for solitary reflection on their wrongdoing. Though the differential between exploitation and rehabilitation appears stark, and underscored by individual cell dimensions of only 8'x4' in New York and 10'x12' in Pennsylvania, the virtues of the latter were quickly undone by overcrowding and understaffing (with each inmate fixed permanently in his quarters, guards had to operate essentially as a concierge service).

NOT HOME, BUT ALONE

But the fact of it was I liked it out there, a ruin devoid of human vanities, clean of human illusions, an empty place reclaimed by the weather...[36]

JOAN DIDION ON ALCATRAZ

NO PRISONS built in the Cold War period, and certainly no single prison designer, could be said to have reconfigured the problem of incarceration as thoroughly as Kahn's museums recast the architecture of exhibition.[37] Before the surging growth of both building types in the last thirty years, the number of US prisons and museums grew haltingly. The need for each grew slowly after WWII, but especially so for prisons. Until well into the 1970s, new holding space was simply not in demand. The federal prison population actually fell between 1940 and 1980.[38] The many construction projects of the New Deal — including the bastions of Attica, Alcatraz, and Rikers Island — and, after WWII, the conversion of decommissioned military bases such as Leavenworth, created a glut of cell space that lasted until new drug laws began to flood the federal and state systems in the early 1970s.

Those New Deal prisons, like much WPA architecture, depended on advances in concrete construction, especially its trucked delivery, and the cheap or free labor required for massive form-work and quarrying. Prisons built in the first half of the 20th century were stolid cast containers, redundant in plan and devoid of ornament, save for occasional Classical colonnade or Moderne banding that aided in or resulted from the cement form-release. Even as glass and steel grew more accessible in the 1950s, American prisons remained mostly lapidary projects, often still involving forced inmate labor in their realization. Most of this prison building relied on replication, which produced cellblocks and compounds of unforeseen scale as designs were simply enlarged or multiplied on site for greater capacity.

Isolation is compounded at all scales. The federal system of penitentiaries often makes a fetish of location: Fort Leavenworth; Alcatraz; Terminal Island; and Florence, Colorado, are all remote by geography or circumstance, to say nothing of the holding facilities we now operate beyond our borders — adjoining Cuba, throughout Iraq, and elsewhere. As Alexis de Tocqueville observed on his first journey to the United States to assess our prison system in 1833, the American enthusiasm for incarceration reflected our collective distrust of the exceptional as much as it did the brotherly love of Philadelphia Quakers.

In 1908, Adolf Loos wrote a series of articles that called for the elimination of all decorative augmentation of modern buildings, remarking that "the evolution of humanity goes hand in hand with the ordinary object's moving away from embellishment."[39] Most early 20th century avant-gardes — in all media and disciplines — struggled to pare away at problems of representation and figuration, and many of those movements demanded profound aesthetic renunciations. However, only in Minimalism is the negation of the tabula rasa raised to an ideal in its own right, not a transitional procedure before new additive possibilities. There is no shortage of Loosian extremism in the competitive exclusions that now define most architectures for ornament and for crime.

LIBERTY IN THE NEGATIVE

And in its midst, one notices an evenly lighted 'cell' that appears
crucial to making the thing work: the gallery space.…Through the
fifties and sixties, we notice the codification of a new theme as it
evolves into consciousness: How much space should a work of art
have (as the phrase went) to 'breathe'?[40]
BRIAN O'DOHERTY

Brian O'Doherty describes how the "White Cube" of the Minimalist gallery led to the super-graphic isolation of the work of
art, especially painting, in a plane of designified cultural reflection. He laments that hallowed museum walls — bands of white
between skylights and hardwood flooring — consign all objects
in their expanse to an ethereal plane fit only for the contemplation
of form, rather than engagement with their production, origins,
or intent. O'Doherty believes we have transformed our houses
of culture into containers of containment itself. As he put it, "As
modernism gets older, context becomes content. In a particular reversal, the object introduced into the gallery 'frames' the
gallery and its laws."[41]

We now presume that museums can take any shape, so why
so many unadorned boxes? The answer lies in the assumption:
stripping the exhibitionary box to its bare minimum was essential to realizing its current flexibility. Contemporary museums
offer themselves first and foremost as theaters of freedom,
and as such, the least resistant of environments to extremes of
expression. But before the free-for-all of contemporary museum
design could escalate, a host of distractions, impediments, and
"distance" between artist and audience had to be eliminated.
Reduced here were barriers and limits, precisely the most essential components in incarceration. But this distinction is largely
rhetorical. The spaces of "freedom" granted by late modern
museums usually present themselves as free in the sense that
they avoid semiotic distraction, hierarchy, or differentiation from

YALE UNIVERSITY ART GALLERY, CEILING DETAIL

other gallery spaces, not free in terms of an audience's route through or behavior in those spaces. (The constrained freedoms of artists who install or perform in contemporary art space are another matter.)

LESS IS THE LAW

It remains to be seen if art exists anywhere else than on the level of negation.[42]

MARCEL BROODTHAERS, 1974

Prison is asceticism without end.[43]

BERNARD STIEGLER, PHILOSOPHER, INCARCERATED FROM 1978–82

THE INCURSION of penitential aesthetics into buildings for exhibition also reflects the heightened role of renunciation in late-modern architecture and Minimalist art. By 1960, the prewar avant-garde priorities of transformation — through dynamic modelling in Futurism, or fracture and recombination in Cubism, for example — had ossified into a Minimalist canon of fixities: reduction, repetition, neutrality. Chief among these, and the most tied

45

to carceral precedent, is reduction. Cold War innovations in both building types may be framed very differently, but almost all can be read in terms of subtraction, simplification, removal, absence, and abstraction. Time and space, and their trappings, are never more palpable than in confinement. Mid-20th century prisons and museums are in fact catalogs of reduction and negation, toward a *literally* bare minimum.

A distinction between the Modern and the Minimal is critical for this study — and the subject of fast-growing scholarship. For many years, *modern* and *minimalist* were confused in histories of 20th century architecture, in which many post-WWII buildings are described by the terms interchangeably.[44] Especially among the late masterpieces of the High Modern generation including Le Corbusier, Ludwig Mies van der Rohe, and Frank Lloyd Wright, one must acknowledge both tendencies, and, in certain respects, the inspiration for Minimalism in the Modern, and vice versa. However, with Louis Kahn and his generation a distinction can be drawn consistently. Vincent Scully argued that Kahn had abandoned the painterly bias of the High Modern generation and is "never pictorial," but former *ArtForum* editor Joseph Masheck clarifies that Kahn's architecture is at least as aligned with contemporary *sculpture* as it is with Scully's notion of a renewed Modern Classicism:

> "That [Scully's pronouncement] seems too sweeping, but it could well apply to the once denoted 'Primary Structures' of the minimal art that paralleled the florescence of Louis Kahn's decidedly inorganic architecture. Mies was no minimalist, despite the generalizations of the anti-modernists; but the uniform and continuous poured concrete triangular clustering-into-hexagonal coffers of Kahn's Yale Gallery ceiling, dark and chunkily faceted, practically adumbrate the extreme formal single-mindedness of American minimalist sculpture in the 1960s."[45]

Examining the early work of Kahn, John Hejduk, and Frank Gehry, Mark Linder maps a fast-evolving relationship between architecture and art in the 1960s in *Nothing Less Than Literal: Architecture After Minimalism*.[46] Through a series of what Linder terms transdisciplinary "improprieties" in that decade, architects came to produce more "medium-specific" buildings, and artists deployed architecture — its parts, representational techniques, scale — as a basis for their work.[47] A generation of artist-theorists

TOKYO MUSEUM OF WESTERN ART, Le Corbusier, Tokyo, Japan (1963)
Opposite: NEUE NATIONALGALERIE, Mies van der Rohe, Berlin, Germany (1968)

led by Donald Judd and Robert Smithson reject *any* discussion or allusion outside the physical, material properties of a given work — work that need no longer allude to its discipline of origin. As Linder condenses it, " 'This is this' is the axiom of Literalism." It is a defining Minimalist mantra both more stringent and more open-ended than Mies' famous "Less Is More" and categorically apart from it. Minimalists sample the natural and built environment, extinguishing the metaphorical distance between objects and their representation. This quest for the unmediated "real" in art leads to both extremes of openness — Smithson's null spaces and non-sites — and closure — the containers of Judd, Robert Morris, and LeWitt. In almost all Minimalist scenarios, however, site, volume, and structure are segregated and reduced to their barest components and geometry.

Linder cites a 1981 essay by Christian Bonnefoi that draws out Kahn's Minimalism in specifically carceral terms.[48] Bonnefoi defines the issues central to Minimalist, as opposed to Modern, architecture in terms of renunciation: the question of mounting and support rather than the internal modulation of a work's content, and a refusal of expressive and dynamic qualities of volumetric permutation:

> "(I)t should be noted that the question [in Kahn's work] is one of renewals and transformations of properly formal, i.e. pictorial and sculptural effects, not to be confused with the effects of volume, such as can be seen, for example, in the work of Le Corbusier.... These formal and conceptual effects are precisely those which have become established in the pictorial and sculptural work on Minimalism from the sixties up to the present time."[49]

Bonnefoi also sees a clear reciprocity between the strategies of presence employed by Minimalist artists and those of Kahn, continuing:

> "The volume must not struggle with the space surrounding it through simultaneous relations of penetration and retrac-

tion, but rather must fill it at once, *with a single gesture*, so that the object introduced into the space becomes to some extent its parallel and, finally, its model. This means that in Kahn, as in Minimalism, the object has, through various devices, the function of opposing to space a wall [whether opaque or transparent] on its four sides, thereby 'retrenching' and protecting itself against possible aesthetic or phenomenological comparisons."[50]

The cellular operation that Bonnefoi describes above, in which "the object" becomes walls fashioned to fill, retrench, and protect itself on four sides, has a longer pedigree in American architecture, dating back to our nation's 19th century (and continuing) obsession with solitary confinement.[51]

RIVAL SPIRALS

A museum can be anywhere, collect anything — an architecture independent of the ground and of culture, a nomadic architecture for a globally networked world. The spiral museum travels just as easily as the architect.[52]

BEATRIZ COLOMINA

WHILE THE 1940s, '50s, AND '60s were not as prolific for museum building as subsequent decades would prove, at least six major buildings for art were completed in those years. Three of these were culminations of major Modernist careers — those of Frank Lloyd Wright, Le Corbusier, and Mies van der Rohe, all of whom were born well before 1900; another three marked the attempts of a 20th century generation, Louis Kahn (born 1901), Marcel Breuer ('02), and Philip Johnson ('06), to join their pantheon. The first trio by the "Masters" marks both the apogee of Late Modernism and the cusp of Minimalism: Wright's Guggenheim, begun in 1947 and completed in 1959, Le Corbusier's Museum of Western Art in Tokyo spanning 1959 to 1964, and Mies' Neue Nationalgalerie in Berlin, begun in 1962 and opened in 1968. All three museums were a result of intense pre-WWII design research and proto-typing: Wright's Auto Destination of 1938 and many prelimi-nary versions of the Guggenheim, Le Corbusier's sketches for an "endless museum" or *Musée Mondial* through the 1930s, and Mies' study for a Museum for a Small City, published in 1942.[53]

Wright's Guggenheim, to which I will return in greater detail in Chapter 03, was one of two "rival spirals" invented in the 1930s for museum design. The other, Le Corbusier's *Musée Mondial*, was most exactly realized in Tokyo, as the Museum of Western Art. A maze-like, abstracted nautilus, the *Musée Mondial* was Le Corbusier's last foray into ideal geometry, a plan diagram that could be interpreted as either a level or ascending structure. His Tokyo museum is a spiral composed of boxes within a larger box, all with proportions based on the Golden Section and meant to atomize the experience of various artworks while forcing a cir-cuitry of historical passage. He repeated this *parti* in museums for Ahmedabad and Chandigarh, as well, though both were part of larger cultural complexes. One can find traces of the *Musée Mondial* in almost every one of Rem Koolhaas' early public build-ings, but especially his Kunsthal in Rotterdam (a collage of dis-crete orthogonal spaces stacked around a switchback core), the Dutch Embassy in Berlin (like Tokyo, a taller spiral in a box), and the 1997 Educatorium in Utrecht (a spiral of ramps between offset plates).

While Wright and Le Corbusier vie in their internal geome-try, Le Corbusier and Mies are more kindred in terms of the siting and presence of their new museums. Both punctuate large urban plazas with definite, square volumes. Neither is a "push-pull" urban composition, neither blends nor bleeds into its surround-ings. They share a reliance on cellular organization, of spaces in Tokyo and structure in Berlin, as well as monolithic elevations — *brut* concrete panels in Tokyo, and bounding curtain walls in Berlin. The universal gridding and transparency of Mies' Neue

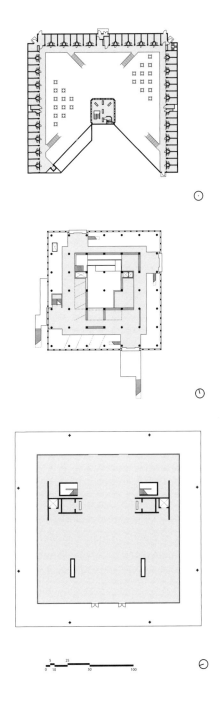

NEUE NATIONALGALERIE+MUSUEUM OF WESTERN ART, TOKYO+"270" PRISON BLOCK. Plans at common scale, upper levels shaded

5 25
0 10   50   100

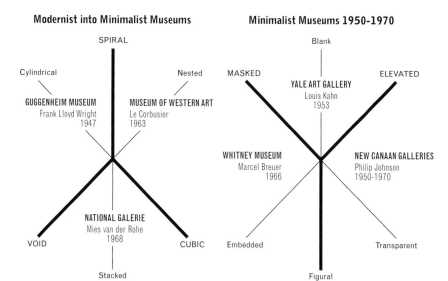

Modernist into Minimalist Museums

SPIRAL

Cylindrical — Nested

GUGGENHEIM MUSEUM
Frank Lloyd Wright
1947

MUSEUM OF WESTERN ART
Le Corbusier
1963

NATIONAL GALERIE
Mies van der Rohe
1968

VOID — CUBIC

Stacked

Minimalist Museums 1950-1970

Blank

MASKED — ELEVATED

YALE ART GALLERY
Louis Kahn
1953

WHITNEY MUSEUM
Marcel Breuer
1966

NEW CANAAN GALLERIES
Philip Johnson
1950-1970

Embedded — Transparent

Figural

MODERN > MINIMAL MUSEUMS, ddd llc (2012)

Nationalgalerie proved both more iconic and controversial, as it relegated art to partition walls clearly subordinate to the open, almost-infinite continuum of space compressed below a deep, hovering waffle of roof-plane.

In all three cases, the long sojourn of the war years from major public building led these leading Modernists to extend a single exhibitionary conundrum into a literal spatial proposition: for Wright, the "gallery as Art itself"; for Corbusier, the "gallery without end"; and for Mies, the "gallery without walls." All three transition between Minimal and Modern forms of architectural expression. All share a unified legibility, a blankness — gone are the ribbon windows of MoMA, the pinwheel, almost de Stijl layout of the Bauhaus — but none is a simple container. Wright and Mies both refuse to box their holdings: Wright extrudes gallery walls beyond recognition; Mies eliminates them as solid armature entirely, at least above ground. The location and situation of the buildings that finally evinced these ideas were presumably secondary for the architects, though in every case crucial for their lasting significance. Masterworks by Swiss and German, but now emphatically international designers, and paid for in US dollars, the Museum of Western Art and the Neue Nationalgalerie were also exercises in Cold War diplomacy and the crowning achievements of former-Axis Reconstruction.[54] Though Wright's building trumped both as a global destination, all three are still linchpins in a global art network they presaged.[55]

20TH CENTURY MEN

I never found him [Kahn] the great lovely guru-type. I couldn't stand all those long monologues about belief in truth. I can't stand truth. It gets so boring, you know, like social responsibility....
    And I never talked much to artists. They don't talk much. The better the artist, the less they are able to verbalize. So I prefer critics.... One communes with artists, quite properly, by means of grunts.[58]
PHILIP JOHNSON

THE OTHER TRIO OF MUSEUMS, all in the United States by architects born in the "new" century, build on the reduced parameters of their elders, but without their burdens of life-long modernist trajectories: Philip Johnson's Glass House and surrounding galleries (1949–70), Louis Kahn's Yale Art Gallery (1953) and Marcel Breuer's Whitney Museum (1965). Kahn's Yale Art Gallery dispenses even more radically with the articulation of facade and institutional legibility than does Le Corbusier in Tokyo; Breuer takes up Wright's figural challenge and delivers a more audacious logo-building, a Surrealist/Brutalist cyclops only blocks away from the Guggenheim. Johnson's campus in New Canaan, Connecticut, spans these three decades, and likely forms one side of a long-running dialogue with Mies that led both to build glass exhibition pavilions above much larger subterranean gallery spaces.

Johnson's complex is often viewed exclusively through the lens of his Glass House of 1949. While this vitrine-for-living foregrounds the relationship between exhibition and exhibitionism, the Picture Gallery and the Sculpture Gallery he built nearby in the 1970s are more original investigations, positing modest but new architectures for art. Each is precisely calibrated to the medium on display. The Picture Gallery takes its cloverleaf shape in plan from the three wall-height, radial rolodex used to rotate over thirty wall-planes into a single gallery space. Naturally lit from above, the Sculpture Gallery steps down through multiple levels and terraces so that artworks of varying scale, orientation, and installation can be seen in the round and in relation to one another. As Francesco Dal Co describes, "Johnson's art collecting is united with architectural collecting. But it is, precisely, an encounter between two different tendencies.... The need to decodify is combined in Johnson's work with the eclectic experimentalism of his formal research, [and] with the autobiographical narcissism which is one with the innate penchant for collecting."[57]

Dal Co's essay concludes an issue of *Lotus International* devoted entirely to museums of architecture, one that begins with discussions of both John Soane's museum completed in 1837 and the Isabella Stewart Gardner Museum of 1903. Like these earlier essays by enlightened "amateurs," Philip Johnson's New Canaan complex hinges vitally on his dilettantism, his willingness to transgress across disciplines at no small cost to his credibility. Although many have examined Johnson's likely sympathies for Mies, Nazi Germany, and various post-WWII "-isms" in architecture, too little attention has been paid to the art collection he amassed with his partner David Whitney, as well as his adherence to the stringent formalist teachings of art critic Clement Greenberg. Johnson answers Greenberg's call for "medium-specificity" in painting and sculpture with architectures exclusively tailored to each.

All six exhibition spaces are contentious projects, and all have slid in and out of favor with the public. Each has at one time or another been considered deeply flawed as a space for viewing art. (Having visited each of them recently, I would argue that Le Corbusier's museum is perhaps the least redeemable in this sense.) All, save Johnson's private retreat, have played pivotal roles in urban development and in the civic recovery of beset cities. Interestingly, even those by the high Modern generation eschew industrial imagery and detailing in favor of continuous, planar surfaces and monolithic presence. All are buildings of paradox: austere and luxurious, simple and complex, often ordered in structure but perverse in their organization.

Despite their similarities, however, these two generations are engaged in very different modes of cultural production. Though their museums play out over a shared time frame, in the first three by Wright, Corbusier, and Mies, modernists may be forecasting Minimalism, but their shared, very Modern, aim is the invention of new spatial paradigms. In the second three, Minimalists actually *suppress* differences in spatial experience in favor of structural and expressive distillation. Kahn, Breuer, and Johnson develop a new grammar to refine and unify a received,

SCULPTURE GALLERY, Philip Johnson, New Canaan, Connecticut (1970)

but previously colloquial, language of poured concrete, panel-
ized facades, and steel-frame construction. The Guggenheim,
Tokyo, and Berlin established that the "high game" of abstraction in architecture would be played out in institutions for art,
while the next generation codified the rules of that game.

MINIMALLY INVASIVE?

(S)ome of the symptoms as to what's going on in the area
of museum building are reflected somewhat in Philip Johnson's
underground museum, which in a sense buries abstract kinds of art
in another kind of abstraction, so that it really becomes a negation
of a negation. I am all for this kind of distancing and removal. [56]
ROBERT SMITHSON

A MUCH LESS REPORTED, but far more radical alteration of
New Haven's skyline than the renovation of Kahn's art gallery was
the 2006 demolition of the New Haven Veterans Memorial Coliseum by Kevin Roche and John Dinkeloo, imploded just weeks
before the YUAG was reopened.[59] I actually liked Roche and Dinkeloo's long-condemned coliseum — a mammoth, hovering cage
of decomposing CorTen steel on New Haven's most prominent
southern edge — for its resemblance to Constant's New Babylon,
and once imagined a student project hanging off a corner of its
cantilevered parking levels. Completed in 1972, the coliseum
had been ill-starred since its opening, structurally suspect and
never well attended, but it at least wore its misguided ambitions proudly. The coliseum and adjoining Knights of Columbus
Tower, also by Roche and Dinkeloo, spoke much more eloquently
to nearby Interstate 95 than lowly New Haven, and delivered a
message without compromise: Utopia Now, Blight Be Damned.
    Sadly, many of the architects who cut their teeth in the '60s
and '70s were undone later by the criticism they endured for their
doctrinaire simplicity in those years. Before his coliseum, Kevin

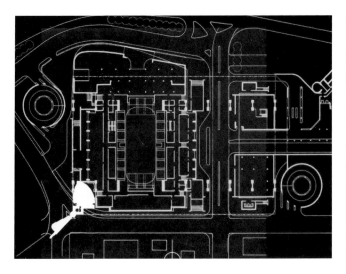

MONITOR STATION HUNG FROM NEW HAVEN COLISEUM, Joe Day, student project, Yale College (1988)

Roche also designed the stringent Oakland Museum (1961–68), in which a city block's worth of exhibition space is completely subsumed underground, below terraced landscape trays. Both projects show Roche developing a voice apart from Eero Saarinen, whose practice he inherited on Saarinen's untimely death in 1961, and within an emergent Minimalist cohort. But after completing the Temple of Dendur (1976) at the Metropolitan Museum of Art, a project that finally delivered some epic space and light into post-WWII gallery space, Roche too felt the pull of postmodernity. As the house architect for the Metropolitan Museum of Art in the 1980s and '90s, Roche churned out a slew of donor-driven pavilions cut to suit their benefactors. Both the restoration of Kahn's tiny museum at Yale and the demolition of its enormous cousin by Roche and Dinkeloo reflect not only the fickle tastes and rabid appetites of US urban dwellers, but also the rising lot of Minimalism in architectural discourse. Kahn's building is now canonized for being Minimalist *avant la lettre*; the coliseum might have paid for its authors' later apostasies against that sensibility.[60]

The generation that separates Kahn from Roche and Din-keloo, and the twenty years between the Yale Art Gallery and both his Center for British Art and their New Haven coliseum, matter a great deal. They bracket America's first major surge of post-WWII urban expansion. By the 1970s, Minimalist architecture had become the default in large-scale American building. Kahn's first gallery posed an ideal of radical austerity for new American civic buildings, simultaneously modest and monumental; the next crop of American architects dispensed with understatement and mag-nified basic forms to gargantuan ends. Some would argue that the only shortcoming of Kahn's museum was the unintended and unforeseeable inspiration it held for his many acolytes like Roche, I.M. Pei, Philip Johnson, and others. But architectural ideas almost always decline in refinement as they increase in scale, and the coliseum amplified its Kahnian features — sheer brick fascia, hovering floor plates — to a point of radical difference. The archi-tectural "collage" comprising most US cities usually combines the prototypical and the overplayed, and it is the latter, as often as not, that has a more formative role in urban life.

In fact, Connecticut proved a surprisingly fertile testing ground for Minimalist architecture. Kahn's museums, Roche and Dinkeloo's coliseum, SOM's corporate campus for GE, Philip Johnson's many pavilions in New Canaan, as well as Breuer's megalithic towers for Perelli and Yale all look closer now to the works of Donald Judd, Robert Morris, and Frank Stella than they do to the contemporary compositions of the CIAM architects or the emergent New York Five. For all their differences, one sees in both the Architects' Collaborative and the NY5 a common resort

NEW HAVEN COLISEUM, Kevin Roche, New Haven, California (1972)
Opposite: OAKLAND MUSEUM OF CALIFORNIA, Kevin Roche, Oakland, California (1969)

to formal habits of pre-WWII modernity, and in particular, strategies of collage. The Connecticut Minimalists, by contrast, are
no longer composing their way to a pleasing "balance of form,"
but are instead distilling their discipline, architecture, to what the
postwar art world might see as its formal prerequisites — structure, enclosure, surface — and living with the stark results.

All of this might not amount to more than a regional preoccupation — except that it was immediately exported. Connecticut
incubated a new post-WWII formalism in architecture akin to the
new painterly formalism pioneered in Long Island in the 1950s,
and as was the case for Abstract Expressionism, the effects of
those Minimalist forays may have been felt more profoundly at a
distance. A third museum by Kahn, in Fort Worth, Texas, signaled
a shift from urban to suburban circumstances, and from unified
to expandable notions of Minimalist architecture. Connecticut
played a central role in product-testing Minimalism in architecture, but Western states would host the rollout.

02.REPEAT

15 UNTITLED WORKS IN CONCRETE,
Donald Judd, 1980–1984, detail

WITH A NEWLY SIMPLIFIED architectural vocabulary, institutions of constraint and display began to multiply quickly in the
1970s. Many economies of scale were achieved through repetition
of spaces and structural elements in a single building, as well as
the massive expansions in networks of exhibition and discipline
as standardized forms were replicated in many locations. Serial
organizations become ends in their own right in "telephone-
pole" prisons, where any number of cellblocks are strung along
an extruded service corridor, and in survey museums that extend
in all directions to house ever more curatorial specializations.

I □ JUDD

A good building, such as the Kimbell Museum, looks the way a Greek temple in a new colony must have looked amongst the huts....The temple looks like civilization. The Kimbell is civilization in the wasteland of Fort Worth.[61]

DONALD JUDD

Don't mess with Texas

A VOLUME OF LOUIS KAHN'S work and writing, interleafed with a note from the Kimbell Museum, rests today on Donald Judd's kitchen table. Preserved for posterity in The Block, Judd's compound in Marfa, Texas, the scene divides one of two hangars that Judd converted into gallery spaces for his earlier work. Another identical hangar includes more exhibition space and a library for his 5,000-volume collection of books, and a nine-foot adobe wall bounds the square complex. Truly a cloister of Minimalism, Judd's residential retreat acts simultaneously as a repository of the artist's interests — forty feet of shelving devoted to Native American tribes and modern architecture, each roughly twice what he allotted to contemporary art — and a clear demarcation of the increasingly stringent limits he set for producing his own

KIMBELL ART MUSEUM, Louis I. Kahn, Fort Worth, Texas (1972)

work. Judd's Block, like all of his holdings in Marfa, manages to be both monastic in its rigors and somehow decadent in its mania for simple geometries.

Though The Block opened to visitors only in 2006 after Judd's death, his nearby studios, composed of a dozen barracks and other structures on a defunct Air Force base, have welcomed pilgrims since 1986. The fact that a west Texas town with a population of 2,121 owes its current welfare to a cycle of art-worldly hajj to Judd's retreats, and now to many smaller arts venues, is an irony not lost on the locals. That cosmopolitan frisson deepens with the realization that much of Judd's former military installation had been built in the '40s to house WWII prisoners of war. Stenciled signs in German, advising prisoners to stay in line, still adorn walls in the sheds now holding Judd's array of aluminum boxes.

Though many of Judd's container-like constructs could be likened to holding spaces, he seems to take on that theme and scale most directly as you leave his complex in Marfa. Running along the eastern edge of the Chinati parcel are fifteen discreet structures composed of open-sided "cells" of roughly 8'x8'x16" constructed entirely of 12" thick concrete slabs and spaced at 100-meter intervals. Approaching the Chinati from the south on Route 67, these *15 Untitled Works in Concrete* lead to the Marfa town line, and to a federal Border Control station.

In almost every respect — in their linearity and materiality, repetition and variation — these cellular structures offer an exacting microcosm of carceral Minimalism. The many nuances and scales of variation within this and Judd's other serial constructions spur one's search through Marfa: Are all the barracks identical? When did Judd shift from color to structure to encode differences in his series? What rules govern the changes from one aluminum or concrete composition to the next, given that all are of a common wall thickness, and all reach common outer dimensions? Is Marfa really like any other town in Texas?

A similar litany of questions structures this chapter. How and why did we build so many cultural and correctional institutions so quickly in the last quarter of the 20th century? What architectural "economies of scale" made such multiplication possible, and by what internal variations are these buildings to be judged effective or interesting? Finally — and this is a question that arises from seeing so many machine-produced art objects by Judd, Dan Flavin, and John Chamberlain in a rural setting so devoid of industry — how did Late Modern prisons and museums become the postindustrial "factories" and "warehouses" of late 20th century lament?

The Lone Star State is home to a disproportionate number of groundbreaking holding spaces for art and people. In addition to the Kimbell Museum and the new Modern Art Museum of Fort Worth by Tadao Ando, Houston has examples by Mies van der Rohe, Gunnar Birkerts, and Rafael Moneo — and Dallas and Austin are close behind. One could argue that there is even a "Texas typology" in contemporary art museums, based on standardized structural bays, modular skylighting, and pat-

ISNTALLATION OF ALUMINUM WORKS, Donald Judd, Marfa, Texas (1984)

terns of linear repetition. Through linear repetitions of another sort, Texas also now leads the country in numbers incarcerated. George W. Bush's four-year term as governor marked the apex of the Texas prison boom, and the state is now the nexus of a peculiar internationalism, one in which foreign architects routinely design innovative buildings for art in our most aspirant cities, while its contractors, such as El Paso-based NH Hunt Justice Group, export American prison know-how abroad. With Arizona, Texas is also on the front line of immigration-related detention.

Not unlike a Dallas debutante sent on her Grand Tour, we will need to visit New York, with stops in London and Paris, to put these local developments in proper perspective.

SUITS AND BOOTS — OIL MONEY, INSTANT CULTURE, AND SWIFT JUSTICE

On drugs, anyone who pushes gets life in prison. And I mean life — no matter what amount. No more of this plea bargaining, parole and probation.[62]
NELSON ROCKEFELLER, 1972

The giants of the art world were not remote deities to Nelson Rockefeller. Rather, they were more like gifted subjects whom a young nobleman admires and patronizes.[63]
JOE PERSICO

WITHOUT REALLY AIMING TO — and often while not on speaking terms with one another — three brothers initiated the explosive growth in both prisons and museums over the last forty years.

Developments in incarceration and exhibition were fitful between the end of WWII and 1970, but thereafter they accelerated rapidly and evenly in the United States, with politics priming the pump in both cases. On the one hand, a revolution in criminal sentencing virtually automated the imprisonment of far more people for far longer terms; on the other, subtle shifts in tax codes made it far easier for wealthy Americans (though, oddly, not artists) to support cultural institutions. Three Rockefeller brothers drove a decade's worth of precedent-setting legislation related to prisons and museums, from principle to nuance, at city, state, and federal levels.

Between 1930 and 1950, the Rockefeller heirs to Standard Oil took over the reins of New York cultural patronage from the Vanderbilt clan, whose fortune dated to the original Great Lakes shipping cartels and Manhattan's first real estate boom. The shift from a Gilded to Glistening Age in New York's noblesse oblige was personified by Abby Rockefeller, who co-founded and largely underwrote the Museum of Modern Art for its first decades. However, it was three of her five sons — John, Nelson, and David Jr. — who ensured the hyper-expansion of both corrections and collections in the last quarter of the 20th century.

The criminal side of this story is easier to tell than the cultural. "Rockefeller Republicans" are considered the lost centrists of that party now, but those urbane GOP stalwarts were prescient and hard-line in their "law and order" positions. Few aspects of "Rockefellerism" have proven as politically hardy and broadly appealing as the idea of mandatory minimums. In the 1980s and '90s, Republicans of all stripes, joined by most centrist Democrats including Bill Clinton and even New Labor "Blairites" in the United Kingdom, pushed for harsher sentences and less negotiable terms for almost all offenses, but especially for drug-related convictions.

As governor of New York, Nelson Rockefeller oversaw the passage of the so-called Rockefeller Drug Laws in the first half of the 1970s, a series of statutes that established draconian terms for drug-related charges, the precursors for other state and then federal sentencing guidelines.[64] The tenfold increase in US prisoners between 1970 and 2000, and the myriad facilities to house them, have no more obvious point of origin than the Rockefeller

MUSEUM OF MODERN ART, Philip L. Goodwin and Edward Durell Stone, New York, New York (1939)

Drug Laws. As the quote above suggests, Governor Rockefeller was not just signing his name to laws coined by more reactionary aides — he demanded the legislation. As Rockefeller speechwriter Joseph Persico recounts in *The Imperial Rockefeller*, Nelson Rockefeller's inner circle was stunned when the governor delivered his Life-Without-Escape ultimatum at his State of the State address on January 3, 1973, and then appalled in May when he browbeat the New York Legislature into passing the 1973 New York State Drug Law, which attached a life sentence to trafficking in "hard drugs" including LSD, heroin, and amphetamines, and curtailed all plea bargaining, parole, and commuted sentencing.[65]

The motivation for Governor Rockefeller's hard line on controlled substances turns out to be personal. After a close family friend, William Fine, then president of Bonwit Teller department stores, struggled with a son's addiction, Rockefeller suggested to the aggrieved father that he tour other countries in search of the most effective policies to thwart drug use. In Japan, Fine found a prototype for "zero-tolerance" laws that removed drug users from society indefinitely to prison clinics, and drug sellers to prison for life. He failed to note how rarely such measures were taken

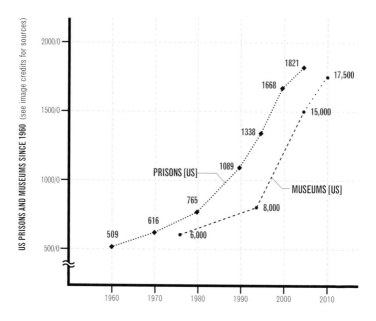

US PRISONS AND MUSEUMS SINCE 1960 (see image credits for sources)

in Japan, where incarceration rates were, and are, a fraction of ours. What would be widely interpreted in the United States as a pretext for mass incarceration could have been read instead as an argument for the selective, if legally over-expedient, hospitalization of addicts. Speechwriter Persico recounts how Rockefeller kept Fine from sharing his advice with Ronald Reagan, then governor of California, at a fundraiser in 1972, and concludes, "Thus the law under which thousands of narcotics cases would be tried in the courts of a great state had been something of a family affair, a neighborly improvisation without the deadening hand of over-sophisticated professionals."

Nelson's oldest and youngest brothers, John and David Jr., on the other hand, helped draft at least two tax policy changes that altered the way Americans, and especially wealthy families like the Rockefellers, could support cultural institutions with tax-free gifts. The Tax Reform Act of 1969, ushered through Congress by John D. Rockefeller, went so far as to make cultural giving *to other nations* tax deductible, a feat that led the French to award President Richard Nixon the Legion of Honor in recognition of American donations to the refurbishment of Versailles.[66] The Reform Act made even more generous provisions for US museums, making a greater share of their revenues tax exempt and expanding the provisions for donation. These changes to the tax code effectively privatized much of the Great Society cultural funding that Kennedy and Johnson had enacted through the creation of the NEA and NEH in 1965.

Another salient innovation for American cities was the solution that David Rockefeller Jr. and his fellow MoMA trustees arrived at for the development of Museum Tower, a 44-story condominium development in the air rights over MoMA, designed by Cesar Pelli and completed in 1984. In order to circumvent the non-profit requirement for the museum below, lawyers for the MoMA trustees drafted legislation for The Trust for Cultural Resources of the City of New York, which allowed for-profit development to hold nonprofit "tenants" in trust. MoMA now rents its premises for $1 a year from the Museum Tower Corporation, and receives a share of the profits generated by leases and sales in the tower.[67] Prefiguring many "stealth" towers to come in the 1980s, Pelli's tower retreats from the street and from the exhibition spaces below. As David Jr. observed in his 2003 memoir, "Inside the museum one is totally unaware of the tower rising over it."[68]

Neither could David, Nelson, nor John Rockefeller have been aware how many prisons and museums would rise according to the policies they framed in the 1970s and '80s. Between 1975 and 2005, the number of both institutions in the United States *tripled*, with a jump from 616 to 1,821 in prisons and jails and a leap from an estimated 6,000 to 18,000 museums. As prison literature specialist Bruce Franklin noted in 2000, "Since 1976, we have been building on average one prison every week." By the same math, a new museum could have opened *every day* of that quarter century.[69]

Two tendencies of post-Rockefeller institutions are worth noting: their verticality and their westerly bias. In Chapter 05, we will look more specifically at the vertical turn that the MoMA tower and a concurrent series of Metropolitan Correctional Centers brought to American inner cities. Given the source of their fortune in wildcatting and oil exploration, it's perhaps appropriate that the effects of Rockefeller politicking were more immediate and resoundingly felt in the West. Though Nelson Rockefeller didn't let Reagan steal his thunder, California quickly followed New York's model in establishing mandatory minimum sentencing benchmarks, and proved far more scrupulous about enforcing them than New York in the 1970s and 1980s. Governor George W. Bush led Texas into the fray of mass incarceration in the 1990s, stiffening penalties and issuing prison construction bonds. Texas had a staggering 236% increase in its prison population between 1990 and 2004, recently overtaking California for total inmates confined.[70] Sun Belt cities also turned out to be the favored location for major new cultural philanthropy, especially for donors — often other oilmen — who wanted to express their generosity in new, self-named, ground-up monuments.

BATTLE OF THE SKYLIGHTS

As the medieval cleric saw signs of regeneration in the intense local competition to erect the most spectacular basilica, we may perhaps interpret the simultaneous emergence of a striking number of outstanding temples of culture throughout America, but especially in the Lone Star State, as a sign that something extraordinary is happening.[71]

BARBARA ROSE

Paradoxically, the Menil Collection with its great serenity, its calm, and its understatement, is far more 'modern,' scientifically speaking, than Beaubourg. The technological appearance of Beaubourg is parody. The technology used for the Menil Collection is even more advanced (in its structures, materials, systems of climate control), but it is not flaunted.[72]

RENZO PIANO

I WAS THRILLED when I saw Kahn's monograph at the Block, but also reminded that Kahn was, at least while he lived, almost a secret — long respected by architects and then artists, but unknown to their supporters. As museum director Aaron Betsky pointed out to me recently, Kahn himself had almost no influence on or connections to donors or patrons of the arts when he was alive. Kahn's influence on museum design, even his securing of museum commissions, flowed almost entirely through fellow architects, such as Philip Johnson, Philip Goodwin, and I.M. Pei, who often gave him jobs they had won for themselves, and who popularized his work through their own. For that matter, Kahn showed scant interest in the art of his time.

Kahn's Kimbell is nevertheless a critical beachhead between Minimalist art and Late Modern architecture. Composed completely of nearly identical barrel vaults, run side-by-side and segmented to provide entry and a relief of small courtyards, the Kimbell neatly dispenses with both the radial logic of older

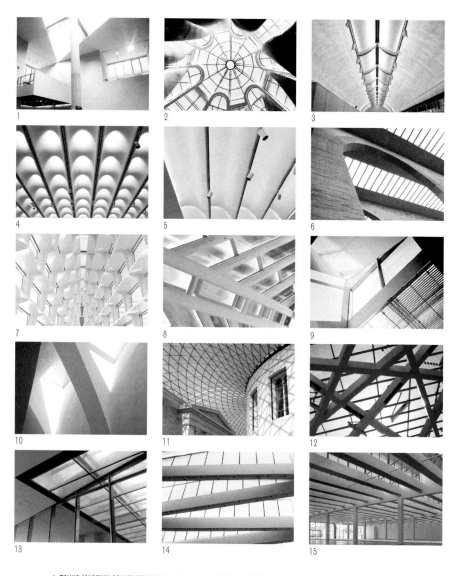

1. TOKYO MUSEUM OF WESTERN ART, Le Corbusier (1963) 2. GUGGENHEIM MUSEUM, Frank Lloyd Wright (1959)
3. KIMBELL ART MUSEUM, Louis I. Kahn (1972) 4. HIGH MUSEUM OF ART, Renzo Piano and Richard Meier (1983)
5. MENIL FOUNDATION, Piano (1987) 6. MUSEUM OF ROMAN ART, Raphael Moneo (1984) 7. MILWAUKEE ART MUSEUM,
Santiago Calatrava (1994) 8. SAN FRANCISCO MUSEUM OF MODERN ART, Mario Botta (1995) 9. MUSEUM OF
MODERN ART, New York, Yoshio Taniguchi (1997) 10. KIASMA MUSEUM OF CONTEMPORARY ART, Steven Holl (1998)
11. BRITISH MUSEUM GREAT COURT, Foster and Partners (2000) 12. JEWISH MUSEUM BERLIN, Daniel Libeskind (2001)
13. SEOUL NATIONAL UNIVERSITY MUSEUM, OMA (2006) 14. BLANTON MUSEUM, Kallman McKinnell Wood 15. BROAD
MUSEUM OF CONTEMPORARY ART, Piano (2007)

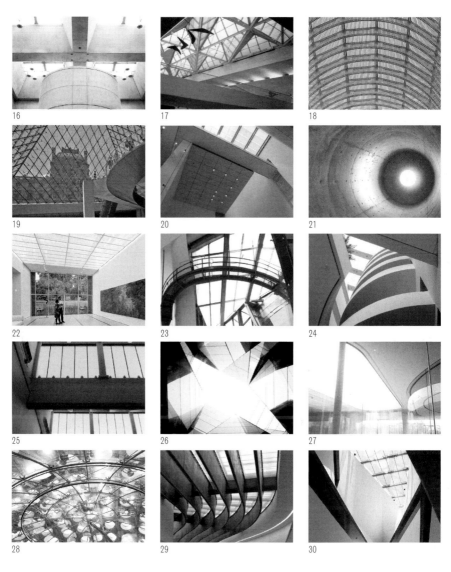

16. **YALE CENTER FOR BRITISH ART,** Kahn (1974) 17. **EAST WING, NATIONAL GALLERY,** I.M. Pei (1978)
18. **WEST WING, MUSEUM OF FINE ARTS BOSTON,** Foster (1981) 19. **LOUVRE PYRAMID,** Pei (1989) 20. **CARRE D'ART,**
Foster (1993) 21. **CHIKATSU ASUKA HISTORICAL MUSEUM,** Ando (1994) 22. **BEYELER MUSEUM,** Piano (1997)
23. **GUGGENHEIM MUSEUM BILBAO,** Gehry Partners (1997) 24. **AROS MUSEUM,** Schmidt Hammer Lassen (1997)
25. **DIA: BEACON, RIGIO GALLERIES,** Robert Irwin/OpenOffice (2003) 26. **BARCELONA FORUM,** Herzog & de Meuron (2004)
27. **GLASS PAVILION AT THE TOLEDO MUSEUM OF ART,** SANAA (2006) 28. **CALIFORNIA SCIENCE CENTER,** Piano (2008)
29. **MAAXI MUSEUM,** Zaha Hadid (2009) 30. **TEL AVIV MUSEUM OF ART,** Tel Aviv (2011)

Minimalist Museums after Kahn

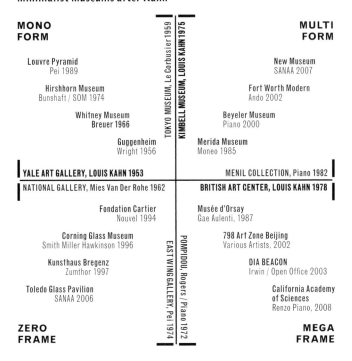

MONO FORM — **MULTI FORM**

ZERO FRAME — **MEGA FRAME**

Louvre Pyramid
Pei 1989

Hirshhorn Museum
Bunshaft / SOM 1974

Whitney Museum
Breuer 1966

Guggenheim
Wright 1956

New Museum
SANAA 2007

Fort Worth Modern
Ando 2002

Beyeler Museum
Piano 2000

Merida Museum
Moneo 1985

YALE ART GALLERY, LOUIS KAHN 1953 — MENIL COLLECTION, Piano 1982

NATIONAL GALLERY, Mies Van Der Rohe 1962 — BRITISH ART CENTER, LOUIS KAHN 1978

Fondation Cartier
Nouvel 1994

Corning Glass Museum
Smith Miller Hawkinson 1996

Kunsthaus Bregenz
Zumthor 1997

Toledo Glass Pavilion
SANAA 2006

Musée d'Orsay
Gae Aulenti, 1987

798 Art Zone Beijing
Various Artists, 2002

DIA BEACON
Irwin / Open Office 2003

California Academy
of Sciences
Renzo Piano, 2008

TOKYO MUSEUM, Le Corbusier 1959

KIMBELL MUSEUM, LOUIS KAHN 1975

POMPIDOU, Rogers / Piano 1972

EAST WING GALLERY, Pei 1974

museums and the gridded expanse of most modern ones. Donald Judd singled out the Kimbell as the only piece of American architecture worthy of the term, and the affinity that Kahn shares with Judd and his peers in terms of the orchestration of space through repetitive geometry is self-evident.

If the Yale Art Gallery and the Center for British Art rely on the blank plane and neutral frame for their power, respectively, Louis Kahn's Kimbell Museum is a celebration of the extruded, repetitive bay. A more primitive building in many respects than either of his museums in New Haven, the Kimbell was nonetheless far more broadly and immediately influential. By distilling the gallery spaces down to a single, sky-lit and human scale extrusion, the Kimbell offered something neither of the Yale museums did: a serial logic for expansion. Although Judd saw the Kimbell in Greek terms — it is beautifully sited and composed — it was its Roman pragmatism that made it a systemic model for so many museums so quickly. For many art collectors, the Kimbell's synthesis of classical forms and modern finishes made it possible to imagine dignified, privatized monuments for contemporary art.

Though a common opposition is drawn between minimalist and "maximalist" museum architecture — boxes and baubles — one can trace the arrival of the latter from the former. Formalism in museum design descended first from a consideration of light: specifically, the challenge of illuminating works of art with natural light without direct exposure of those works to the sun's damaging rays.

When Kahn substituted longitudinal slivers of glazing for the keystone of his barrel vaults at the Kimbell, his substitution of light for structure would quickly escalate in the '70s and '80s to include all varieties of clerestory protrusions and intrusions. I.M Pei's East Wing for the National Gallery and Kahn's Center for British Art at Yale were both considered astoundingly expensive buildings, driven by custom skylights and the pristine concrete husks needed to support them. Arata Isozaki portrayed LA's MoCA as nothing but a landscape of pyramidal light wells rising above the datum of Grand Street. The argument could be extended to lower portions of a building as well. Richard Meier and Aldo Rossi, among many others, used elaborately shaded section studies to reveal how staggered wall-planes were in fact elaborate, exactingly calibrated light filters: walls stay blank, neutral, uniform; light, and then *form,* erupt above.

A vast (and surprisingly Latin and Asian) alliance of architects extends Kahn's legacy to the present day. Tadao Ando's recent Modern Art Museum of Fort Worth, catty-corner to the Kimbell, and his Pulitzer Foundation for the Arts in St. Louis read almost as inspired sequels to the Kahn original. Aldo Rossi and Rafael Moneo head a long list of Italian and Spanish adherents, but the most prolific of these is Renzo Piano, whose current popularity springs from two contradictory projects, his Centre Pompidou of 1975 and the Menil Pavilion of 1981–86. In the latter he paid penance for many of the perceived sins of the former, working from inside out and focusing his attention on the display of art rather than the generation of spectacle. The wave-shaped reflectors that hover over and modulate the light entering the Menil opened an entire cottage industry of skylight design for art (though they do not completely protect paintings from ultra-violet damage). In recent interviews, Piano claims that the Menil rather than the Pompidou set the pattern for his career, what he describes as a constant striving for better spaces of viewership. Museum trustees flock to him for this latter-day humility in the face of art; architects remember him for rivaling art in the Pompidou.

THE NEW NEWNESS

The order is not rationalistic or underlying but is simply order, like that of continuity, one thing after another.[73]
DONALD JUDD

THROUGH THE 1600s AND 1700s, London's Fleet and Newgate prisons set standards of infamy, persecution, and lawlessness that had no sequel until recently. The first and second Newgates, both eventually torched by London's rioting poor, offer an interesting scalar comparison with Louis Kahn's museums, and cautionary lesson in penal "progress."

The "Old" Newgate dated from 1630 and was in fact the oldest prison in London, shoehorned into a massive gothic gate through an older inner ring of the city wall. More than 300 debtors, felons, thieves, and thugs were packed away at a time, along with their families and livestock. Turnkeys and highwaymen ruled the various wards for profit, demanded bed rent (each shared by as many as five), fleeced and preyed on younger inmates. Hang-

THE GRAVEYARD, New Newgate Prison, George Dance the younger, London, England (1768)

ings, routinely performed atop the jail for spectacle, had to be moved inside when the plague in 1752 forced keepers to replace the gallows with a windmill to drive bellows that in turn pumped a modicum of fresh air into the fetid wards below. Once burned in 1660 and twice closed by famine, Old Newgate was finally abandoned in the 1760s.

Designed for an open site near Old Newgate by George Dance the Younger in 1768, the second or "New" Newgate rode a tide of reformers' goodwill. Orderly rows of cells surrounded three open-air courtyards and allowed inmates to be separated by age, gender, and seriousness of crime — major signs of progress in the eyes of Christian activists driving for new, more monastic, or "penitential" settings. All, however, was not about reformation. The rough-hewn arches and long, oppressive lines of Dance's New Newgate were based explicitly on the hallucinatory scenography of G.B. Piranesi's *Carcere*, or *Prisons*, printed in 1761. Though the cellblocks were emptied and incinerated in the Gordon Riots of 1780, the husk of Dance's Newgate was preserved until 1902, ostensibly to remind Londoners to behave.

The New Newgate and the Kimbell differ from their predecessors most in their serial arrangements. Linear galleries and cellblocks boast the greatest spatial efficiency, in terms of numbers of inmates held or works of art on display. Behind its sublime facade, Dance's more "modern" Newgate is composed entirely of single-loaded corridors — not quite cellblocks, but close. In 19th century prisons devised soon afterward, a proto-

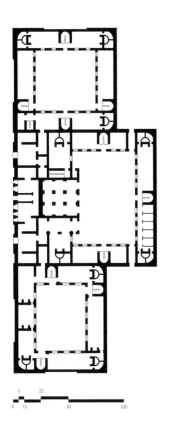
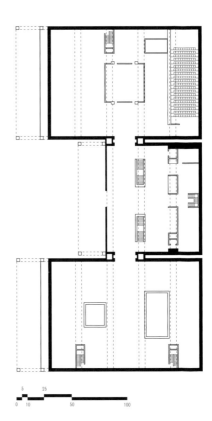

5   25
0 10   50   100

5   25
0 10   50   100

typical cell design is first mirrored, then multiplied into longer and longer cellblocks. As is the case in Kahn's Kimbell, a single well-resolved section can yield a limitless extrusion, bound in its length by managerial, rather than structural, demands.

For François Truffaut's lovers in *Jules et Jim*, sprinting through the Louvre's long galleries in 1962, as for guards taken hostage at Attica in 1970, the precise extent of a single, crowded wing of an institution can matter quite a bit. It also matters how linear elements are combined in the larger composition of an institution. Much of the typological evolution of reformative prisons, beginning with the Penitentiary Competition of 1782, has explored this question exclusively. No less an architect than John Soane proposed two model designs in the competition, one for male convicts and another for women, both essays in linear cell-block arrangement. Sixty years later, the Model Prison at Pentonville by Joshua Jebb established a fanning template still in effect for much of the former Commonwealth.

Early in the last century, the "telephone-pole" plan — with parallel rows of cellblocks joined by a long spine of circulation — became the organization default in prison layout. Although their configurations varied little, "telephone-pole" designs held a generally Cartesian appeal for architects, and a more specifically Corbusian potential for vertical extrusion into rows of orderly modernist slabs. Many of the most cinematically notorious prisons are Californian versions of this type, such as those at Folsom and Vacaville, which are easy for film crews to reach, and appear to extend and repeat infinitely on screen.

Though telephone-pole arrangements were common in mid-century prisons (and remain so in hospitals and housing developments), radial organizations turned out to be the more efficient template for prisons, while courtyards favor museums. Radial or "hub-and-spoke" prisons consolidate staff and oversight at their centers and hold inmates in each branch, thus limiting the need for officers to circumnavigate the facility. Governor Rockefeller and other officials bear considerable blame for the riots at Attica in 1971, but the prison's four-square plan, with long stretches between guard stations and enormous yards ripe for inmate takeover, didn't help. For museums, by contrast, running lengths of gallery around shared courtyards has the virtue of a more "collegial" atmosphere for curators and visitors, and greater variety in the direction and quality of light entering the galleries. The Louvre and the Eastern State Penitentiary are early realizations of this differential in type, and the Met and Leavenworth more recent examples. That isn't to say the opposite isn't still often built: the courtyard prison in Muret, France, completed in 1965, established a monastic paradigm now common

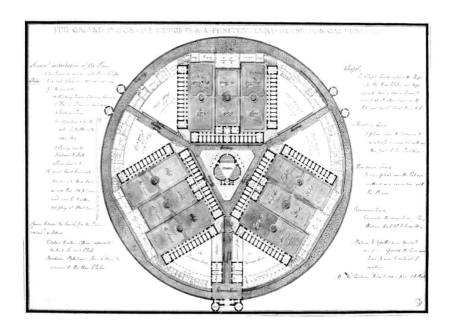

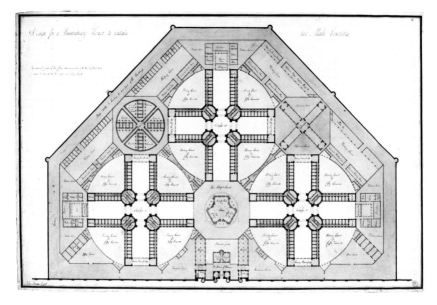

in much of the European Union, especially the Netherlands, and the success of Frank Gehry's radial *parti* for the 1997 Guggenheim Bilbao may lead to more along similar lines.

Cast in any pattern, linear, serially organized prisons and museums underscore a basic tenet of institutional planning: *sometimes, nothing succeeds like more of the same.*

FREEDOM FACTORIES

The first sighting of the Pompidou Center in the late 1970s may rank with the moon landing among the epiphanies of our time.... In a century when the engines of both education and the post-industrial economy are beginning to liberate the middle class from the suffocating insularity of low-paid, unskilled labor, the arts have become common property. The enduring legacy of the Pompidou Center is this: that it signified this fact before it became common knowledge.[74]

DOUGLAS DAVIS

The Men's block feels as if it's a machine.[75]

BBC REPORT ON FLEURY-MÉROGIS PRISON, FRANCE, THE LARGEST PRISON IN EUROPE

A RICH LITERATURE is devoted to the mechanization of punishment, and an almost as extensive one bemoans the industrialization of culture. In both cases, the leading authors were French, and of the *soixante-huit* generation. While the counterculture protested industrial-strength modernity, Europe's first mega-prison was completed in 1968 on the periphery of Paris, and an equally record-setting museum complex was imagined in the next year for its center.

Fleury-Mérogis Prison and the Centre Pompidou, which would open in 1977, are the largest institutions of their kind in Europe. Designed to hold a then-unprecedented 3,000 men and

81

FLEURY-MÉROGIS PRISON Aerial View; Guillaume Gillet, Fleury-Mérogis, France (1964)

Opposite: CENTRE POMPIDOU, Renzo Piano, Richard Rogers, Gianfranco Franchini, Paris, France (1977)

women in a tessellated network of tripod wings bounded by a hexagonal ring wall, Fleury-Mérogis is, from above, the most impressively space-age correctional composition ever realized, a dystopian homage to Marcel Breuer's UNESCO master plan, on one hand, and the Starship Enterprise on the other. It is also, by general agreement, an abject peneological failure, with perhaps the sole virtue that it tends to consolidate almost all French prison scandals within a single institution. In the 2008 BBC coverage cited above, the warden of Fleury-Mérogis, now bursting with 3,800 inmates, counsels then Justice Secretary Jack Straw in Britain against his plans for three "Titan" super-jails, each to hold 2,500. Those remain on hold.

The Pompidou, by contrast, enjoys cycles of popularity and lament. At this point, the Pompidou has considerable competition within the fabric of Paris. I.M. Pei's glazed pyramid at the Louvre reverses Piano and Rogers' nearby Pompidou exactly, and in terms at least as technologically extravagant. Piano's escalators and space-frame lift Parisians up over their city; Pei's skylight illuminates the catacombs of a nation. The Pompidou echoes the switchback stairs in Schinkel's Altes Museum in Berlin, while the

pyramid alludes to Boullée and Ledoux's primal geometries. Both "shock" the antique city, but by updating architectures of empire rather than subverting them.

Perhaps the most articulate reflections on the Beaubourg Effect are by Jean Baudrillard, who gave name to that phenomenon in 1982, and Sanford Kwinter's recent *Requiem for the City at the End of the Millennium*, which he opens with a recollection of Gordon Matta-Clark's *Conical Intersect*, cut into a building about to be demolished for the Pompidou. Baudrillard's first rendering of a "museum effect," however, remains bracing:

"Beaubourg is a monument of social deterrence.... That's the supreme irony of Beaubourg: the masses rush there not because they slaver for this culture which has been denied them for centuries, but because, for the first time, they have a chance to participate, en masse, in this immense work of mourning for a culture they have always detested. If, therefore, we denounce Beaubourg as a cultural mystification of the masses, the misunderstanding is total. The masses fall on Beaubourg to enjoy this execution....

And two pages later:

> "(I)n presenting an idealized miniature model, they hope to produce an accelerated gravitational pull, an automatic agglutination of culture as an automatic agglutination of the masses. The process is the same: the nuclear chain reaction, or, the specular operation of white magic."[76]

Baudrillard's concluding nuclear analogy is nicely telling. In France, the fascination with mega-scale mechanization also marked a turn from petrol to fissile power. Fleury-Mérogis and the Centre Pompidou were erected in tandem with France's "nuclear embrace" after the oil crisis of 1974, a shift that today accounts for 78% of the electricity in France, via fifty-eight reactors (most built by Westinghouse). Though most US politics still reflect a post-Rockefeller landscape of wealth and political will based on resource extraction, much of the developed world hopes to move to other energy models, or in the case of much of Asia and the Middle East, up the ladder of consumption. The "New Economy" shift in metaphor from assembly line to turbine is worth bearing in mind as we will look next at a countervailing, and more concentric, tendency in prison and museum design in the post-WWII period in which rotation, rather than repetition, animates the logic of institutions.

■ OBSERVER   ▨ OBSERVED

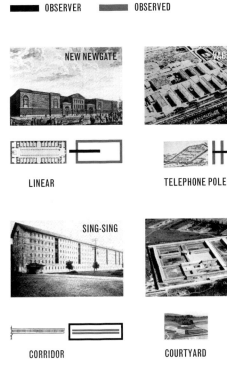

NEW NEWGATE

LINEAR

VACAVILLE

TELEPHONE POLE

270

PODULAR

SING-SING

CORRIDOR

MURET

COURTYARD

LANCASTER

CAMPUS

PRESIDIO

PANOPTIC

LEVENWORTH

RADIAL

MDC

TOWER

↑ 1800s - EXTRUSION   ↑ 1900s - PATTERN   ↑ 2000s - AGGREGATION

Common Prison Partis

POST-MINIMAL

Chapters 03, Rotate, and 04, Proliferate, ask how effective Minimalist strategies of simplification proved, and note a "turning of the tables" in exhibition and incarceration from object to subject, and viewer to viewed. Post-Minimalist strategies shifted both the nature and rationale of incarceration and exhibition, fostering an even more accelerated proliferation of both. Chapter 03 examines how we have consolidated the tasks of surveillance and exhibition into single, concentric volumes after the models of Jeremy Bentham's Panopticon and Frank Lloyd Wright's

Guggenheim, respectively. This reassessment led to an array of podular prisons and nominal "centers" for contemporary art that ask to be read as templates for personal and collective transformation, rather than mere institutions of containment. Central here are the "easy" spaces and flexible gestures that Frank Gehry pioneered in his trajectory from the repurposed industrial shells of his early Aerospace and Temporary Contemporary museums through the civic convolutions of Bilbao and later proposals.

03.ROTATE

Only in one field did Bentham ever sow the teeth of dragons.
He had the logician's passion for order and consistency; and he
wanted to impose his ideas of tidiness, not only upon thoughts
and words, but also upon things and institutions. In human affairs
the extreme of messiness is anarchy; the extreme of tidiness,
an army or a penitentiary.[77]

ALDOUS HUXLEY

To show that an architect could hold his own with the most
advanced representatives of the Romantic tradition, and on their
own ground, was the primary function of Wright's art museum, a
function that the Guggenheim's absurd and glorious form followed
to precise perfection.[78]

HERBERT MUSCHAMP

MULE CREEK STATE PRISON in California's Central Valley has the feel of a military garrison made permanent. As in most of California's prisons, many of the officers are recently decommissioned from the armed forces, and, as in war, the correlation between higher-risk assignments and promotion is clear. The few older guards at Mule Creek, remnants of a less martial time, bulge out of police-issue blues as they roam the medium security yards and the cafeteria; newer recruits sport wraparound glasses, paratrooper jumpsuits and many-pocketed and -padded vests as they quickstep like Navy SEALs to their assigned cellblocks.

A tour of Mule Creek concludes in the AD-SEG block, a lockdown unit for gang members held in "Administrative Segregation" from warring factions. The atmosphere is tense, but subdued. Guards eager for promotion vie for the assignment, it turns out, and one could easily imagine the team on duty performing special ops in Fallujah (to say nothing of better managing Abu Ghraib, though more on that later). Inmates can leave their cells only once a day, in shackles and triple-flanked by officers, so cleaning chores that usually fall to inmates are here performed by guards. The floors have a high sheen. We were allowed into the second-floor command center, which resembles a miniature air-traffic control tower. An interior three-sided glass window surveys all three sides of the square cellblock, while Lexan panels in the floor allow a top-down view of inmates entering the block through a sally port directly below. A horseshoe-shaped panel of red LEDs indicates which cells are open and which are locked. As we were leaving, an officer explains the organization of the unit in terms of its universal sightlines and concluded, "We were taught in training, these units are like the Pop-ticon."

If the shift from warrior to keeper now involves only slight wardrobe modifications for California prison guards, consider instead the complications that artist Matthew Barney endured as he completed his famous *Cremaster* film cycle by scaling the interior rings of the Guggenheim Museum in a kilt, bagpipes, wig, and prosthetic ears. Video of the climb shows Barney lunging onto the outer face of the ramping spiral and shimmying up to the next ring, and then the next. Though Barney's ascent underscores his distinctive sartorial instincts and physical prowess — he was a football recruit and J.Crew model as a Yale undergrad — it also reconfirms the centrality of the Guggenheim rotunda as the single most sacred space in the contemporary art world. Though the Tate Turbine Hall may now give it a run for its money, the privilege of producing site-specific work in the Guggenheim atrium often sums up an entire career: consider the emblematic installations of Ellsworth Kelly and Dan Flavin, or more recently, those of Daniel Buren and Zaha Hadid. The hagiographic potential of one's Guggenheim arrival was not lost on Barney — he went so far as including his precursors bodily in his own canonization. While Barney scaled the spiral, sculptor Richard Serra awaited at the coil's end, slinging Barney's signature material, frozen Vaseline, as he, Serra, once had molten lead.

Dress codes and casting seem oddly relevant in many of today's museums and prisons, as if all parties were on display and costumed for their role. For this, perhaps we must thank Jeremy Bentham and Frank Lloyd Wright, the inventors of two distinctly tailored theaters-in-the-round: the Panopticon and the first Guggenheim. Both buildings foreground the act of viewing itself, as much as those on view, while staging in miniature all the dramas central to each of their disciplines. Both are transformative designs that, after marked controversy, altered the rules of the game for each field.

Jeremy Bentham struggled with the design of the Panopticon Prison from 1787 to 1798, and Frank Lloyd Wright fought to realize the Guggenheim Museum from 1943 until 1959, the year he died and the museum opened. In their time, both were regarded as eccentric projects, objects of obsession and folly for their authors. After developing a summary of panoptic or "all-seeing" principles for a Russian naval factory with his brother Samuel, Jeremy Bentham compromised his otherwise stellar intellectual reputation as an economist and philosopher in a long, bitter and

THE CREMASTER CYCLE
Installation at the Guggenheim, Matthew Barney (2003)

unsuccessful twenty-year campaign to see a Panopticon prison built in Britain. Correspondence between Wright and the Guggenheim Foundation reveal that Wright and his wife literally *gave their eyeteeth* to secure the commission, only to have the sixteen-year project picketed by the leading artists of the day on its inauguration.[79]

Both designs and their authors seem uniquely out of step with their respective times, at odds with contemporary notions of progress that they themselves sought so avidly to define and embody. The Guggenheim and Panopticon were experimental structures that have been treated as cautionary tales for most of their histories. Complaints about the Guggenheim persisted for thirty years, and it was at least that long after Bentham's death before a Panopticon was actually built — in the Netherlands. Far from vindicating Bentham, those first Dutch Panopticons, and

later ones in the United States and Cuba, were deemed failures of unusual cruelty to both inmates and their keepers.

After long periods of eclipse, however, both the Panopticon and the Guggenheim have surged back into fashion. In the 1970s, Michel Foucault and others resurrected the Panopticon as a template for critical thought and a prototype for contemporary prison design; the Guggenheim became a touchstone for its blurring of bounds between art and architecture and its inauguration of the museum as civic event. Their perceived "failures" — of the Panopticon as a modern penitentiary, and of the Guggenheim as a museum for modern painting — only compound the irony of their current popularity. The Panopticon and the Guggenheim bracket and defy most conventions of Modernism, and, in doing so, foreground crucial postmodern developments in both building types. As we will see, the Panopticon is the basis for the smaller, self-contained, and nonlinear cellblocks of "Podular" Direct and Indirect Supervision, the DNA of "New Generation" prisons.

The Guggenheim poses at least four hugely influential strategies for engaging contemporary art practices: its dramatic silhouette inaugurates the "signature museum"; its appropriation of Central Park reasserts the model of the cultural plaza; its interior spiral prefigures the prescriptive paths or "infotestines" of most contemporary exhibition design; and its rotunda, the first single-space distillation of the museum experience, foreshadows both the anything-goes formalism of Deconstruction as well as the many "readymade" museums of adaptive reuse. It is the last of these strategies that most clearly links the Guggenheim to the Panopticon, and its parallel feat of all-in-one incarceration.

Like a target or gearwheel, the plan of the Panopticon is composed of concentric and striated rings, varying in density and definition. An outer manifold of cells encircles a central viewing area, so that the focal points of surveillance all emanate from a single origin. At the perimeter, human beings are separated, framed, and doubly gridded for view by the rectangles of each cell opening and then by the crisscross grating of cell bars. At the center, an observer may take in every nuance of the surrounding tableau, while concealed from the incarcerated. Most commentators, architectural historian Robin Evans and Foucault prominent among them, have concentrated on the efficient subjugation of the inmates within the individual cells lining the outer ring of the institution. In each cubicle a single criminal pays a precisely calibrated price in time and activity for his crimes, under the omnipresent gaze of a nameless and shapeless overseer hidden in the central domain of the prison.

It has become a rote assumption in contemporary architecture that *program*, or the spatial allocation of functions, no longer drives design. Things can and do happen anywhere in most commercial buildings now, thanks to omnipresent electrical and plumbing services, continuous glazing and climate control, acoustically dampened floors and ceilings, and most of all, the open plan. The free-plan environmental evolution in work space has carried over into residential and retail design, where "loft-style" and "big-box" are the latest wall-free formats, but stalled to some degree in major public amenities such as stadiums and terminals, which still have to deliver a specific experience or passage to large numbers of people. In much of what Dutch critic Hans Ibelings terms "Supermodern" architecture, for example, it is less an elision than a magnification of program that creates the impression of evacuated, abstract non-space. Not much attention has been paid to either the slow erosion, rather than erasure, of programmatic demands in most building types or to their stubborn persistence in certain typologies. Museums and prisons offer instructive, if diametric, evolutions in this regard. Museums have become the most "free" of institutions, testing the outer envelope of volumetric and organizational license with each new mega-form building and massive installation, whereas prisons remain among the most internally intractable.

The Panopticon and the Guggenheim implode their respective typologies by isolating and recomposing their premodern components. Neoclassical museums and prisons were both almost universally axial in their design, meaning that they were composed of two parts: *points* of entry or transition and *lines* of viewing space. Entry porticos and rotundas gave onto double-loaded *enfilade* gallery or cellblock wings radiating from central, domed enclosures. Wright's Guggenheim molds one element out of the other, forming a rotunda out of a spiral extrusion of gallery wall. In Bentham's reformulation, the rotunda is magnified until it will absorb the length of its wings in its circumference. In both, the bilateral symmetry of the traditional viewing spaces — think of the Metropolitan Museum's galleries or the endless corridors of the Eastern State Penitentiary — have been filleted down their center and spun into an open, multilevel continuum, to be viewed both from near and far. In opposition to 200-year histories that imagined both prisons and museums as sequential, if not always hierarchical, passages through a cadence of grand and intimate spaces meant to recalibrate an individual's understanding of and relationship to society, the Panopticon and the Guggenheim force all of those transitions, and all of their respective transformations, to occur simultaneously within the confines of two very differently appointed 100' cylinders.

Though the Panopticon and the Guggenheim form complementary paradigms for contemporary architectures of discipline and display, more than 150 years separate the projects. The very different historical origins of both, to either side of architectural modernity, are worth a brief recounting. Neither design began as the type of building it would become; each was an exercise in transcultural diplomacy; both had very long periods of gestation and a pair of unlikely midwives.

BACHELOR MACHINE

Samuel was building a sizable manufactory around a core of directors' rooms from which the whole establishment could be easily overlooked. This caught his fancy and while he waited for Catherine the Great to pay him court, Jeremy Bentham enlarged on the idea and gave it a name — Panopticon: the all-seeing eye.[80]
ROBIN EVANS

THE PANOPTICON was not initially envisioned as a prison, but as a factory. Jeremy Bentham visited his younger brother Samuel Bentham, an engineer, in St. Petersburg in 1787, where Samuel had been contracted the previous year by Prince Potemkin to overhaul Russia's navy. A more speculative venture in every sense, Jeremy Bentham's journey to Russia was at his own expense. While he waited in vain for an audience with Catherine the Great, with whom he hoped to discuss a thorough Utilitarian transformation of the czarist state-run economy, Jeremy reappraised his brother's innovative solution to monitoring the imported, unskilled laborers building a new Russian fleet.

Much of the centripetal logic of the Panopticon is already clear in Samuel Bentham's manufactory plan of 1787, which shows a circular building with a circumference carefully subdivided by fin walls into individual work areas. The 1787 scheme designates the central area "GOVERNOR" but does not specify a centralized enclosure. This design by Samuel Bentham is often cited as the first Panopticon, however it went through critical modifications over the next five years. Although the "cells" lining the exterior of the building vary only slightly in number and

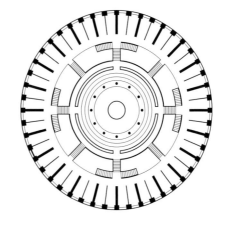

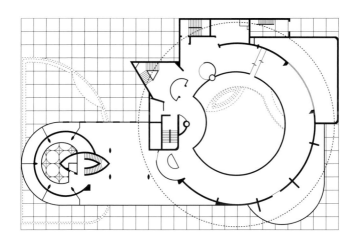

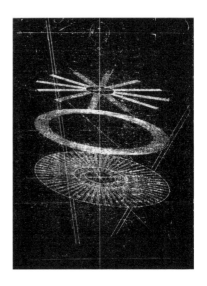

OCULIST WITNESSES, Marcel Duchamp (1920)

dimension in the different permutations of the design authored by Jeremy Bentham between 1787 and 1791, the central viewing station was radically reworked at least four times.[81] His first plan provides for a complex of "director's rooms" in the middle, a loose collection of offices and meeting rooms without obvious orientation to the surrounding cells. The second scheme imagines an entire house for the director and his family at the core of the institution, a domestic nucleus encircled by annular, laboring peons. The penultimate scheme is perhaps the most radical. Dispensing with all the interpersonal complications at the center of the previous two schemes, Bentham hangs a single inspector down into the panoptic cylinder of cells in a device he called "the lantern." The lantern is a skeletal chamber shrouded in translucent muslin and shaped much like a tailor's bust. Inside a single inspector would sit unseen, staring out in all directions through peepholes.

This penchant for secrecy carried over into the final version, published as the "Panopticon Penitentiary" in 1791. Inside, the prisoners are duly consigned to an outer ring of cells, but the core has been refashioned once again. The surveillance lantern of the previous scheme is now a larger bulb, wrapped in Venetian blinds to conceal its occupants, and hovering over a pulpit from which a Director was to address the inmates in a theater-in-the-round. Outside the cones of amphitheater seating in this final plan, guards were to race in circular halls to monitor inmates in their cells, then report back to the Director. An ingenious but self-defeating exercise in centripetal and centrifugal planning, the final design in many ways exactly refutes the ends of the original scheme. As the amphitheater blocks much of the view of the cells, no viewing position surveys the whole — no "I" is all-seeing.[82]

Bentham posed the Panopticon as a benign laboratory of human desires and deterrents, a system for testing a central Utilitarian principle that calculations of pleasure and pain, unique to each individual, govern all human interaction. Most of Bentham's peers, however, read the Panopticon as a merciless joke, a device for suspending the autonomy of its charges for the voyeuristic gratification of the Inspector, a role Bentham too eagerly offered to fill himself.

Bentham lobbied for his prison's construction in the British House of Lords until 1820 — so long that, though they never took up his design, the lords voted Bentham a personal stipend for his trouble. All of his efforts on behalf of the proposal went nowhere, but had the net effect, within his lifetime, of undermining the credibility of his formidable earlier achievements as an economist and advocate of liberal internationalism.[83] The few Panopticons that were built in the 19th century would be roundly derided over the next 100 years.[84] Popular for much of his life for his enlightened renderings of emergent concepts of individuality and citizenship, Bentham is now remembered principally for inventing spatial persecution. It's an irony that many Benthamite scholars enjoy — along with tales of his preserved but often misplaced head on display still at University College London — but one that Jeremy Bentham would have found considerably less flattering than Marcel Duchamp's possible homage to the Panopticon in the *Oculist Witnesses* of 1920.

ARCHITECTURE EQUAL TO, OR GREATER THAN, ART

As you feel the ground, the sky and the 'in between' you will perhaps feel them too; and find the way. I need a fighter, a lover of space, an agitator, a tester and a wise man.…I want a temple of spirit, a monument!

HILLA REBAY TO FRANK LLOYD WRIGHT, JUNE 1, 1943

IF THE PANOPTICON was invented to make workers of disparate and often displaced men — to bring rigor to the random — the Guggenheim began in the imagination of Hilla Rebay, a Russian curator and lover of Solomon Guggenheim, as a refuge from orthodoxies. Rebay championed the work of Wassily Kandinsky and what she termed Non-Objective painters as an antidote to both the representational styles of the 19th century and the geometric abstraction of Cubism. As she explained her preferences and terminology to Wright in an early letter,

> "I feel that each of these masterpieces should be organized into space and only you so it seems to me would test the possibilities to do so.… Functionalism does not agree with non-objectivity.… I do not think these paintings are easel paintings. They are order creating order and are sensitive (and corrective even) to space."[85]

She continued in her next correspondence, "Such a building as I am planning takes endless thinking, planning, testing." And indeed it would take seventeen years to bring her ambitions, distilled and transformed by Wright, to fruition. Neither Rebay nor Wright nor their patron Solomon Guggenheim would survive to see the finished building.

Rebay and Wright imagined a space for art in which contemplation and movement were in constant tension. Much has been made of Wright's disdain for the art to be housed in "his" museum, and, in all likelihood, the rotunda's design harkened back not to temples of art and an "inverted ziggurat," but to neighboring parking ramps in Manhattan and Wright's own spiral "Auto Destination" monument of the previous decade. Hardly precious with his innovation, he would repeat the spiral on Park Avenue, just thirty blocks south of the Guggenheim, in a 1954 Mercedes dealership. However, Wright appears to have taken some of Rebay's principles seriously, at least to the extent that the official museum write-up could easily conflate Wright's rhetoric of "organic" architectures based on pure but non-orthogonal geometries with hers for non-objectivity: "The Guggenheim Museum is an embodiment of Wright's attempts to render the inherent plasticity of organic forms in architecture. Even as it embraced nature, Wright's design put his unique stamp on Modernist Architecture's rigid geometry. The building is a symphony of triangles, ovals, arcs, circles, and squares."[86]

In most respects, though, the Guggenheim is preoccupied less with patterns in plan than with spatial experience, and with a volumetric proposition that moves in and out of specific and general encounters with art, and across creative disciplines of art, architecture, and music. Again, as the official description continues:

[Wright] dispensed with the conventional approach to museum design, which led visitors through a series of interconnected rooms and forced them to retrace their steps when exiting. Instead, Wright whisked people to the top of the building via elevator, proceeding downward at a leisurely pace on the gentle slope of a continuous ramp. The galleries were divided like the membranes in citrus fruit, with self-contained yet interdependent sections. The open rotunda afforded viewers the unique possibility of seeing several bays of work on different levels simultaneously.

The meticulous vision took decades to be fulfilled. Originally, the large rotunda was to be accompanied by a small rotunda and a tower. The small rotunda (or monitor building, as Wright called it) was intended to house apartments for Rebay and Guggenheim but instead became offices and miscellaneous storage space....

Some people, especially artists, criticized Wright for creating a museum environment that might overpower the art inside. "On the contrary," he wrote, "it was to make the building and the painting an uninterrupted, beautiful symphony such as never existed in the World of Art before." In conquering the static regularity of geometric design and combining it with the plasticity of nature, Wright produced a vibrant building whose architecture is as refreshing now as it was 40 years ago. The Guggenheim is arguably Wright's most eloquent presentation and certainly the most important building of his late career.

I quote this description at length for two reasons. The Guggenheim is arguably the first "signature" museum, and its hagiography of Wright is the first of many tales that museums now tell of their architects overcoming barriers of cost, civic reluctance, artists' naiveté, and even philistinism on the part of the patron to see a Vision realized. This language, which pits designer against circumstance and presents the finished building as a victory over the powers that be, rather than a manifestation of their largess, has had the effect both of equating the architect with an archetypal struggling artist, and of endowing the entire enterprise of museum building with a self-congratulatory, countercultural mythology. The second reason is its echo of Bentham's own description — often more a sales pitch — for his Panopticon. Certain passages could describe either building: galleries segmented "like the membranes in citrus fruit, with self-contained yet interdependent sections"; an open rotunda affording "viewers the unique possibility of seeing several bays of work on different levels simultaneously"; and even the "small rotunda [or *monitor building*, as Wright called it] intended to house apartments."

TARGET PRACTICE: POST-PENITENTIAL PRISONS AND POST-PAINTERLY MUSEUMS

It was only with the expositions of the 19th century that the marvels of the year 2000 began to be announced.[87]

TONY BENNETT, QUOTING UMBERTO ECO

The Guggenheim and Panopticon have hauntingly similar *partis*, circular plans and cavernous, atriated sections that could almost pass one for the other. However, they differ radically in every subtlety. Where the Guggenheim spirals up in a seamless ground/wall-plane, the Panopticon layers segregated rings of cells. Wright wants his viewers daunted, overcome by his sculpting of space and distracted from what he viewed as decadent, second-rate art. And he wants them moving. Bentham opts for a clarity and fixity — inmates in their cells, inspector in the tower, with their radial and vertical locations dictated by the optical limitations of a central viewer. Backlighting in the Panopticon ensures that each inmate is reduced to a clear two-dimensional silhouette, where the Guggenheim has a sliver of banded skylight running along the top of the exhibition walls, bathing all planar work in unbroken, undifferentiated frontal light.

The two buildings are most polemical in their reversal of typological expectations, and their adoption of the other's priorities: museums were historically the most reassuringly ordered of buildings, and prisons the most chaotic and random. Wright's sublime, encompassing atrium punctuates a century of redundant, linear, sequenced galleries based distantly but consistently on the logic of the Louvre. The Panopticon's clarity runs exactly counter to the labyrinthine Bastille and myriad premodern jails. However, the vertigo of the Guggenheim is not so unlike that of Piranesi's *Carceri*, and the viewer's primacy in the Panopticon offers in plan what the Louvre (or most pre-20th century collections) offers in section: salon hanging, in which paintings are tiled up the walls and then tilted down toward the viewer, is a

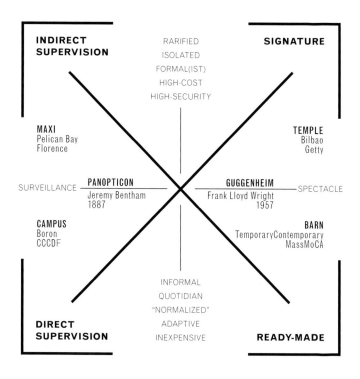

INDIRECT SUPERVISION

SIGNATURE

RARIFIED
ISOLATED
FORMAL(IST)
HIGH-COST
HIGH-SECURITY

MAXI
Pelican Bay
Florence

TEMPLE
Bilbao
Getty

SURVEILLANCE ——— PANOPTICON
Jeremy Bentham
1887

GUGGENHEIM ———SPECTACLE
Frank Lloyd Wright
1957

CAMPUS
Boron
CCCDF

BARN
TemporaryContemporary
MassMoCA

INFORMAL
QUOTIDIAN
"NORMALIZED"
ADAPTIVE
INEXPENSIVE

DIRECT SUPERVISION

READY-MADE

PODULAR / NOMINAL INSTITUTIONS. ddd llc (2012)

proto-panoptic tactic to maximize the number of images on view and perpendicular to the viewer.

To the degree that the Panopticon illustrates Utilitarian precepts and the Guggenheim draws (however forced) inspiration from theories of non-objectivity, the buildings stem from two minor, but surprisingly complementary, schools of modern philosophy. Equal parts libertarian and mechanistic, Utilitarians like Bentham and John Stuart Mill saw the world as an endless matrix of cost-benefit assessment by individuals always seeking to maximize their pleasure and minimize their pain. Utilitarianism arrived at a novel, and for neoclassical economists quite useful, conclusion that individuals are both *rational*, as they operate consistently in their self-interest, and *incomparable*, because their interests, and the degrees of their passion, are utterly peculiar to each.

Non-Objectivity, at least as Rebay interprets Wassily Kandinsky's term, seeks pictorial "truths" that distill reality into visions both essential and personalized. Kandinsky's paintings, which remain the core of the Guggenheim's collection and raison d'être, create a paradox of forms and space that both multiply and refute representational interpretation. Non-Objective art claims to reach new Platonic universals, not through received geometries, but by way of an individual painter's invented, transcendent iconography.

Both Utilitarianism and Non-Objectivity thus grapple with the individual and exceptionalism: people share a will to freedom and pleasure, but by no means equal aptitudes or appetites for their realization. According to both Utilitarianism and Non-Objectivity, there is no accounting (literally) for extreme dispositions, only a recognition that "genius" must be sifted out and celebrated as exemplary for those of lesser drives. Utilitarians and Non-Objectivists share a distinct, almost Panglossian optimism borne of their faith that, while some people succeed spectacularly, all people are trying their best at all times, within personal limitations. Bentham believed that by offering an array of human subjects to view simultaneously, his Panopticon would open both their shared humanity and their diverse drives to public purview. Though far more judgmental and dismissive himself, Wright designed the Guggenheim in accord with Rebay's inclinations, even going so far as to show how excellent, middling, and subpar work (in his estimation) could be displayed in the same spaces, not excluded or ranked. In this light, Bentham's solicitation of Catherine the Great and Prince Potemkin, and Wright's engagement by Rebay appear less serendipitous than strategic. Although both the architects and their patrons invite Romantic caricature, their well-documented "excesses" — libidinal, urbane, geometric — are symptomatic of a shared hunger for and belief in individualized, orderly gratification. Like Potemkin's famous villages, the Panopticon he financed was societally naive, but also a complex exercise in statecraft as stagecraft.[88]

The Panopticon and the Guggenheim are less architectures of reform than devices of assimilation. Both buildings were designed to control the expression and behavior of foreigners, to stage and understand a non-Western "other." Unlike his many faith-based contemporaries who imagined penitentiaries as quasi-monasteries, Bentham sees his Panopticon as a mechanism for inculcating generic "civilization" rather than specific religious conversion. Because Non-Objective art refused representation, it required a host space to prepare its audience and deliver its promises. In Rebay's estimation — and in marked contrast to the formidable post-WWII Abstract Expressionist canvases they presage — the abstractions of Kandinsky, Paul Klee, and German Expressionism must be seen as fragile, introverted, and easily misapprehended. If the Panopticon in the end is more concerned with providing a theater of evidence to an Inspector than it is with transforming its charges, then the Guggenheim is designed less to flatter art than to shape an encounter with the unknown.

The Guggenheim and Panopticon are unique in their fields for their constant modulation of viewing, rather than their spatial efficiency in collecting. Neither design maximizes the number of inmates or works that could be held within their bounds by compounding or extruding galleries or cellblocks. Both instead introduce major, mediating void spaces to distance the viewer from the viewed, to deepen perspectives, and to multiply sightlines. This emphasis on the viewing subject is out of step with both neoclassical institutions that choreograph a march of periods or parade of offenders, and with most modern examples that concentrate on the flow of crowds, in effect accelerating the classical model but not breaking from it. The Panopticon and Guggenheim engender intense self-consciousness in all of their participants: artists, curators, visitors; inmates, guards, warden. As diverse and inequitable as their roles may be, all are constantly on stage, enacting continuous dramas of transgression and catharsis. Although this state of simultaneity may occur by chance in other prisons and museums, these two designs are the first to elevate the visual transactions between their constituencies to an organizational absolute. By refocusing the architectural emphasis on the orchestration of interpersonal experience, rather than on the economies of enclosure, Bentham and Wright set the stage for a post-Minimalist reassessment, and turbocharged expansion, of both building types.

PODULAR PRISONS —
DIRECT AND INDIRECT ENGAGEMENT

Smaller, generally less violent county jails are often proving grounds for new carceral models. In two separate facilities in the late 1970s and early 1980s, Contra Costa County in California pioneered Podular Direct Supervision, perhaps the single most important penal design milestone in fifty years. Much of the penal commentary in the 1980s begins with the same anecdote, a recitation of a visiting administrator's amazement during tours of the Contra Costa County Detention Facility, where inmates casually relax in their cellblocks and guards circulate freely among them, unprotected by any secure control room for retreat. In Contra Costa, living-room-like common rooms are surrounded by private bedrooms that inmates may leave and return to at will. Not since Napoleon retreated to Elba has confinement looked so plush. But, as those 1980s assessments always went on to say, the innovations at Contra Costa were just *sensible*, all in the name of safety and cost savings.

Podular blocks like those in Contra Costa owe a debt to behavioral psychology, and in particular to "functional units" pioneered for drug and alcohol rehabilitation in the 1960s. US mental health facilities were a terrifying mix of prison, hospital, and madhouse, with patients of many diagnoses, treatments, and levels of pathology often held together. Ken Kesey's *One Flew Over the Cuckoo's Nest* portrays the state of psychological asylums in the

GLENN E. DYER DETENTION FACILITY, Oakland, California (1984)

post-WWII period with only slight sensationalization. Studies of the mentally ill in the late 1960s found that when held separately, a smaller number of similar patients proved easier to treat, both more docile and more conveniently monitored. Functional Units arose first as a managerial and then a spatial subdivision: a basic separation of one kind of malady from another so that they could be "functionally" treated.

Unlike older hospital wards, these units were imagined as isolated therapeutic settings, designed to ease both administration and anxiety. Functional units domesticated the environment of treatment and established the optimal head count for treating people in recovery. Though these findings would be applied only sparingly in our mental health system — especially after it was broadly defunded at the federal level in the 1980s by Ronald Reagan — they proved the basis for many of the prisons and jails imagined thereafter. Podular cellblocks, based on these functional units in psychiatric wards, have become a national norm and house between thirty and sixty inmates in a cluster of cells surrounding an open living area. In contrast to a vast majority of prisons designed to provide "negative" surveillance down long, empty corridors, the neo-panoptic Podular prisons rely on constant visual and often physical contact between inmates and guards. The "Podular Revolution" extends from lowest to highest security prisons, and from the smallest to the largest of new institutions. Though in all podular cellblocks prisoners are allocated and arranged like patients in a functional unit, the role, location, and even the title of the guards monitoring those units can take polarized forms.

Each pod or module is isolated from the remainder of the facility of which it is a part, meaning that specific demographic, disciplinary, and medical classifications can be held and treated separately. Its basic hallmark is the organization of inmates into groups or "pods" of twenty to sixty held collectively and apart from other inmate populations. These groupings may be defined by almost any variable: gender, level of security risk, age, term of sentence, and seriousness or variety of offense. For example, sex offenders — or "J-Cats" in the parlance of the California Department of Corrections and Rehabilitation — are often held together, as they are often targeted for assault in the general population. Recently, podular segregation has been used in Los Angeles County facilities to separate rival gangs, group inmate populations by psychotropic medication, even to capitalize on inmates' shared experience of former military service.[89]

Podular design can be tailored to provide the most lenient and the most brutal of conditions for prisoners. At Contra Costa detention facility, all surfaces are carpeted or brightly painted, TVs and a pingpong table anchor living-room-like common areas. The biggest concerns of jail management in the 1980s were depression and obesity among inmates they referred to as "clients." By contrast, solitary confinement at Pelican Bay State Prison (PBSP) is also organized in podular fashion, with twenty-odd cells forming a cruciform Secure Housing Unit or SHU. In this modern-day dungeon, inmates are confined to bare, constantly lit cells, appointed with only a combo sink/toilet and concrete sleeping platform. They remain there for twenty-three hours a day, with any movement outside the cell brief, shackled, and usually court ordered. Numerous cruel and unusual punishment lawsuits have

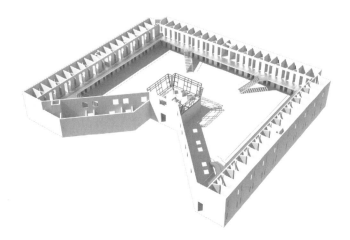

been brought against **PBSP**, alleging sensory deprivation, negligence, and wanton abuse. In one particularly medieval case, an inmate was left horribly scarred from the neck down after being boiled alive in a cauldron, with guards claiming the scalding bath had been necessary to remove weeks-old fecal matter from the violently incoherent prisoner.

Podular Supervision is defined by how surveillance is orchestrated, and by how boundaries are erected, dissolved, and negotiated between inmates and their overseers. Two podular approaches have evolved, known as Direct and Indirect Supervision, with increasingly stark carrot-and-stick differences between them. Direct Supervision, in which officers and inmates mingle freely most of the time in shared living space, deinstitutionalizes the incarceration of low-risk offenders and opens the possibility of infinite subcategorization of inmates. Indirect Supervision, in which guards oversee inmates from a secured booth, governs almost all higher security imprisonment up to and including SuperMax isolation units, where much of the panoptic surveillance is via video feed. Crucial to both is the relatively small number of inmates held in any one space — a limit that ironically has made it possible to contain unprecedented numbers in one larger facility. Many new campus prisons house more than

5,000 inmates, but because each podular housing unit holds fewer convicts, violent outbursts in new prisons rarely engulf an entire institution at once. The California State Prison system has developed two basic podular formats, the 180 Unit and 270 Unit, so named for the angle-span of their sightlines, which surpass Bentham in his own terms. The 270 Unit, in particular, is likely the highest volume, fastest built, least obstructed, most efficiently staffed panoptic cellblock ever conceived.

NOMINAL MUSEUMS — SIGNATURE AND READYMADE EXPERIENCE

It might be true that the most abject forms of public housing and cities were formulated upon the Modernist conception of continuous, homogeneous space. But the very qualities that prove it to fail as outdoor public space (undifferentiated, scale-less, delocalized) are some of the ideal conditions for viewing art. The space of the gallery is one of the few successfully liberated social abstractions.[90]

SHUMON BASAR

THE EVOLUTION OF MUSEUMS since the Guggenheim is by no means as uniform as the refinement of Podular prisons has been for the last thirty years. However, the diversity of new museums and the "envelope-testing" that marks each new opening — bigger, higher, simpler, stranger, etc. — point to the shared liberation all these institutions enjoy from any single ideal notion of architecture for art. Contemporary museums illustrate the present tautology that, without shared aims in terms of human improvement, the mission of museums "to edify" is often reduced to the construction of an unlikely edifice. If post-Minimalist Podular prisons divide into Direct and Indirect Supervised variations, concurrent Postmodern museums are similarly bifurcated

between bespoke signature buildings and readymade conversions of existing structures.

Both signature and readymade designs become museums by the same nominalist alchemy that Marcel Duchamp employed in naming both his custom productions and everyday objects, Art. Duchamp underscored that it was his judgment as an artist (and perhaps its display in the context of other art) that ratified the work of art as such, not its material qualities, nor evidence of representational skill, nor temporal investment on the part of the artist. Like much of the art they house, museums of contemporary art ask visitors to suspend their preconceptions of what art and architecture are, and to participate in naming what they might become. Visitors, curators, and artists are challenged to invent their own means and rationale for triangulating between art object, art environment, and their own status relative to both, just as Duchamp asked his audience to "complete the work" by accepting his signature as proof of the sculptural status of "Fountain," or by entering into the hermetic complexities of the "Large Glass."

Frank Gehry's museum trajectory from industrial repurposing in the Temporary Contemporary in Los Angeles (1984,

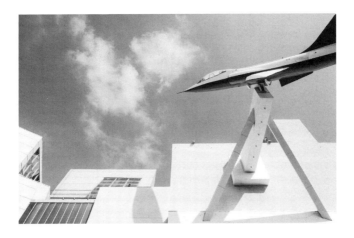

now the Geffen Contemporary), through the *merengue*-like gyra-
tions of the Guggenheim Bilbao (1997) illustrates this nominalist
dialectic in a single career. In the context of their times, Gehry's
more radical contributions to museum design are to be found in
the early renovations he performed for the California Aerospace
Museum and MoCA's Temporary Contemporary in Los Angeles.
Both were briefs calling for the redeployment of industrial buildings with new circulation strategies around and through existing shells, and little else. What unites all these projects are the
"easy" spaces and flexible gestures that Gehry invented first
to lure people into defunct structures, then to pull people into
neglected corners of cities.

The California Aerospace Museum was earlier and more
prosaic, given a fixed collection of aging aircraft to display. The
hangar-like space tied directly to the planes' previous housing,
but suspending them aloft shifted tenses toward the past-per-
fect of whale and dinosaur skeletons in natural history curation.
Still, this wasn't uncharted ground after the National Aerospace
Museum, a far more seductive museum of technology, and, one
suspects, that Gehry set out to demystify and deglamorize.

NEO-DUCHAMPIAN

NOMINAL

POST-INDUSTRIAL
RECUPERATION

URBAN MALAISE
AS MEDIUM

TATE MODERN

MOMA QNS

Paul McCarthy

Douglas Gordon

Liam Gillick

Matthew Barney

Dan Graham

Mike Kelly

TEMPORARY CONTEMPORARY

PS1

Weiner, Asher

Matta-Clark | Robert Morris

PRODUCTION — Smithson — Rauschenberg — Ruscha — POLEMIC

Warhol | Beuys

POMPIDOU | 60s | Haake

Lichtenstein | Polke | DOCUMENTA

Koons, Hirst | 80s | Broodthaers

Beecroft | 90s | Hirschorn, Pardo

GUGGENHEIM VEGAS | DIA, MAK

CIVIC/CONSUMER
SPECTACLE

FRAME FOR PERSONAL
/POLITICAL STATEMENT

PERSPECTIVAL

READYMADE MUSEUMS

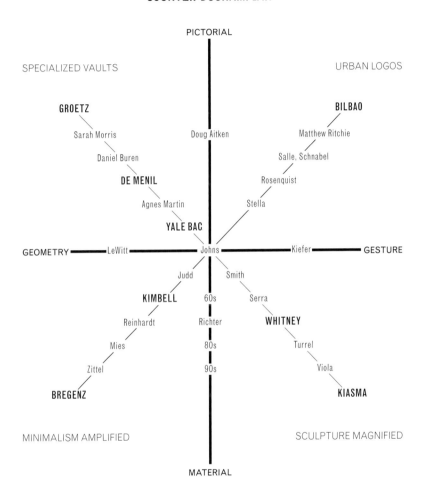

COUNTER-DUCHAMPIAN

PICTORIAL

SPECIALIZED VAULTS   URBAN LOGOS

GROETZ   **BILBAO**

Sarah Morris   Doug Aitken   Matthew Ritchie

Daniel Buren   Salle, Schnabel

DE MENIL   Rosenquist

Agnes Martin   Stella

YALE BAC

GEOMETRY ━━━━ LeWitt ━━━ Johns ━━━━ Kiefer ━━━ GESTURE

Judd   Smith

KIMBELL   60s   Serra

Reinhardt   **WHITNEY**

Mies   Richter   Turrel

Zittel   80s

BREGENZ   90s   Viola

KIASMA

MINIMALISM AMPLIFIED   SCULPTURE MAGNIFIED

MATERIAL

MUSEUM AS ART OBJECT

Abstract Expansionism

For Gehry, the type, inclination, and "disposition" of the fighter plane cantilevered over the entrance of LA's aerospace museum became the driving issue of the design, if not a cautionary allegory for public sector compromise. Interestingly, it is the most exactingly literal of Gehry's sampled imagery, and unlike the fish, snakes, and binoculars, the least recurring. Drawn first as a vaguely expressionist German Stukka diving toward visitors, Gehry described in a BBC documentary how in the client meetings the plane quickly became an actual American F-15 fuselage in meteoric ascent. Optimism not optional.

In the 1980s, the Temporary Contemporary was as much a poster child for readymade museums as Bilbao would be for signature museums at the end of the following decade, but both approaches were common throughout the 1980s and '90s. MoMA Design Curator Terence Riley noted that many major museums embraced both strategies simultaneously in what he called the "Temple and Barn" approach to expansion. The densest twenty-year period of museum construction in history, spanning from 1985 to 2005, is rife with proposals that almost gratuitously test the limit of what could be designated museological space, beginning with the challenges of Gehry's Temporary Contemporary and Peter Eisenman's signature Wexner Center (1987), and concluding, respectively, with the Herculean extremes of Robert Irwin and OpenOffice's conversion of a vast Nabisco printing plant into Dia:Beacon and Santiago Calatrava's Milwaukee Museum of Art, which redirects a river in its sculptural excess.

The fact that none of these buildings precisely resembles the Guggenheim does not detract from the latter's role in making all of them *possible* as museums. The Guggenheim's spiraling void opened the field to almost any open-span geometry as a home for art, and its counterintuitive silhouette, underscoring how its architecture *defies* the art within, made any structure — old or new, grand or minute, ruled or free-form — a viable candidate for future aesthetic encounters. After Wright's coil, we know to watch one another, and the museum, as closely as we do the art.

THE CONCRETE STOMACH

ALLAN KAPROW:

Our comparison of the Guggenheim, as an intestinal metaphor, to what you've called a 'waste system' seems quite to the point. But this of course is nothing more than another justification for the museum man, for the museum publicist, for the museum critic. Instead of high seriousness it's high humor.

ROBERT SMITHSON:

High seriousness and high humor are the same thing.[91]

BENTHAM AND WRIGHT are both 19th century reformers in their zeal and in their distrust of cities, but what they offer isn't countryside or religion, but a more radical abstraction of human relations than those within metropolitan norms. The Panopticon and Guggenheim re-conjugated relationships of viewing and viewed, figure and ground, desired and despised in ways that defy both Classical and Modern notions of hierarchy and symmetry. Both operate less by extrusion and repetition than through an asymmetrical understanding of the gallery "wing," one in which a viewer no longer centers a room giving onto paired, symmetrical views or cells, but is understood as an individual assessing singular "events" in the form of pictures and prisoners.

Neither as tidy as the Modernist trajectory that extends in parallel, nor as random in their dispositions as many contemporary theorists would describe them, postmodern spaces of incarceration and exhibition are surprisingly dialectical in their evolutions. Both Direct and Indirect Supervision prisons, as well as Signature and Readymade museums, share presumptions foreign to the bulk of modernist institutions: all-in-one spatial configurations for their "holdings"; a nesting, micro-within-macro organizational logic; a faith that behavioral transgressions — whether criminal or cultural — are best apprehended through the specific tailoring of sightlines and interaction; and finally, an

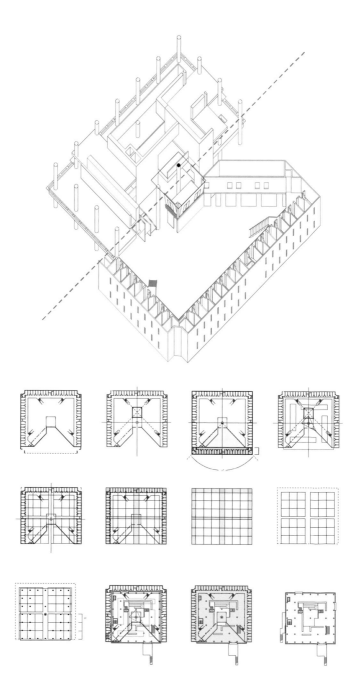

overarching confidence that acts of naming — the constant classification and reclassification of works, subjects, processes — carry transformative, demystifying powers in their own right.

It is in this sense that the Panopticon and the Guggenheim laid the groundwork for architecture's engagement with Conceptual Art over the last fifty years. Obviously, the relationship between museums and these currents in fine art is better documented. Prisons, however, reveal how deeply certain aesthetic developments have penetrated society. Together, they register the evolving notions of *discipline* that continually reshape the criteria for both aesthetic and penal systems.

If, as installation artist An Te Liu recently opined, "everybody's making rumpus rooms," then museums both accommodated and facilitated that shift. It's worth noting that for all its fraught history with Abstract Expressionism, the Guggenheim was host to more, earlier, and larger Minimalist and post-Minimalist shows than MoMA (fifty-one shows to MoMA's forty-one), and arguably found its mission as an institution exhibiting that later work.[92] It may come as more of a surprise that many within our justice system see the new forms of incarceration in a similar light. Bemused or bewildered by the Podular Direct cellblock he was assigned to at the LA central jail, inmate Lorenzo Thompson, serving 180 days for possession, described it thus: "This is *Romper Room*, this is the *New Zoo Revue*."[93]

04.PROLIFERATE

Chapter 04 explores how more efficient podular and nominal institutions multiplied and escalated into far-flung, internodal networks, championed by proselytizers such as Thomas Krens of the Guggenheim Foundation and Donald Novey of the California Correctional Officers' union. Both prisons and museums are now franchised according to tested prototypes, conceived as iterations in a larger skein of strategic planning. Krens and Novey pioneered new management regimes of constant expansion, pooling old and new institutions, as well as readymade and signature buildings, under the yoke of a single brand.

MASS MOCA, Bruner Cott Architects, North Adams, Massachusetts (1999)

DOUBLING DOWN

You're behind walls in this line of work. Most in our profession
never think outside the walls.[94]
DON NOVEY, 1996

Krens could not have succeeded were it not for a general social
bias that favors architecture over art....Critics once predicted
that the age of reproduction would fill the world with a surfeit of
images and spawn 'the museum without walls,' as Andre Malraux
put it. But instead we have the opposite phenomenon: the museum
that is just walls.[95]
DEBORAH SOLOMON, 2002

TWO LARGER-THAN-LIFE FIGURES emerged in the 1980s to
recast the basic mathematics of incarceration and exhibition in
the United States and beyond. Don Novey and Thomas Krens
began their lives on opposite coasts, with radically different
apprenticeships in the guards' ranks at Folsom Prison and the
curatorial Art History program at Williams College, respectively.

122

Save for its rate and trajectory, Novey's sharp-elbowed, navy-blue-collar ascent to lead the California prison guards union bears little resemblance to the well-calibrated arc Krens traversed from Williams, to Yale's School of Management, then on to lead the Guggenheim. However, Novey and Krens implemented many of the same principles for revitalizing their fields: define new constituencies and secure new patrons; leverage, expand, and update existing collections; fill old buildings and insist on new ones to hold the latest acquisitions as well as archived treasures. In short, fight for more walls than you need, fight for more "content" than you can hold, and use success on either front to demand more of the other.

Novey and Krens are dramatic, bullish extroverts in very different but equally introverted worlds. Each has been profiled in the pages of *The New York* or *Los Angeles Times*, as well as in more specialized terms by the art press, legal journals, and local papers, but the correlation of their accomplishments has not been explored. Both ruled for twenty years. Over Novey's two decades as president, from 1982–2002, the California prison guards' union (now the CCPOA, for California Correctional Peace

THOMAS KRENS | Opposite: DON NOVEY

Officers Association) became the most potent force in California state politics, rebalancing the state's budget from higher education in favor of prisons in less than two decades. Krens led the Guggenheim through its most expansionist period from 1988 until 2008, when he relinquished his general directorship to oversee the completion of the largest of his satellite projects, the Guggenheim Abu Dhabi.

Both might wince at this comparison: Krens for having his stewardship of the avant-garde compared to incarceration; Novey for having his political savvy and success at empire building likened to "pie-in-the-sky" cultural speculation.

But the early similarities are flattering to both. Don Novey famously rebranded guarding prisons as the "Toughest Beat," a job entitled to all the benefits and pay scale of other peace officers. His success in selling this argument in Sacramento — especially vis-à-vis the other statewide corps of officers, the Highway Patrol — made him a quick legend within his own ranks. (As did his inventive and ambitious political patronage: an officer at the state prison in Susanville recalled that Novey once sent fifty

FOLSOM STATE PRISON: C-BLOCK, Represa, California (1880)

pounds of prison-smoked Kielbasa sausage to thank Governor George Deukmejian; he later had the CCPOA contribute a record $3 million to Gray Davis' failed attempt to stave off a recall.) The other, even more politically potent forces he unleashed were victims' rights groups.

Thomas Krens, in like fashion, recognized that his long-overlooked and underappreciated constituency was not the Guggenheim's curators or visitors, but its board of trustees. His care and feeding of "neglected" board members, and his nurturing of art world newcomers with more freshly minted and active fortunes, became a new paradigm for ambitious museum leadership. But Krens' best advocates of all were architects. Whether banking on Frank Gehry's integrity or Rem Koolhaas' intellect, no one harnessed the long untapped cultural currency of our field as profitably.

Geographical reach is an important difference between Novey and Krens. As Solomon continued in her *New York Times Magazine* profile, Krens is credited with inventing "the global museum" and seeking Guggenheim branches and partnerships around the world. Novey's domain is more circumscribed — limited (with some interstate contracting) to the boundaries of California — but by no means dwarfed in this comparison. Twenty of California's thirty-three state prisons opened during Novey's presidency of the CCPOA, and those twenty new facilities run to a total of 15,872 acres, *or 24.8 square miles,* of new penal real estate. For a sense of scale, the land area of the borough of Manhattan is just 23.2 square miles. Almost any one of California's new prison campuses could amply encapsulate all of the Guggenheim museums, built and unbuilt, before and after Thomas Krens.

RURAL REVOLT

An anti-LA righteousness, which turned on an almost patriotic notion of duty, cloaked the eagerness of small-town delegations who came to Sacramento looking for prisons to revive isolated, flagging economies.[96]

RUTH WILSON GILMORE

(A)rt museums are an 18th century idea (the encyclopedia) in a 19th century box (the extended palace). The extended palace is a collection of rooms that fulfilled its structural destiny sometime towards the end of the 20th century; which is to say, the rooms got filled — they weren't adequate to the imaginations of contemporary artists who began to work with notions of scale.[97]

THOMAS KRENS, 1997

AN IMPORTANT FEATURE of Krens' and Novey's strategies for expansion stems from their shared rural pedigree. Novey is a proud sixth generation son of Sacramento and a second generation prison guard, beginning his career in 1971 at Folsom, the most "up-river" of California's early prisons. As Ruth Wilson Gilmore notes in her survey of the California prison system, *Golden Gulag*, Novey also arrived as Reaganite law-and-order politics tipped into the statewide mainstream: "The Uniform Determinate Sentencing Act of 1977 was California's formal abdication from any responsibility to rehabilitate, stating neatly: '(T)he purpose of imprisonment for crime is punishment.'"[98]

Folsom was a hotbed for the counterrevolution in Novey's early years, home to both the leadership of the Aryan Brotherhood among its inmates, and the origin of the first anti-discrimination case filed by white employees, in which Anglo officers alleged they had been passed over for promotion in favor of minorities and women. In December 1978, Novey co-founded and edited *The Granite*, a monthly newsletter to guards to promote running prisons the old-school "Folsom Way."[99] Johnny Cash aptly sums up the basics of that worldview, both for inmates and their keepers, in *Folsom Prison Blues*: "I know I had it coming, I know I can't be free. But those people keep a moving, and that's what tortures me...If they freed me from this prison, if that train out there was mine, I'll bet I'd move it farther down the line..."

Thomas Krens is a New Yorker by birth, but upstate by training and Harley-touring disposition. Both Krens and the curatorial program at Williams that spawned him are a circuitous consequence of the success of Kahn's first museum at Yale (a university that Krens would later matriculate from with not an art history PhD but a business degree). By the 1970s, New England was awash in great collegiate micro-museums, far more challenging on a curatorial level than the major New York and Boston institutions they fed — and also more daring in terms of the architecture they sponsored. Krens, as well as his Williams colleagues Joseph Thompson and Michael Govan, was a beneficiary of the collegiate art museum boom of the '60s and '70s that provided not only Williams, but also Bard, Syracuse, and a host of other schools (some, like Pomona, even farther-flung) with the gallery training grounds for today's hotly contested ranks of Museum Men.

Though his tastes and ambitions now seem definingly cosmopolitan, Thomas Krens' first great museum idea was to convert the outsized remnants of small-town industrial America into gallery space, leaving a leasable remainder. As Rosalind Krauss relates in a 1985 interview with Krens, "Suddenly, he said, he thought of the huge abandoned buildings in his own neighborhood of North Adams, and he had the revelation of MASS MoCA."[100] A series of industrial closures had left a vast tract of factory space dormant in North Adams, and Krens suggested to the governor a huge cultural retrofit, transforming the tract into a vast art complex — at thirteen acres and more than 100,000 square feet of exhibition space, still among the largest art spaces in the world. His colleague Thompson led that effort, and protégé Govan would follow suit with Dia:Beacon a decade later.

In 1988, Thomas Krens found the Guggenheim at what he chose to see as a crossroads. His arrival coincided with the completion of an addition by Gwathmey Siegel that barely eased the museum's need for space — only 3% of the Guggenheim collection could be on view in 1992.[101] Krens usually frames his case for what he calls "satellite" Guggenheims in terms of spreading the wealth of a single museum's collection, not replicating the structure of the whole in each location. In this respect, Krens sought to build on the model of MoMA by engaging the Trust for Cultural Resources of the City of New York to underwrite the Gwathmey construction and later an expansion downtown. Almost all of his partnerships, with governments and corporations, follow a similar pattern in which the partner fronts the costs of land and construction of the new museum, while the Guggenheim offers content, coverage, and brand identity. It was principally in this sense that Krens "collateralized" the collection, though he also sold off some major works, including some by Kandinsky considered inviolate.

Krens' ventures overseas also borrow liberally from the Rockefeller model. As the Rockefellers aided in the reconstruction of Versailles, then received US tax relief for their late, informal contribution to the Marshall Plan, Krens developed a plan for partnering with the Hermitage that, at least briefly, signaled an impressive post-Cold War cultural rapprochement. But "partnership" and "franchise" are controversial terms in museum parlance, likely because they suggest elements of crass commercialism, or imperial overreach. When Napoleon consolidated the spoils of his military campaigns in the Louvre to form the first "encyclopedic" museum of European art, he also imagined a network of provincial or *"envoi"* museums through which those treasures would circulate.[102] These were never built. The temptation to not only fortify a collection but, having done so, to project it outward, thus has an august pedigree, if not a great track record.[103]

THE BILBAO ASPECT

In the Middle Ages, when someone came to the city from a village, they had never seen buildings with more than one story before and then they stood in front of this massive cathedral. That's the effect I wanted to achieve. It's technology, cosmology, science and religion, all thrown together. Breathtaking.[104]

THOMAS KRENS, 2008

Thomas Krens resonates more with buildings than with pictures.[105]

PETER LEWIS

THE GUGGENHEIM REFLECTS the *arriviste* politics and aspirations of Solomon Guggenheim, whose fortune was made in grocery chains supplying the new suburbs of the Midwest. As Herbert Muschamp explored in *Man About Town*, his study of Frank Lloyd Wright's conflicted feelings about urban space, Solomon Guggenheim's museum in New York was less a site-specific response than prototypical "solution" to what both Wright and his client likely viewed as claustrophobic, convention-bound cityscape. Under Krens, the Guggenheim has pioneered the global franchising of its collection and identity, at what many now feel was dire cost to the operational viability of the New York hub.[106] From the perspective of Solomon Guggenheim, however, Krens may well have projected his intentions accurately, and ensured the Guggenheim name a much higher profile than it would have had otherwise, simply on the basis of Krens' one broadly acknowledged success: the Guggenheim Bilbao.

As mixed as his legacy may prove in terms of the steward-ship of works of art, Thomas Krens was without rival as an impresario of contemporary architecture in the 1990s. His vacillations between Rem Koolhaas and Frank Gehry mirrored that decade's defining dialogue between American formalist and European conceptual approaches. Krens' well-documented passions for Koolhaas and Gehry, in that chronological order, as well as his bracketing flirtations with Hans Hollein in the '80s and Zaha Hadid in the 2000s, suggest a spectrum of possibilities within what Rosalind Krauss described as "The Cultural Logic of the Late Capitalist Museum."

Like many of his peers, but, as he might have it, at a larger scale, Krens matured from Ready-Made museums such as MASS MoCA, the Deutsche Guggenheim, and the Guggenheim Soho, to Signature museums epitomized by those in Bilbao and Abu Dhabi, as well as most of the speculative projects between those two. From working with Hollein on a frustratingly unrealized branch in Salzburg, Krens likely learned that his tastes are not as precious as those of some Austrian architects (it will be interesting to see whether Michael Govan learns a similar lesson from Swiss architect Peter Zumthor at the Los Angeles County Museum of Art). The projects designed by Koolhaas often tested the possibilities of cross-programming to breaking point. Neither a Guggenheim-plus-Prada in Soho nor a casino-plus-Guggen-

GUGGENHEIM MUSEUM, BILBAO. Aerial View; Frank O Gehry, Bilbao, Spain (1997)

heim in Vegas panned out, but their daring failures cast Krens in
an intellectually flattering light.

The Guggenheim Bilbao will certainly stand as Krens'
crowning achievement, though Gehry may have surpassed
himself elsewhere, or, at least, built as well in more traveled cities.
Indeed, the many efficiencies of geometric rationalization Gehry
Partners pioneered to achieve a surface of 80% compound cur-
vature over the Guggenheim Bilbao — the translation of his loose
swoops into a mesh of perpendicular fasteners supported by a
wire frame of straight steel sections on a 3m grid, for example —
now factor into most advanced international buildings through
software offered by Gehry Technologies.[107] The continuing
debates surrounding Bilbao, regarding both its internal efficacy
(echoes of the Wright protests) and its civic impact (how well is
Bilbao really doing?), have left its titanium skin less tarnished
than burnished by the collective concern.[108] Though fewer tourists are making the pilgrimage each year, the Guggenheim Bilbao
remains the benchmark against which all culturally based urban
renewal schemes are judged, and its near simultaneous opening
with the stolid and far more costly Getty Center in 1997 was a
bruising coincidence for the latter. A recent accord reached with
Basque separatists should deter further schemes to blow up the
mammoth topiary puppy by Jeff Koons near the entrance of the
Guggenheim Bilbao, as a radical faction of the ETA had hoped
but failed to the week of the museum's opening.

More ambitious plans followed. MoMA and the Guggenheim, in partnerships with the Pompidou and the Hermitage,
respectively, are still vying for their cut of the staggering sums
earmarked for the redevelopment of Hong Kong's old airport
island as Kowloon West. Though it's been delayed until 2016, the
scale of this $3 billion project guarantees that Asia will enjoy its
first comprehensive trove of Western art and artifacts, and, by
the same token, that a huge portion of the patrimony of Europe
and the United States will continue its westward migration off
our shores. No matter the outcome, Kowloon West will broker

GUGGENHEIM MUSEUMS WORLDWIDE
1. **NEW YORK: FIFTH AVENUE** (F.L. Wright) 2. **NEW YORK: SOHO** (OMA) 3. **BILBAO** (Gehry) 4. **BERLIN**
(Richard Gluckman) 5. **GUADALAJARA** (Norten) 6. **LAS VEGAS** (Koolhaas) 7. **VENICE** (Peggy Guggenheim)
8. **ABU DHABI** (Gehry) 9. **VILNIUS** (Hadid) 10. **HONG KONG** (Norman Foster) 11.**TAICHUNG** (Hadid)
12. **RIO** (Nouvel) 13. **SINGAPORE** (Hadid) 14. **EAST RIVER, NEW YORK CITY** (Gehry)
15. **URDAIBAI** (mooted site)

the largest transfer of cultural wealth from Occident to Orient ever recorded.[109]

Even so, these plans were quickly eclipsed by those for Saadiyat Island in the United Arab Emirates. One of three colossal museums planned for a man-made island off the emirate, and *twelve times* the size of Wright's Guggenheim, the Guggenheim Abu Dhabi will be a record-setting institution in many respects, but at least two factors may complicate its reception.[110] First, there is the often whispered, but rarely articulated, charge of reactionary Islamic cultural politics, at once puritanical toward much representation and philistine toward abstraction. Presumably Krens and his patron, Sheikh Khalifa bin Zayed Al Nahyan, have taken this straw man into account and will bank on defying expectations in unexpected ways — but these presumptions may set the curatorial bar to a low and populist common denominator.

A more worrying issue may simply be the weather. Recent scholarship on other Guggenheim satellites turned up this prescient concern in 2002 regarding the prospects of the short-lived Koolhaas-designed vault in Sin City, co-founded with the Hermitage: "For Tom Krens' new Guggenheim museum branch in Las Vegas, the regression gives a mixed prediction: Based on tourist beds, Las Vegas looks like a good site; based on January temperature, Krens may have a failure on his hands."[111] It turns out tourists (like undergrads) retreat to museums in cold weather. January is the coldest month of the year in both Las Vegas and Abu Dhabi, with the latter hotter, on average, by almost ten degrees Fahrenheit.[112]

SUPERMAXED OUT

Consistently, from 1982 to 1996, the CDC had six to ten new prisons in some stage of planning, design or construction, at an average cost per establishment of a quarter-billion dollars.[113]

RUTH WILSON GILMORE

I didn't open the floodgates.[114]

DON NOVEY, 2010

IN FACT, HE CLOSED THEM. Pelican Bay is Don Novey's Bilbao. The first SuperMax prison ever, Pelican Bay State Prison was sited in remote Crescent City, at the most northwesterly corner of California, and completed in 1989. Though the federal Super-Max at Florence, Colorado, has garnered more press in the last decade, Pelican Bay was its template, and in many respects remains a more doctrinaire essay in carceral absolutism.[115]

　　The heart of Pelican Bay, and later Maxis, is the Secure Housing Unit, or SHU. SHU blocks are like other podular cell-blocks in their basic scale and occupancy, but without the premise of intermediate, shared common space, as inmates are confined to their individual cells for all but state-mandated showers and outdoor exposure totaling less than one hour a day. So little space is required for interaction, in fact, that the SHU plan has simply reverted to the old cruciform of 19th century peni-tentiaries. They are New Generation, but the Folsom Way.

　　The design of Pelican Bay reflects every demand and passing fancy of Novey's rank-and-file constituency. A space-age new environment of video feeds and automated lockdown capability, Pelican Bay promised total segregation of inmates from staff, and from one another. PBSP also underscores the messages Novey most wanted politicians, citizens, and inmates to hear in the 1980s: Corrections is "the toughest beat," and the prison system is dominated by felons so incorrigible and gang-infected that a separate death star of a prison must be built to

134

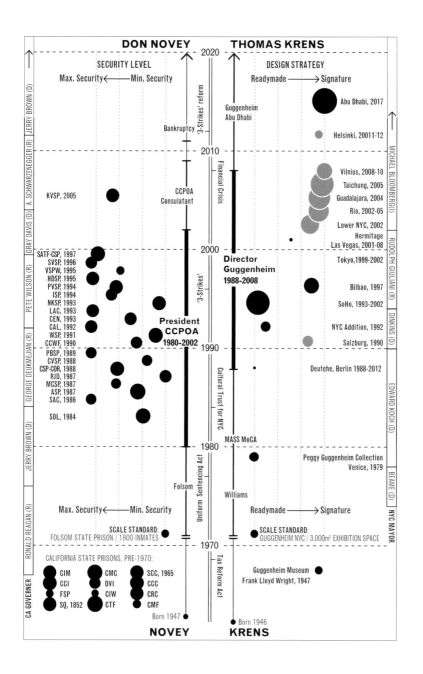

DON NOVEY   THOMAS KRENS

SECURITY LEVEL   **DESIGN STRATEGY**

Max. Security ⟵⟶ Min. Security   Readymade ⟶ Signature

2020

Guggenheim Abu Dhabi   Abu Dhabi, 2017

'3-Strikes' reform

Bankruptcy   Helsinki, 20011-12

JERRY BROWN (D)

2010

A. SCHWARZENEGGER (R)

Financial Crisis   Vilnius, 2008-10

CCPOA Consulatant   Taichung, 2005

KVSP, 2005   Guadalajara, 2004

GRAY DAVIS (D)   Rio, 2002-05

Lower NYC, 2002

Hermitage

Las Vegas, 2001-08

2000

SATF-CSP, 1997   **Director**   Tokyo,1999-2002
SVSP, 1996   **Guggenheim**
VSPW, 1995   **1988-2008**
HDSP, 1995
PVSP, 1994   Bilbao, 1997
ISP, 1994
NKSP, 1993   SoHo, 1993-2002
LAC, 1993
CEN, 1993
CAL, 1992   NYC Addition, 1992
WSP, 1991   **President**
CCWF, 1990   **CCPOA**   Salzburg, 1990
    1980-2002

PETE WILSON (R)   '3-Strikes'   DINKINS (D) / RUDOLPH GIULIANI (R)

PBSP, 1989   1990
CVSP, 1988
CSP-COR, 1988   Deutche, Berlin 1988-2012
RJD, 1987
MCSP, 1987
ASP, 1987
SAC, 1986

SOL, 1984   Cultural Trust for NYC

GEORGE DEUKMEJIAN (R)   EDWARD KOCH (D)

MASS MoCA

1980

Peggy Guggenheim Collection
Venice, 1979

JERRY BROWN (D)   Uniform Sentencing Act   BEAME (D)

Folsom   Williams

Max. Security ⟵⟶ Min. Security   Readymade ⟶ Signature

SCALE STANDARD: **SCALE STANDARD**:
FOLSOM STATE PRISON / 1800 INMATES   GUGGENHEIM NYC / 3,000m² EXHIBITION SPACE

1970

RONALD REAGAN (R)   NYC MAYOR

Tax Reform Act

CALIFORNIA STATE PRISONS, PRE-1970:

Guggenheim Museum
Frank Lloyd Wright, 1947

CIM	CMC	SCC, 1965
CCI	DVI	CCC
FSP	CIW	CRC
SQ, 1852	CTF	CMF

CA GOVERNER

Born 1947   Born 1946

NOVEY   KRENS

Institutional Protagonists

straitjacket the worst of them and scare the rest. Pelican Bay also has more subtle fiscal virtues: by isolating the highest security, most costly offenders, PBSP acts as a "loss leader" for the rest of the state system, consolidating Level 4 maximum security inmates, who cost $59,000 per year to hold, and thus reducing cost-per-inmate calculations at all other facilities.

Whatever controversies it generated — and they are ongoing — Pelican Bay brought a wealth of downstream advantages for those hoping to expand the state system in general. With the "worst of the worst" accounted for separately, older maximum-security redoubts such as San Quentin and Folsom could be rebalanced toward lower-risk populations rather than refurbished for more dangerous ones. And the advances of Pelican Bay could be replicated elsewhere. Single AD-SEG or SHU housing units, such as the one described earlier at Mule Creek State Prison, provide localized deterrence at many of the new state facilities. While more ambitious guards and hardened inmates fill those Level 4 arenas, medium security convicts (at least, those lucky enough to "program" with a work assignment) still stamp license plates and sew chambray "prison blues" at mid-level campuses, while low-risk Level 1 "trustees" clean up California highways and help put out the state's many wildfires. At only $12,000 a year to detain in dormitory tents, prisoner firefighters are probably the best bargain in the system — and one of the reasons the CCPOA fought so hard in the 1980s and '90s for laws maximizing terms for low-end offenders.

Don Novey kept everyone moving on down the Line.

WILD, WILD WEST

But as Susanville has discovered, a new prison requires that the community adapt to a rapid leap in a specific kind of population — those drawn to and associated with the work of corrections, an industry for whom the raw material is the systemic incapacitation of despairing human beings, in this case, over 10,000 of them.[116]
JOELLE FRASER

Incarceration is very abstract in Sacramento.[117]
ROSE BRAZ

THE ADVENT of postmodern prisons and museums would be of little interest outside the field of architecture had those innovations not factored so effectively into broader strategies for massive institutional expansion. While Krens sought new channels for the export of Western art, Novey redefined the western landscape.

In California prisons, however, the shifting colors of that landscape meet with expressionist violence, even in those sited in the plein-air hinterlands. I've toured seventeen operating prisons and jails in California, nine of them state prisons and the majority of those built in the Novey era (the others were five county jails and three federal penitentiaries, institutions that either feed into or supersede the state system). Though the new California prisons blur into one another when seen from above, they meet their surroundings, and their neighboring communities, uniquely. In Susanville, for example, two side-by-side state prisons quadrupled the county's population and overtaxed their municipal services enough to justify the first successful lawsuit against the California Department of Corrections, or CDC for its urban impact.[118]

The current extent of carceral California is better grasped as a shadow infrastructure than as an "archipelago," the nature of which is most legible at its urban extremities. The largest of these, both in terms of intake and "pooling" within the network, is Los Angeles County.

On January 18, 1996 — the same week Tupac Shakur's "California Love" welcomed us to the Wild, Wild West — race riots erupted at Pitchess Detention Center, a Los Angeles County-run holding camp in Castaic, California, and reverberated through the county's jail system, engulfing 5,700 inmates in five days of mayhem. In highly orchestrated attacks by Latino prison-gang members on black inmates, the latter suffered 75% of the 150 casualties, and an old order toppled.

Californians, especially those now kept or keeping others behind bars, learned with brutal alacrity how dependent the rapid expansion of the state's correctional empire was upon a demographic anomaly. Because black inmates long formed a narrow but consistent plurality of the institutionalized population, African-American prison gangs dominated California's correctional system for decades, well into the 1990s. A head count conducted on New Year's Eve 1990 by the CDC, showed the state prison population to be 35.5% black, 30.0% Hispanic, 29.8% white, and 4.7% Asian or "other." But the mix within the system shifted dramatically, "favoring" Latinos, who by March 1995 had grown to 33.8% of the state prison population while blacks fell to 31.9%. The numbers were more radically imbalanced at the county level, where the *LA Times* reported that Latinos were 45% of the LA County jail population in the same year.

At the state level, shifts in population can be managed and absorbed. Some of the thirty-three state prisons will be black-dominated and some "brown," but by shuffling the numbers at each of their 5,000-inmate "campuses," wardens will concoct a new equilibrium among prison gangs of differing races, as they have juggled intra-ethnic rivals such as the infamous Crips and Bloods, or the Sureños and Norteños, the two major statewide Hispanic affiliations. However, bound by their proximity to the courts to receive all accused and hold those awaiting trial under a presumption of innocence, county jails and holding facilities have neither the time nor the luxury of alternative venues to continually swap warring factions.

Traditionally, jails control the flow into and out of larger, more alluvial state prison systems. If each of the 5,000-inmate state prisons is designed as a "reservoir" in the correctional ecology, then county jails, detention centers, and "honor ranchos" run by local sheriffs are suppose to serve as the dams and filters of the system. California is reversing these roles, and the levees have begun to give way. Down from record highs in the early '90s of more than 250%, state prison populations are at 180–205% of capacity (varying by facility), a surprisingly convenient level of overcrowding for facility planning and staff promotions. Gymnasiums in state prisons, long used as packed dormitories with beds stacked up to three bunks high (all gyms, save one under court order at California Medical Facility, were converted), are now emptying for the first time in a decade.

Compounding these factors in 1996 (shortly after the longest baseball strike ever), Californians endorsed "three-strikes" legislation: three felony convictions mean a felon is "out," or locked up for twenty years to life. Three strikes paradoxically lightened the state prison load in the short term by pushing inmates back down to the county level for longer and longer periods. Defendants facing a second or third "strike" are now far more likely to take their case to a full jury trial rather than cop a plea and bargain for less time as most did before. Many more accused are appealing every decision, and must stay close to city courts to do so. Local facilities are now overtaxed to bursting, none more so than the county jails of Los Angeles. When Pitchess erupted, its twelve dormitories held 1,700 inmates, more than three times the allowable number.

CALIFORNIA, UBER ALLES

I'm the Governor Pete Wilson you know
Baddest governor to ever grab the mic and go boom!
I'm so proud to know the Great Communicator
Want to be known as the Great Incarcerator...
California, über alles, California, über alles...[119]
MICHAEL FRANTI, DISPOSABLE HEROES OF HIPHOPRISY, 1992

Today we want to talk a little bit about prison reform....
Now we are at the point where if we don't clean up the mess, a
federal court will do the job for us. And that is bad news because
they will order the immediate release of criminals and they will
dig into our general funds....
CALIFORNIA GOVERNOR ARNOLD SCHWARZENEGGER, VIDEO ADDRESS,
DECEMBER 21, 2006

141

CALIFORNIA DIDN'T CLEAN UP the mess. A federal consent decree to fix the state's prisons came due in 2008, with a *$7 billion* price tag. And, note, that is simply what the receiver thinks it will take to patch up prison health care facilities, deemed in the report to be "in an abysmal state of disrepair," not to improve or reform any other aspect of the 100,000-bed system, holding 172,000 convicts that year.

Though Governor Schwarzenegger called for prison reform in 2006 and onward, one would have had to parse the term carefully to find any relation to the way it was employed during his first term in office. "Reform" no longer means an actual overhaul of the way we incarcerate our record 172,000 state inmates, nor any reassessment of the sentencing guidelines that have taken us to close to 210% of capacity in our thirty-three state prisons. Rather than actually changing policy, the governor's 2007 correctional budget of $10.9 billion simply promised new facilities and new staffing targets for an already bloated, dangerous, and poorly supervised bureaucracy. That $10.9 billion included $2.5 billion for health care, so the federal receiver's recommendations will in fact add only $4 to $5 billion to the tally. A total of $14.7 billion in new prison construction is planned over the coming years.

Though he successfully lobbied to lengthen the agency's name, and ostensibly, its mission, to the California Department of Corrections *and Rehabilitation* in 2005, Governor Schwarzenegger ran up against stiff opposition to any directive that might alter the way inmates are warehoused, or stem their influx. Though the federal court order has effectively pulled health care provision out of the hands of state officials, the prospects for real improvement in the lives of the incarcerated — or a reprieve for California taxpayers — seem more remote than ever. A report issued in the wake of the governor's proposals on January 26, 2007, by the Little Hoover Commission, a nonpartisan review board for state agencies, described a system in "tailspin" and concluded that "the state's correctional policy is politically bankrupt."[120]

One must at least credit Schwarzenegger for testing how indentured California politicians have become to the state's prison empire, before painting his capitulations as reform. His predecessors of both parties, Gray Davis and Pete Wilson, proudly fed the CDC (now the CDCR) and its rank-and-file at every opportunity.

Through the '80s and '90s, prisons managed to be all things to all people, save prisoners. Republicans, usually miserly toward state programs, invested heavily in law-and-order fantasies of mass incarceration, and Democrats, all too true to form, saw a state employees' union (and an astoundingly aggressive and well-financed one) to accommodate at every turn. Between 1984 and 1994, Republican Pete Wilson and a Democratic state legislature presided over the largest, fastest expansion of a prison system ever undertaken, and then Governor Gray Davis, a Democrat, added $680 million in raises for those patrolling all those new yards. Both supported draconian initiatives and legislation that guaranteed an ever-expanding and longer-held pool of inmates, securing ever more prison construction and staffing.[121]

With no provisions for reduced sentencing, the 2008 proposals from the governor's office promised a host of expensive stopgaps: the completion of two of four long-planned prisons, and an overhaul of the parole guidelines. Their most innovative proposition actually did not address the state prison system, but the grossly overtaxed county and city jails that feed it. In a rare acknowledgement of the burden that our state laws and detention system place on local governments, the governor earmarked $5.5 of the $10.9 billion in funding for jail additions and expansion. It is money that will at least go to urban areas, and county jails in California have proven the most architecturally ambitious in the country, often for both better and worse. As Sheriff Lee Baca is fond of pointing out — often on his way to explaining why something terrible happened while no one was looking — the largest prison in the free world is the 12,000-bed LA County Jail and Twin Towers complex under his supervision.

CALIFORNIA STATE PRISONS
1. SAN QUENTIN STATE PRISON (1852)   2. FOLSOM STATE PRISON (1880)   3. CALIFORNIA INSTITUTION FOR MEN (1941)
4. CORRECTIONAL TRAINING FACILITY (1946)   5. CALIFORNIA MEN'S COLONY (1954)   6. CALIFORNIA CORRECTIONAL
INSTITUTION (1954)   7. CALIFORNIA MEDICAL FACILITY (1955)   8. DEUEL VOCATIONAL INSTITUTION (1953)
9. CALIFORNIA REHABILITATION CENTER (1962)   10. CALIFORNIA CORRECTIONAL CENTER (1964)   11. SIERRA CONSERVATION
CENTER (1965)   12. CALIFRONIA STATE PRISON, SOLANO (1984)   13. CALIFORNIA STATE PRISON, SACRAMENTO (1986)
14. AVENAL STATE PRISON (1987)   15. MULE CREEK STATE PRISON (1987)   16. RICHARD J. DONOVAN CORRECTIONAL
FACILITY (1987)

17. CHUCKAWALLA VALLEY STATE PRISON (1988)   18. CALIFORNIA STATE PRISON, CORCORAN (1988)
19. PELICAN BAY STATE PRISON (1989)   20. CENTRAL CALIFORNIA WOMEN'S FACILITY (1990)   21. WASCO STATE
PRISON (1991)   22. CALIPATRIA STATE PRISON (1992)   23. CALIFORNIA STATE PRISON, CENTINELA (1993)
24. CALIFORNIA STATE PRISON, LOS ANGELES COUNTY (1993)   25. NORTH KERN STATE PRISON (1993)   26. SALINAS
VALLEY STATE PRISON (1996)   27. HIGH DESERT STATE PRISON (1995)   28. VALLEY STATE PRISON FOR WOMEN (1995)
29. CALIFORNIA SUBSTANCE ABUSE TREATMENT FACILITY AND STATE PRISON, CORCORAN (1997)
30. KERN VALLEY STATE PRISON (2005)

TEMPORARY/CONTEMPT

Everyone in this room right now can be a beacon of love.[122]

SHERIFF LEE BACA, ADDRESSING LA MEN'S CENTRAL JAIL INMATES

Designed by Albert C. Martin in 1963, the LA County Men's Central Jail is one in a string of correctional facilities laced up Alameda Boulevard on the eastern edge of downtown Los Angeles. Together with the abandoned Lincoln Heights Jail to the north, now leased for movie shoots, and the Metropolitan Detention Center, a sleek 588-bed federal fortress across Alameda, the Central Jail and its offspring the Twin Towers form what urban historian Mike Davis dubbed "LA's own Gulag Rim."[123] (The truss-shrouded recreation decks of the federal MDC, once rappelled with a rope of knotted sheets by an escaping inmate, appear on the cover of Davis' *City of Quartz*.)

The same architect that gave the May Co. Building of 1940 its iconic five-story, faux gold-leaf entry tower on Wilshire Boulevard's "Miracle Mile" extended his gift for oversimplification to the Central Jail. Though cast completely in concrete, the Central Jail's one public space has a generic, late-modern elegance closer in its proportions, if not its opacity, to A.C. Martin's nearby Water & Power Building than a house of corrections. The grassy, arcaded entrance court at Men's Central ably masks a spiraling limbo of despair worthy of Dante.

Touring the Central Jail took just eighty minutes, the last seventy-five without any directional orientation to the outer world. Not one in a class of twenty architecture students could point toward the entrance of the jail after passing through the labyrinthine intake sequence that began the tour. One of the three officers escorting our tour explained that the disorientation we had experienced was central to the jail's management.

Like Disneyland, the Central Jail seeks to establish an alternate reality within its walls, a reality with its own code of ethics and conduct, and a reality that can be serviced by secondary and tertiary circulation routes known only to the keepers. Short-term inmates are overseen by deputies on eighteen-month tours of duty before they are promoted out to the streets. The margin of facility knowledge separating a "fish" or new inmate from a hardly more seasoned deputy-recruit is critical to maintain. Myriad stairs and mall-style escalators bind the six floors of the Central Jail in a confounding web.

Unlike the Magic Kingdom, however, which depends on the consistent, cartoonishly blue skies of Anaheim and Orlando to transport its visitors out of the everyday, the Central Jail blocks out the sky entirely. With the exception of a few filthy white-glass skylights high over cellblock catwalks, there are no windows into the inmate-occupied portions of the Central Jail. Instead, caged fluorescent tubes burn everywhere night and day, turning all faces — all races — a sickly purple-blue. Unlike the other fifteen facilities toured by our class, the Central Jail allows many inmates to wander freely, while deputies collect in groups at the sally ports. Deputies wear mustaches and muscle-hugging khaki. Their

270 HOUSING UNIT UNDER CONSTRUCTION, Susanville, California
(student photo: Carceral California Seminar, 1995)

badges, buckles, and batons glint in the blue light, but the officers seem narrow-eyed and vulnerable without the reflective sun-
glasses they'll soon wear outside. The inmates come in a wider
array of ensembles. Lightweight coveralls, much like surgical
scrubs, color-code the arrival status, security level, job assignment, as well as the physical and mental health of all inmates.

New arrivals wear orange before classification; most will
soon be issued the standard royal blue daily-wear "County
Blues." Inmates in lighter blue have medical needs, served in a
300-bed hospital wing, and those with yellow tops are under psychiatric supervision. Low security, working inmates, usually classified as "trustees," wear tan. Mismatched coveralls, one sleeve
blue and the other white, are reserved for state prison convicts, in
Central Jail only for trial dates. All inmates wear white go-ahead
slippers — no laces, no metal, no soles.

Though 1,300 state cons and other more ambitious gang-
land stars are held on the fifth floor in solitary and two-man
cells, the majority of those confined at Central Jail share space
with between four and 400 other inmates. Three vast tanks on
the first floor for intake and release and an equal number on the
top floor for holding can absorb up to 2,000 new arrivals, who
will be detained here an average eight to eleven hours for processing. Cordoned off by long runs of steel bars and grating,
the pens allow a rough separation of hostile parties in crisis,
but more often serve to keep the intoxicated from falling prey to
other inmates. There are a few bunkbeds and open-air toilets in
each. Many passing through the Central Jail for minor offenses,
DWIs (driving while intoxicated) or D&Ds (drunk and disorderly)
for example, will never pass beyond the tanks. As the influx has
escalated over the last twenty years, one- to three-day sentences
are routinely held and released without full processing.

Upstairs on the second through fourth floors, cellblocks
follow a linear pattern endemic to US prisons from the 1930s
through the early 1970s. Four-, six-, and eight-man cells run down
either side of long, two-story corridors with chain link "suicide

148

TWIN TOWERS CORRECTIONAL FACILITY, HOK, Los Angeles, California (1997)

screens" along the upper level balcony and a glassed-in surveil-lance cat-walk above. As one shuffles down the narrow length of the catwalk, each cell opens beyond the wire-reinforced glass like a full-scale diorama, each its own dim, purgatorial *tableau vivant*. A student asked about the many inmates curled up on the bare linoleum. "Some of them really prefer sleeping on the floor," explained a deputy. Just as we were leaving Men's Central after a tour in 1995, another deputy asked whether we had seen the "White Elephants" across the street.

Adjacent to the Central Jail stands the Twin Towers Correc-tional Facility, then a perhaps aptly silent eye in California's penal hurricane. The jail addition was complete but vacant, a mammoth on ice, for three years. Sheriff Sherman Block refused to open the 2,024-cell addition for lack of funding. The Twin Towers cost between $239 million and $373 million to build (the contractor's figure and the county's figure vary by more than $100 million in change orders and wage inclusions), and the sheriff told the *LA Times* that $90 million to $110 million more was needed to open and staff the facility for one year. According to a source close to the project, at least $200,000 was spent on useless fire doors alone. This impasse was finally resolved in 1997.

Designed by Hellmuth, Obata & Kassabaum Inc. (HOK) over a two-year period in the mid-'80s, the towers make a more self-consciously "correctional" statement than their precursor across Bauchet Street. The Twin Towers are linked to the Central Jail via a 450-foot enclosed overpass, an extruded and window-less airport gangway supported by miniature freeway caissons. Contrary to the low-slung, reticent Central Jail, the two capsule-planned wings of the Twin Towers rise emphatically into the LA skyline. Though clad completely in stucco, the towers have a believably lapidary presence. Following the neo-Medieval lead of the federal MDC down Alameda, the Twin Towers employ a wealth of "old school" prison iconography. A constant staccato of five-inch sliver windows slice across each facet of the facade, under-scored by six-foot maroon bands encircling both towers at every floor level. The bands are corbeled to resemble half-lapped brick coursing, here magnified to grotesque overstatement. The dark hues and odd scale-play recall French Enlightenment schemes such as those by Jean-Charles Delafosse, in which chains as big around as human thighs secure massive colonnades and mon-strous keystones teeter over tiny dark portal doors.

The Twin Towers have no front door. Inmates enter by bridge from the Central Jail or by bus through an eighteen-foot razor-wire wrapped control gate tucked behind the north wing. It is a vast facility, huge for even a prison and unthinkable for a jail. Built on 9.5 acres opposite the Central Jail, the Twin Towers run to 1.2 million square feet, with 175,000 square feet — almost four US football fields — in intake and release areas alone. Following the demands of the Sheriff's Department, the intake areas spin all newcomers through a vast maze. A schizophrenic series of interview banks, shower rooms, and briefing stations serpentine into classroom-planned holding areas with low cement block toilet stalls where the teacher should sit.

Above the processing levels, the towers are identical in plan, with five split-level stories of cellblock apiece. Designed like a Q-tip, each floor has a bar of offices, medical rooms, "chapels," and storage that separate and support two bulbous housing units at either end. Following Jeremy Bentham's original 1791 Panopticon plan almost to the letter, the Twin Tower blocks form concentric zones radiating outward: observation decks look directly into two bare holding areas, which in turn give into dayrooms and finally a band of forty-eight solitary cells lining the perimeter (a second bunk was added to each cell before opening).

High-rise structural requirements and the faceted exterior of the Twin Towers, however, wreak minor havoc with panoptic principles. Larger, irregular cells wedge into the towers' hexagonal corners, and these favored cells are further privatized by the three-foot structural piers that block the view from the observation deck. When the inequity of this arrangement was pointed out, our tour guide explained that the internal hierarchies of prison gangs would be harnessed to help in jail management with a reward system including marginally better accommodations. The huge glass panes framed in almost every door in the housing units was downgraded late in construction to tempered glass. Though it won't shatter into blade-like shards, tempered glass fractures into a sharp granular powder that if packed into a sweat sock, would pack the lethal wallop of tear gas.

When the deputy at the Central Jail called the Twin Towers White Elephants, he meant first that they had cost too much, but also that they might not work as a jail. Designed after the model of new state prisons, the cellblocks of the Twin Towers are meant to hold convicts after classification, not the random assortment they are more likely to receive. Private cells, blind spots behind structural columns, and a door configuration explained with some chagrin during our tour as "Triangles of Death" all breed opportunities unseen in a bare holding pen. (Because some of the swinging cell doors are less than four feet apart, a triangle big enough to trap one or two inmates can be formed by opening two doors into the dayroom from two adjoining cells until their outer, knob-side edges meet.)

POSTSCRIPT, 2005: A brief follow-up visit to the Twin Towers in use revealed a dystopia in which Huxley abets Orwell. The six panoptic wedges of the housing unit we visited were each dedicated to a different mood-altering drug regimen — ranging from the antidepressant Zoloft up to quetiapine, an opium-like antipsychotic that 30% of LAMCJ inmates are said to have feigned symptoms to obtain.[124] Usually retailed as Seroquel, but known inside as "Suzie Q" and "Snoozeberries," quetiapine resembles nothing so much as Soma, the miracle drug rampant in Huxley's *Brave New World*. Many of the inmates wandered the common areas in stupors, one of them naked, oblivious, and masturbating in slow motion. We watched from a glassed-in control booth run by a typical two-person team including a female deputy sheriff and an outside computer consultant in his early twenties. Twelve design students on the tour were less fazed by this scene than they were by a window tapping medley they received from (presumably less sedated) inmates at the nearby Metropolitan Detention Center as the class admired that building from across Alameda.

HOW LACMA GOT THE LED OUT

In my past you on the other side of the glass
Of my memory's museum
I'm just saying, hey Mona Lisa
Come home you know you can't Rome without Caesar[125]

KANYE WEST, "FLASHING LIGHTS"

February 2008: the opening gala for the Broad Contemporary Art Museum (BCAM) at LACMA — the one with the Easter egg invitations by Jeff Koons. The night included a lot of surgery, a lot of spectacle, and a lot of speeches — the most telling line of which was Eli Broad's promise that LACMA could have his art as long as it like, *as long as it stayed on display.*

Just before dessert, a Eurasian trio dropped from the ceiling playing a deafening version of Led Zeppelin's "Kashmir" — da, na, na, DA, da, na, na, DA, da, na, na, DA — as the curtain lifted on the new building. Forty violinists, faces painted like the Blue Man Group, but in red, kept the bass line rolling while all of haute LA took in the new building and one another. Edythe Broad rolled her eyes when I asked about the music; LACMA Director Michael Govan (rhymes, it turns out, with Guffman, not Jovan) seemed to know it was Zeppelin, though he was taking no credit for it.

The BCAM is another architectural half-step on the LACMA campus, but Koons and his work, and, Pop more generally, looked good in it. I think the Broad collection will be redeemed in the end for how it fleshes out and reframes all the tangents headed into and out of that movement: how Cy Twombly popped into Basquiat (who'd have thought?); how Rauschenberg and Johns actually needed Warhol to clean them up, how Koons holds up to Hirst; how even Serra's big swoops can be commoditized and boxed for delivery. All the Cindy Shermans look like headshots, of course, and Jenny Holzer's engraved benches reminded me of "The Loved One." An '80s room of neo-Expressionists looks like the pop rehash of AbEx that in fact it is. All BCAM really, desperately needs is Ruscha's "LACMA Burning" on a prominent wall to make the whole place look knowing and in on the joke — a joke that really is no joke. LACMA should be to Pop, belatedly, what the new MoMA decided, equally late, to be for Minimalism.

Mike Davis once dismissed the Getty Center as a "Nordstrom in the sky," but the BCAM simply defers to its superior retail neighbor, the May Co. Building by A.C. Martin. One absorbs that reality from a temporary hangar behind both buildings they've erected for all the parties — a not-very-poor-man's version of Rem Koolhaas' 2001 competition-winning original proposal for the (then bigger) job of fixing LACMA. At least 30' tall and 100'x100' open space, the hangar had most of the gala folk thinking they were in a vast new gallery of BCAM, only to be herded after dinner into the (still super-generous, but nowhere near as big) spaces of the actual building, just dwarfed by their party tent. LACMA really can't help itself. The escalator that's supposed to recall Piano's first move like that for the Centre Pompidou looks more like a cherry red fire escape from the Beverly Center.

URBAN LIGHTS, Chris Burden (2008; Broad Museum at LACMA beyond)

Chris Burden assembled 202 restored streetlamps in a tight square grid out front, which seemed uninspired until I saw it from down the street leaving; from a distance, it looks like a weird peristyle abstraction of all the kitschy Pereira buildings around it (LACMA could have been designed by Mies van der Rohe, who was turned away by the board in the 1960s). As Burden said modestly, "I put the Miracle back into Miracle Mile." True, but in much the same way that the Dude's rug in *The Big Lebowski* tied his whole place together.

Better: a huge Tony Smith space-frame, *Smoke* from 1967, tesselates up through the dim atrium of the old LACMA. It's like stumbling into that dim, cavernous hold on the ship where they kept King Kong (1970s, Jessica Lange version), and having the beast pat you on the head on your way to the restrooms.

POSTSCRIPT, 2012: It turns out that the tent was the future: the Lynda and Stewart Resnick Exhibition Pavilion opened in October 2010, matching the tent's dimensions. To this was recently added Michael Heizer's suspended boulder, *Levitated Mass*. All the monumental striving of architects Pereira, Goff and Piano, as well as the efforts of Burden and Heizer, combine to suggest a certain "Californian Empire Style" that all, save maybe Pereira, would likely disavow. But perhaps the most salient rhyme for LACMA could now be written by Alejandro Zaera-Polo, whose theory of architectural Envelopes has found pristine expression. With the vast, horizontal expanse of the Resnick space joining the stacked Broad cube, Michael Govan has replicated the basic format of dual spaces that the Dia Art Foundation pioneered in Chelsea and Beacon that he left behind in New York. This dyad — of a dense, "spherical" (to use Zaera-Polo's term) core building paired with a sprawling "Mat" at some distance — is the contemporary state of corrections and collections in microcosm.

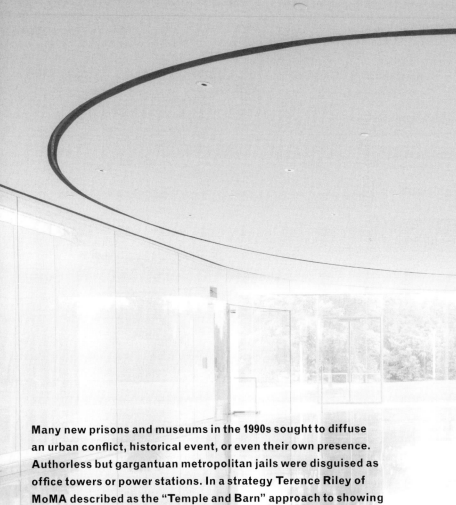

Many new prisons and museums in the 1990s sought to diffuse an urban conflict, historical event, or even their own presence. Authorless but gargantuan metropolitan jails were disguised as office towers or power stations. In a strategy Terence Riley of MoMA described as the "Temple and Barn" approach to showing modern and contemporary art, many museums reclaimed older industrial structures for the latter work, often as they finalized schemes for newly minted main buildings to showcase their modern gems. Diplomacy through design factors in both the many cross-border museum commissions to "global" architects and in the banal facades of tower jails built to appease squeamish urban neighbors. An orchestrated circuitry of viewing and holding spaces, or "infotestines," debrief new arrivals on the lore and future of these networks, and now typify most jails and single-topic museums.

MILLENNIAL

05.NEUTRALIZE

DE YOUNG MUSEUM. Herzog & de Meuron, San Francisco, CA (2005)

Previous image: GLASS PAVILION, TOLEDO MUSEUM OF ART, SANAA, Toledo, OH (2006)

PURPLE WORLDS

It would be plausible to show the link that probably connects
panorama and levitation: sovereinty, euphoria, powerful lightness[126]
ROLAND BARTHES, FROM THE NEUTRAL

January 2008. My first visit to a Planet Hollywood, at Fisherman's
Wharf in San Francisco, and startling for how exactly it met my
expectations: wall-to-wall memorabilia, deafening guitar solos,
a gantlet of faux concert swag. Six varieties of potato skins, and

Coors on tap. Though no doubt meant to reassure, all the familiar songs, fatty foods, and prewashed jersey-knit prove oddly disorienting, as if the entirety of the environment had been branded into my consciousness beforehand by a latter-day Philip K. Dick. A video of Prince's once distantly anticipatory anthem "1999" filled a flat screen over our booth. In a miasma of purple lights and smoke, exactingly choreographed band members perform parts on guitar and synthesizer that, if memory serves, Prince had recorded solo for the album. He is still hypnotically alien to watch, but the analog production values show their age. Lisa and Wendy both gyrate against Prince throughout, as if fending off the Minneapolis cold. Pinched and pegged below, their silhouettes splay upward to wide, triangular shoulders, collars, and hair, identically coiffed for all band members. The stage set, hardly discernable through the smoke and strobes, seems to rake up infinitely to a distant drummer, who pounds away like John Bonham or Keith Moon, but looks more like a sushi chef in training.

As primitive as the camera angles and lighting effects are, "1999" shows us the mechanics of a total video environment, an amorphous merger of performers, space, and technology into a new seamless whole — a whole not greater than a sum of its parts, but one in which, as artist Olafur Eliasson put it in a different context, *surroundings are surrounded*. "1999" is precisely the *shape* — if not the sound, fashion, or message — of things to come.

Twenty-five years later, that video seems as good a place as any to mark the beginning of a *millennial* sensibility in US popular culture (there are of course other standards — theological, geopolitical — that would see most of the 20th century in end-of-days millenarian terms). Just a year before 1984, the milestone for more Orwellian prognosticators, Prince forecast a *fin de siecle* mood pretty accurately and succinctly: an endless New Year's Eve bash, hazy, violet, video-pixelated, depthless, immersive. Though Public Enemy and Nirvana might have had more to say about the states of black and white America in the 1990s, Prince's

"1999" proved an instructive premonition for how we would come to terms with a both momentous and arbitrary date change.

The close of the 20th century brought with it a sensibility that is still being realized at the scale of architecture. On a personal level the coming new millennium rarely meant more than (happily unrealized) concerns about "Y2K" computer malfunctions. As a society, however, we took the turning of the calendar very seriously, by enshrining, commemorating, and edifying as many historical high and low marks of the last 100 years, if not the last thousand, as quickly, grandly, and "experientially" as possible. We also locked up an astounding number of people who arrived too early and too rowdy for the party.

At once encyclopedic and vague, the Millennial ambition to encompass all of something within a single space and time forced a wholesale renegotiation of the relationships between new institutions for constraint and display and the cities they augment, as well as between the interior and exterior of the buildings themselves. The logic of container and contained that carries through Minimal and post-Minimal structures was gradually superseded by a new set of precepts for modulating *surroundings*. How do buildings blur into, re-illuminate, or simply become their surroundings? How can architecture envelop, but not encase, its functionality? How can the orchestrated surroundings required to detain people or exhibit art be nested within, or through, architectures that have become more and more permeable and seamless pulses in the city? The most innovative prisons and museums built in the late 1980s through the early 2000s met these questions by concentrating on a few architectural effects — displacement and disguise, de-scaling and disorientation — and on the isolation of techniques for their realization.[127]

Collectively, these are tactics of architectonic *neutralization*, in which an institution's extent, singularity, and clarity of purpose are rendered indefinite, if not infinite. The form, surface, and organization of millennial institutions are designed both to prefigure the future, and to guard against its uncertainties.

PRE-DIGITAL UNDERGROUND

When I used to play prisoner's base in the Luxembourg, what
I liked best was not provoking the other team and boldly exposing
myself to their right to take me prisoner; what I liked best was to
free the prisoners — the effect of which was to put both teams
back into circulation: the game started over again at zero.…
Perhaps the Neutral is that: to accept the predicate as nothing
more than a moment: a time.[128]

ROLAND BARTHES

PLANET HOLLYWOOD at Fisherman's Wharf is but one among
many institutions in the Bay Area trying to broker between time
frames, and between generic categories and specific specimens,
through strategies of *displacement and disguise*. Since before
Prince's anthem was a hit, San Francisco and its neighboring
counties have played a pioneering role in architectures of urban
inversion. Circling the San Francisco Bay, one can visit prisons
and museums in every conceivable disposition: underground or
elevated, consolidated or campus-planned, in the guise of one
another or myriad other building types. Appropriately enough,
the architects of both **SFMOMA** and the new de Young Museum
happen to be Swiss, but even outside those rarified cases, the
Bay Area turns out to host quite a bit of neutralizing architecture.

Oakland boasts one of the oddest juxtapositions in America:
the first modern museum built underground, designed by Kevin
Roche in 1965, which is located just blocks from *two* high-rise
jails on the city's most prominent lots facing the bay, one dating
from the 1960s and the other from the 1980s. This suppression
of culture and foregrounding of detention — in a municipality
that spawned the Black Panthers as well as recent port-closing
Occupy encampments and protests — signals the deep urban
ironies shaping a city *The New York Times* recently dubbed "a kind
of living museum of 1970s radicalism."[129]

SAN FRANCISCO COUNTY JAIL, AKA "GLAMOUR SLAMMER," Williams & Tanaka / Del Campo & Maru, San Francisco, California (2004)

Nor is Oakland the only outlier in the East Bay. Berkeley has both People's Park — arguably the first museum (or prison?) of lifestyle as performance art — and, until recently, one of the first and best university art museums, a fanning design in concrete trays by Mario Ciampi (1965–70), condemned on seismic grounds. Toyo Ito won a competition to replace the museum *in situ*, but now a less costly Visual Study Center by Diller Scofidio + Renfro is planned nearby.

Just to the north of Berkeley are Contra Costa County's two groundbreaking jails: the Contra Costa County Detention Facility (CCCDF, 1981, now Martinez Detention Facility) where Podular *Direct* Supervision was first employed, in which officers sit in the open common space of the pod *directly* interacting with their "clients"; and the nearby West County Detention Facility, the first experiment in coed podular detention. Following Kevin Roche's lead in Oakland, and perhaps to conceal some of the novel group dynamics within, the architects of West County tried to bury their jail — or at least surround it in a twenty-foot-high earthen berm. (Though markedly less imposing than miles of razor-wire fencing, the berm actually weakened perimeter security, as it provided an elevated launchpad for firing drugs over an inner fence line and into the jail with a crossbow.)

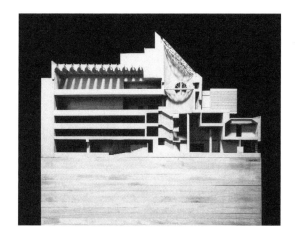

SAN FRANCISCO MUSEUM OF MODERN ART, Model; Mario Botta, San Francisco, California (1995)

Farther to the west, Marin County has both San Quentin (also renowned for its commanding view) and, until their recent demolition, the only jail cells designed by Frank Lloyd Wright in its Civic Center. A jail addition by DMJM, is subterranean, in deference to Wright's Civic Center, and pioneering in its reliance on "borrowed light" — because of its subgrade perimeter, some cells lack windows and must "borrow light" from common areas with relatively ample glazing, an idea that has gained considerable currency in new jail design. And, of course, in the bay itself there is long-abandoned Alcatraz — penitentiary, then movie set, almost casino... now, in part, a museum.

San Francisco proper has an even more complicated recent history. Redevelopment south of Market Street yielded a neighborhood quickly embraced as SoMa — both for the obvious contraction and, as many locals noted with glee, because of Aldous Huxley's so-named intoxicant. In addition to its boho allure, SoMa is the country's most pristine example of "barbell" planning between a new museum and jail. SFMOMA, designed by Mario Botta, and a swooping, cylindrical city lockup known as the "Glamour Slammer" (but technically referred to as SF County Jail #8) bookend the east and west termini of a new cultural district known as Marconi Center. The undulating frosted glass of the Glamour Slammer promises not a jail, but the headquarters for Google's next rival (which, given the panoptic logic of both jails and search engines, might stand to reason). In spite of its location, the jail in SoMa doesn't seem to have the Seroquel issue plaguing the one in Los Angeles, but another opiate for the masses is well showcased in the new Walt Disney Family Museum in the Presidio.

In the last decade, SoMa's civic formula has echoed north with the de Young Museum and science center in Golden Gate Park to the west, and the new San Francisco Federal Building, by Morphosis, at the same latitude to the east. Camouflage and disguise factor into all of these institutions. In an ingeniously literal act of contextual conformity, the Mobius-like galleries of the de Young are wrapped in an embossed and perforated copper skin patterned after a magnification of the local foliage.[130] Both Renzo Piano's science center and the federal building are similarly shrouded, the former in a landscaped roof, the latter in yet more perforated metal. Internally, these buildings present themselves as "flexible," with loose, looping plans and deviated sections, but all prove more prescriptive and sequential on arrival.

Subterranean museums pass for parks; prisons rise resplendently in drag at the water's edge. Few universities enjoy sites as commanding, nor architecture as ennobling (at a distance) as San Quentin and Alcatraz. The Bay Area's legendary tolerance for outlandish ideas and behavior is matched by a contrarian attitude toward institutional architecture. It's not so much that anything goes in San Francisco (that would be LA's role), but that anything might take the form of its opposite. San Franciscans love the frisson of the new inside the old, the daring disguised as convention — the calculated irony of Silicon Valley chieftains living in super-cyberized Queen Anne bungalows. The same elliptical view informs their public buildings: San Francisco has the most prominent prisons, and best-hidden museums, of any American city.

NON-UMENTS: STEALTHY, STACKED, AND ABSTRACT

By far the most provocative nonuments I have ever seen.[131]

GORDON MATTA-CLARK, ON MAYAN RUINS

THOUGH SAN FRANCISCO HAS TAKEN counterintuitive architecture to new extremes, most cities have played against type to
some degree. Before 1980, few imagined prisons would assume
the guise of corporate towers, nor that museums would fill so
many husks of abandoned factories. Yet both have come to pass,
repeatedly, and possibly to the salvation of most major American
cities. Both trends betray a similar civic sleight of hand, a literally industrial strength shell game of urban resource allocation.

In the case of prisons, it took twenty years of government
planning and lobbying to create facilities that appear to vanish;
for museums, the change was more categorical — a landslide of
diamond-in-the-rough conversions followed the realization that
much post-gallery contemporary art didn't demand the stringent
environmental controls of earlier masterworks. In either case,
these new institutions are most remarkable architecturally for
the inverse relationships they pose between vast interior spaces,
often unprecedented in both their scale and complexity, and the
often misleadingly neutral envelopes that encase them.

Jails throughout the United States were in catastrophic
condition by the early '70s, with overcrowding compounding the
failings of many structures built from the '20s through the '50s.
Construction for urban detention stalled between 1940 and 1960,
and even as demand for more holding space began to escalate,
a potent and ideologically broad convergence of belated Aquar-
ian politics, municipal finance crises, corporate resistance, and
urban NIMBYism all stood arrayed against new jail building in
US cities in the early post-WWII period. Few issues have united
the disparate "stakeholders" of urban America like the threat of
nearby prison location or expansion did in the '60s and '70s. To

this resistance must be added the contrary logic of the buildings themselves. For more space within central districts, prisons and museums had to go up, but neither building type rises easily beyond a few floors. Organizationally, it's more convenient for these buildings to sprawl: prisons become less desirable as neighbors and harder to manage the more they loom, and, historically, museum galleries only get emptier the farther they are from street level.

The vertical turn thus required both a redirection of civic will and a reimagining of the buildings themselves. In 1970, the Federal Bureau of Prisons embarked on a building program to clear the impasse for more urban jail space, not only (or primarily) for its wards awaiting appellate and District Court hearings, but to establish a precedent that municipal and county authorities could cite as "good neighbors" when they pressed for their own new cell space. These new federal tower jails, known as Metropolitan Correctional (or Detention) Facilities (MCCs and MDCs), shaped the state of the art in penal architecture through the '80s and '90s.

As is often pointed out during tours of federal prisons, the Department of Justice looks at each new facility as both a *tabula rasa* experiment and as a prototype for lesser state agencies to emulate. This utopian impulse has resulted in an often

problematic, occasionally heroic collection of vaults, including Alcatraz, Leavenworth, and more recently, the SuperMax at
Florence and the airport-adjacent FTC Oklahoma City. Less heralded, but equally groundbreaking, have been their conversions
of immigration and military installations such as Terminal Island
and the Air Force base at Boron, California, into low and medium
security prisons. But the towers were the emblematic achievement of the federal system, redefining both the internal workings of incarceration and the skylines of US cities. The first five
federal prison towers — MCCs in Chicago, San Diego, and New
York and MDCs in Los Angeles and Brooklyn — are arguably the
most radical interventions in American urban space undertaken
by the federal government since the impositions of the interstate
highway system.

With a shared vocabulary of striated concrete fascia, perforated by tall, narrow, deeply set windows, each of the five towers pioneered a new overall silhouette and a new interior organization based on square or triangular Podular housing units. Chicago's triangular template and San Diego's square pods are both developed as discrete double-story volumes, which are then stacked like the trapezoidal beads in Brancusi's *Endless Column* and accessed by elevators that stop only at alternate floors (an idea not lost on Thom Mayne of Morphosis, who used correctional skip-stop elevators for cost savings — fewer lobbies — and spatial variety in San Francisco and LA's Caltrans building). There have been snags in vertical incarceration, especially in later, overtaxed county facilities, but even at the federal level. In both Chicago's MCC and LA's MDC, daring and persistent

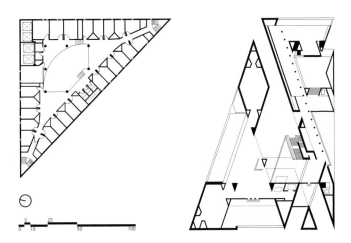

inmates found ways to rappel down from upper levels, though they were quickly caught. A more profound and daily problem has been the elevators — on tours of the MCC in San Diego and MDC in Los Angeles, guards tensed at each floor stop, aware that they, rather than their charges, were backed into the "cell" of the elevator cab if the doors opened to unanticipated circumstances.

In their host cities, however, these new monoliths were received as a bracing tonic: in Chicago the twenty-four-story MCC was completed in 1975 and celebrated as a return to Miesian orthodoxy, if not his transparency;[132] in San Diego, where the eleven-story Metropolitan Correctional Center opened in 1982 and shattered the thirty-foot height limit of old downtown, that MCC set the stage for twenty years of massive high-rise development. In New York and Los Angeles, the square and triangular pods are clustered in plan to generate projections and recesses in the overall massing of those complexes. In all cases, higher profile architecture firms with little or no correctional background were invited to rethink the basic public demeanor of these detention centers, and those firms all took advantage of the relatively closed planar geometry of the building type to develop a dappled pattern of fenestration, composed of vertical bars within the five-

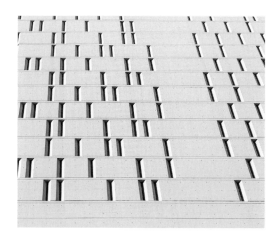

inch width limit imposed by the Federal Bureau of Prisons. The results, especially at twilight when prisoners have some discretion over which cells are illuminated, can be disturbingly elegant.

These effects were not lost on local officials and business owners. County and state agencies lobbied for new, and often exponentially larger, facilities based on the federal success stories, and the increased traffic that these high rises generated around them made them unlikely beacons of civil sector employment and downtown rejuvenation — after all, everyone but the inmates can leave for lunch. The ethnic enclaves of Little Tokyo in Los Angeles and Chinatown in New York, both struggling in the 1980s, now benefit from overlapping economies of art tourism and justice workers. Not to be outdone by Oakland, downtown San Diego now also boasts two tower jails, with a county tower bookending the city's vertical surge in the 1990s, as well as museums that repurpose a train station (the Museum of Contemporary Art San Diego, designed by Richard Gluckman in 2006) and an aircraft carrier (the USS Midway Museum, opened in 2004).[133]

METROPOLITAN CORRECTIONAL CENTER CHICAGO, Harry Weese, Chicago, Illinois (1975)
Opposite: Plan of MCC CHICAGO+NATIONAL GALLERY EAST BUILDING, ddd llc (2009)

MEGA-BOXING

(W)hile you might think that a skyscraper would be memorable, it doesn't work that way in L.A. Big, boxy buildings stay in your line of vision longer...the new cathedral has more in common with the familiar Los Angeles megabox.[134]

PAUL GOLDBERGER

US URBAN GROWTH has been neither strictly horizontal — a pattern of car-and-sign-driven Venturian dispersion — nor vertical — a process of Rem-style densification toward cultures of congestion. More typical are mid-density civic chunks, what Paul Goldberger termed "the familiar Los Angeles megabox."

USS MIDWAY MUSEUM AND MCC SAN DIEGO centered above
Rooflines of other museums and jails outlined

Though many megaboxes are reclaimed structures, they are increasingly built to suit. Megaboxes proliferate both within cities, as Goldberger notes in the cases of the Pacific Design Center, Beverly Center, Sports Club, and new cathedral in Los Angeles, and at their periphery in the form of office parks, malls ("big-box" retail an extreme variant), hotels, schools, and civic institutions. At least two stories but rarely more than ten, mega-boxes usually run somewhere between 200 and 400 feet in their longest dimension and, though they may occupy entire city blocks, more often shy away from zoning envelopes to allow a sea of surrounding surface parking.

As a phenomena, they may be more apparent in a low-rise city such as LA, but they are by no means more common there than elsewhere. Though Goldberger's "mega" term is apt, these boxes actually form a middle landscape of civic space, signifi-cantly larger than historic housing and retail fabric, but dwarfed by the towers and transit hubs of post-WWII expansion. These buildings generally abide by the limitations that governed the sky-lines of most US second cities through the 1940s, tying maximum heights to those of local landmarks (the Washington Monument, for example) once limited by the ladder reach of firefighters. The megaboxes of the last twenty years represent a resurgence of a proto-modern civic scale much closer to Baron Haussmann's Paris than Robert Moses' New York.

Not only have these "big, horizontal masses" predominated in the last wave of urban development, they have also evolved in programmatic terms that neither Venturi nor Koolhaas address. Venturi saw an evolution away from functionally specific build-ings to "sheds" — easily reorganized and redesignated with new signage. Koolhaas saw in the generic, leasable square footage of skyscrapers a liberation from programmatic determinism. As awkwardly leviathan as they are, megaboxes yield not only unprecedented planimetric flexibility, but near-infinite volumet-ric and spatial variation, both fixed and reconfigurable. It is an architecture that capitalizes on hanger-spans and atriated inner

Left: MECKLENBURG COUNTY JAIL CENTRAL EXPANSION. HOK, Charlotte, North Carolina (2009)
Right: PROPOSAL FOR MOMA. Howe & Lescaze, (1930)

courts as much as standardized, stacked open plans. Prisons and museums were the prototypical megaboxes of late 20th century US urban renewal. Both are biased toward consolidated, singular spaces to house their needs, but both can be subdivided into more manageable chunks.

Perhaps most importantly, they are both designed specifically to minimize the number of employees needed within a given volume. Though the cost of building museums often makes headlines, their payrolls are a fraction of similarly sized facilities for the performing arts or sports. Prisons are dense structures, and also costly compared to housing or office space, but even inefficient cellblocks, to say nothing of late-model podular units, require minimal staffing compared to a similar floor area in most building types. Though both professions have made surprising strides in recent decades, neither curators nor correctional officers are highly compensated by comparison with the more plentiful lawyers, brokers, athletes, and office workers who fill neighboring blocks. From a payroll perspective — and after storage and telecom hubs that require even fewer trained personnel to monitor — spaces for exhibition and detention are among the most efficient fixed-use buildings possible.

Though they've evolved into some remarkable forms, museums and jails were the early space holders in moribund US cities of the 1970s and '80s, and they remain among the most predictable bets in urban planning. This chapter focuses on their more gargantuan manifestations in cities, when these architectures of containment are stretched to fill blocks or reach skylines, but their civic advantages lie in their vacant malleability.

Megabox architecture reflects the fact that city leaders can ill afford to choose between Venturi's consumer and Koolhaas' metropolitan, but must try, often at spectacular cost, to lure both as they flee central cities. Commercialized sprawl and congestion have both continued apace, perhaps to the point of formula, but neither is the engine of urban growth that it once was. Whether in the form of museums and jails, or stadia, concert halls, churches, hotels, shopping and sports centers, megaboxes serve primarily to bridge between civic scales, populations, and agendas. Often, they mark a détente more than a division between urban and suburban, as well as private and public, interests.

THE KREMLIN OF MODERNISM —
OR JUST CAPITALISM WITH MODERNIST
CHARACTERISTICS?[135]

The megabox of the moment — and in its various states, for most of the 20th century — is the new MoMA.

As with so much of the Rockefeller legacy, the Museum of Modern Art advances a Hamiltonian faith in American urbanity, a United States led not by popular will and Washington, but by an enlightened, autonomous New York City. For all of the well-orchestrated "outrage" that early MoMA shows may have generated, there was never any real doubt or internal dispute regarding its agenda: MoMA would bring the leading edge of European art to an American audience, and over time ensure that Americans joined, and eventually led, that pantheon of the new. The founders of MoMA — among them Alfred Barr, Philip Johnson, as well as Abby and Nelson Rockefeller — could presume a broadly urbane and forward-looking consensus among moneyed New Yorkers, ready and willing to be shaped to new ends.

For its last upgrade, completed in 2005, the Museum of Modern Art in New York opted for blue-blooded architecture to house its blue-chip art. Yoshio Taniguchi was considered the least adventuresome choice among the five architects invited to charrette for the job, and an expensive capitulation to the notion that modernism must be pristine before interesting. Lost in that assessment are the more serious late-game revisions of 20th century art history now canonized in Taniguchi's scheme. The winners are clearly Cubism and Minimalism, now consolidated as the twin polarities of the 20th century, with other movements including Expressionism, Pop, and Conceptual Art rendered transitional. Major and enormous works by Pollock and Rosenquist now hang like any other pictures in the mega-salon, mere accents on walls so expansive and spaces so vast that even cars and helicopters seem Lilliputian.

The composition of the new MoMA remains essentially Cubist, a push-pull collage of spaces and volumes slipping into and past one another in plan and section. These Cubist or de Stijl compositional strategies govern the enormous atrium and the slotting of galleries around the tower, but give way to Minimalist tactics of scale and articulation: repetitive panelization, "floating" walls and door frames, and the infra-thin mullions and seams for which Taniguchi is renowned.

What cannot be pulled into a Cubist narrative is sorted rather than exhibited. As a number of art theorists noted in an issue of ArtForum dedicated to the new MoMA, two diagonal installations telegraph the general subordination of art to architecture. One of Donald Judd's matrices of colored boxes and a wall section from Gordon Matta-Clark's *Bingo* are both treated as screen wall conditions run diagonally across their respective galleries, when in both cases the artists consistently deployed them frontally. In the case of Judd, the work has been turned on axis with a sightline into the gallery from above, across the atrium.

The disposition of *Bingo* seems to have a didactic role, dividing the contemporary gallery into competing interests in the urban (a cityscape by Gerhard Richter hangs to one side) and the linguistic (a Bruce Nauman neon work pulses to the other). The proximity of Matta-Clark's wall-chunk to Serra's *Cutting Device: Base Plate Measure* (1969) diminishes both pieces to the role of oversized desk fixtures, the latter presumably used to excise the former for later recombination. Post-Minimalist works in general are re-inscribed in the canon as incomplete fodder for curatorial collage, with each gallery an exercise in full-body Cubist recomposition.

MoMA has rebuilt itself three or four times, and at every interval — from Abby Rockefeller's apartment to the streamlined 53rd Street building, through Johnson's and Cesar Pelli's modifications — subtly redirected and narrowed its purview on the canon of 20th century art.[136] Its latest manifestation by Yoshio Taniguchi poses an epic struggle between Cubism and Minimalism as the defining drama of the last century, with a "push-pull" composition of volumes and spaces redolent of the earlier vanguard, but rendered at the scale and in the palette of the latter movement. It's ironic that the losers in this new configuration are the Expressionists, especially the gestural mid-century giants of AbEx that cemented the museum, and by extension, the United States, as the post-WWII capital of the art world. The All-Over really is all over.

In museums, the vertical turn is limited to New York and Tokyo — and, interestingly, primarily to Japanese architects working in both cities. The New Museum on Manhattan's Lower East Side, by SANAA, is a megabox of stacked boxes, almost solipsistic in its delivery of "White Cube" spaces within a totemic pile of the same. The Mori Tower and Museum, high in Tokyo's Roppongi Hills, epitomizes not only the escalation of museums, but also the Icarus-like ambitions of developers through the last two decades.

INFINITY LAMPS

Keep Changing, Connect with Everything, Continue Forever.
TATSUO MIYAJIMA, ARTIST, TITLE OF 1998 WORK INVOLVING 36X48
NUMERICAL LIGHT EMITTING DIODES

THE DEFINITIVE MILLENNIAL SPACE is the endless pixelated
matrix of *The Matrix*, and many museum galleries and even more
installations aspire to that kind of immersive, boundless, hyper-
Cartesian continuity. Inspired by Robert Irwin's many translucent scrim configurations, Peter Zumthor's Kunsthaus Bregenz
Museum (1990–97) employs sandblasted glass shingles outside
and exactingly calibrated translucent ceiling planes within to
create a radically homogeneous, ambient urban presence. In
prisons, podular cellblock interiors have an *Inception*-like feeling
of endlessness and claustrophobia, with a geometrically vague
double-height common area ringed by catwalks and bounded by
a grid of cells. The set design of HBO's *Oz* was based with some
precision on a federal high-security housing unit, and amply
encapsulated that show's many convoluted plotlines without
betraying its actual overall form.

   Zumthor's ambient cube at Bregenz is likely the best among
hundreds of like projects realized to make old cities and exurban

tracts glow anew. Steven Holl's related success at the Nelson-Atkins Museum in Kansas City, in which subterranean galleries break the ground plane only as translucent slivers, bears mention, as does a low-security prison in Austria, the Justice Center Leoben, so diaphanous in its glazing that a blogger recently compared it to an Apple Store, before encouraging American tourists to get locked up for some spa treatments and pingpong. Neither was this analogy (nor those bedeviling the Broad Museum at LACMA and the Getty) the first to equate museums or prisons with retail outlets: in 1995, a review likened the newly opened Botta-designed SFMOMA to a $60 million Ikea.[137]

For many critics after Guy Debord and Baudrillard, museums function less as showcases of cultural artifacts, and more as civic commodities in their own right. But perhaps one

THE NEW NATIONAL ART CENTER. Kisho Kurokawa, Tokyo, Japan (1994)
Opposite: KUNSTHAL BREGENZ. Peter Zumthor, Bregenz, Austria (1997)

late-capitalism simply nests in the other: much of the journalism devoted to museums over the last couple of decades laments the ascendency of the museum store and cafe over gallery space. If commodity culture is in fact the lingua franca of contemporary exhibition, museums have been capitalizing on the shopping impulse since the canvases of Monet and the personal effects of King Tut could be shipped airfreight. If the consumer's tail wags the curator's dog in many museums, entire industries of exhibition and lighting design now ensure that visitors see both art and swag in the most flattering light.

INFOTESTINES

The resulting strain is almost bipolar, with the building aggressively screaming about apocalypse as its exhibition affirms harmonious universalism, with neither making its case.[138]
EDWARD ROTHSTEIN

Quite a few prisons and museums built in the 1990s include mazes. The intake sequences of metropolitan jails routinely move new arrivals through a complex series of stations for behavioral observation and information gathering. During jail tours in both Los Angeles and San Diego, deputies emphasized the useful disorientation that these spatial sequences, often winding through an entire floor level of the building, induced in the newly detained. Museums employ a related strategy to teach linear, historic narratives. Often, these take the form of an Ikea-style forced march through chronologically organized displays, interrupted or culminated by more immersive, "first-person" spaces for empathetic reflection. These circuits of spatial processing harden what used to be a flexible curatorial strategy for organizing a route through a show into a fixed architecture of sequencing in which institutions ingest their visitors and those visitors in turn digest its holdings and mission: the infotestine.

JUSTICE CENTER LEOBEN, Joseph Hohensinn, Leoben, Austria (2004)

The most innovative, if also the most deterministic, genres in this regard are museums dedicated to major watersheds in 20th century history, especially the many devoted to preserving memory of the Holocaust. The tragic urgency of imparting a specific historical narrative, tying the broad sweep of events to the specific losses and suffering of individuals, inspired a series of recent exhibitionary breakthroughs. The United States Holocaust Memorial Museum in Washington, DC, by Pei Cobb Freed opened in 1993 to controversy surrounding the resemblance of its rather exacting brick and steel detailing to the factory-like architecture of concentration camps. As described in a 1993 *Architecture* magazine cover story, "architect James Freed drew from the tectonics of the Nazi death camps to create powerful architecture that prepares visitors for the horrors displayed in the exhibits."[139] Many architects were disappointed with the historicist turn, if not offended by the citation of Auschwitz on the National Mall.

The internal orchestration of Holocaust history, however, was considered revelatory. An early and broad timeline of events leading into World War II gives onto more and more discrete and interactive spaces linking Hitler's war machine to genocide, and to the systematic decimation of Europe's Jewish communities. Two spaces, the multimedia Hall of Witness and the vacated, basilica-like Hall of Remembrance, pull visitors into a larger, collective meditation on the central trauma of the 20th century. Many more anodyne but architecturally diverse single-topic museums, such as the nearby Newseum, devoted to journalism, and Gehry's Experience Music Project in Seattle, followed the internal cadence of the USHMM with precision.

By contrast, Daniel Libeskind's Jewish Museum Berlin is a compelling psychological distillation of the fractured post-WWII condition, but suffers in laymen's comparison with the American museum that preceded it, and in experiential terms with the nearby Memorial to the Murdered Jews of Europe by Peter Eisenman, in which 2,711 concrete monoliths or *stelae* are arrayed in a grid over an undulating ground plane. If Freed's US Holocaust museum makes history legible, and Eisenman's Memorial marks loss via abstraction, the Jewish Museum in Berlin is as haunting in its "failure" as the other two are in their success — Libeskind's is an architecture of incommensurability that doesn't make sense, and perhaps shouldn't.[140] In the last decade, the three memorial strategies of Freed, Libeskind, and Eisenman have given way to a series of labyrinthine, often subterranean ventures (on the model, perhaps, of the information center under Eisenman's Memorial), including those by Moshe Safdie at Yad Vashem in Jerusalem and Hagy Belzberg in Los Angeles. Though a museum of contemporary art rather than of remembrance, Preston Scott Cohen's Tel Aviv Museum of Art, opened in 2011, in which gallery space is braided up from below ground to form a new, amorphous presence above grade, appears to capitalize on and transcend the "infotestinal" trajectory in museum design, having been liberated from its semiotic demands.

The thematic, political, and spatial tactics for choreographing historical lament pioneered in Holocaust museums now extend to a plethora of museums dedicated to preserving evidence of atrocity and genocide, and to celebrating tolerance and

veryhighreconciliation. A more politically nuanced, but to date less architecturally compelling trajectory connects the Simon Wiesenthal Center's sponsorship of a series of Museums of Tolerance in Los Angeles, New York, and Jerusalem, with the last designed, but as yet unbuilt, by Frank Gehry. Of the latter's many-coiled scheme, *The New York Times* quipped in 2004, "Something Israelis and Palestinians can agree on: they hate it." Love it or not, Gehry's proposal suggests that in that context a number of histories, rather than a single master narrative, may need articulation.

Architectural controversy could translate into diplomatic wisdom if, in uniting warring factions in a shared fury over a building, those parties find any new grounds for agreement. Chapter 07, Collide, explores museum/prison hybrids that often combine the twin continua of millennial space, the infinite grid and the information labyrinth, in their reoccupation of historically freighted carceral environments. However, before visiting these conflicted sites, we will turn briefly to the privatized and curious landscapes of single-patron museums and for-profit prisons, the fastest-growing and least predictable of institutional phenomena.

JEWISH MUSEUM BERLIN, Daniel Libeskind, Berlin, Germany (2001)

06.PRIVATIZE

IN THE DECADE preceding the new millennium, the thrust of museum and prison design became both more comprehensive and more particular. Private museums and privately run prisons became testing grounds for new architects and architectural solutions. Usually smaller and more nimbly managed, private facilities of exhibition and detention are hotbeds of innovation, and of eccentricity. As they are often "lite" in their holdings — built for low-risk inmates and less-established art — they enjoy far more latitude in their design and philosophy. This chapter looks first at the surge in "personal" museums, and then at the private prison industry, before assessing the role of the private sector in both fields.

MORI ART MUSEUM. Gluckman Mayner Architects, Tokyo, Japan (2003)

HUBRISPACE

J.G. BALLARD MIGHT HAVE dreamt the Mori. Like the post-industrial megalith of Ballard's 1975 dystopian novel *High Rise*, the Mori Tower dwarfs its surroundings and alters its inhabitants' perceptions in subtle but inescapable ways. Both towers presume and reinforce a direct correlation between altitude and affluence. *High Rise* opens retrospectively with the protagonist, a middle-tier resident, dining on the Alsatian lapdog of the tower's architect. Soon we learn that the apartment block of the title was designed to index wealth, power, and sexual allure by floor level, an arrangement that drives the lowly to scale and defile the upper tiers, and those above to barricade against and then co-opt their inferiors. When an offspring of the lowest floors sullies a rooftop hot tub, a top-floor cabal hurls the woman suspected of allowing the child on the roof to her death. Chaos ensues, as promised on the book jacket, to eclipse *The Towering Inferno*.[141]

An azure-blue, elliptical extrusion pulled from a pristine Tokyo suburb, the fifty-four-story Mori Tower looms over its neighbors like a sinister corporate beacon. As in *High Rise*, most of the Mori Tower is for sale, except for the top two levels, which house the Mori Museum and Viewing Deck.[142] The museum on the fifty-third floor includes 21,500 square feet of "white box" gallery space, a grand exhibition venue at any altitude, but a stupefying expanse in a neighborhood where a 500-square-foot studio runs well over a million US dollars. Much of the time, the Mori Museum curates neither art, as it has no permanent inventory,[143] nor culture, but the promise of pure vacancy. The Mori's popular 360-degree Viewing Deck surveys all of Tokyo, giving constant pride of place to its founders Minoru and Yoshiko Mori's real estate empire, the actual heart of their collection.

From its perch on the crowning floors of a premier property in one of the world's most expensive cities, the Mori distills the current message of the single-patron museum to its essence: "Would that our present could be your future." It is in certain respects a generous vision, inviting all visitors to speculate, in both senses of the term, on Tokyo's future evolution. Here, self-aggrandizement hovers very close to civic goodwill, but with both sentiments magnified, generalized, and abstracted to a point of benign neutrality. The Mori turns an all-seeing eye on a world to which, apparently, we often forget to aspire.

More and more individuals are celebrating their lives and interests through edification, and with good reason. "Personal" museums perform a civic alchemy: they allow those of means to host the city on their own terms, and to share the experience of their largess without forfeiting control over the context, agenda, and credit for their "gift." In return, personal museums and their benefactors can depend on a certain public enthusiasm, even, and sometimes especially, when their missions and manifestations seem completely misguided. And better to have one's name associated in perpetuity with a building, even a really bad one, than with corporate exploitation or malfeasance. As Joan Didion wrote of the original Getty Museum in Malibu, "In the end the Getty stands above the Pacific as one of those odd monuments, a palpable contract between the very rich and the people who distrust them least."[144]

In their architecture, personal museums often prioritize space and site over collection. Many, though not all, aspire to shock and awe their visitors as Versailles does, through an endless, geometric unfolding of indoor/outdoor possibility, with garden follies for scale, rather than following the example of the Louvre in its massive but neutral galleries, anchored by masterpieces. Their emphasis on locale rather than content has made personal museums the butt of much art world ridicule, but has also left them the breeding grounds for a lot of innovative design, especially since Land Art obscured or erased most boundaries between site, art, and building. Even in the staid Midwest, this dynamic has fostered radical, not to say decadent, explorations of form following the pattern of Peter Eisenman's 1987 Wexner Center at Ohio State and Zaha Hadid's recent Rosenthal Center for Contemporary Art in Cincinnati — neither design constrained by a stellar collection.

The diversity of agendas and recognition that now typifies personal museums for art, whether they be named for a patron or an artist, has at least had the effect of radically diversifying the architectural expression of these institutions. Many of the most daring gambles in contemporary architecture are taken first in the housing of private art collections. Indeed, personal museums are by general consensus the petri dish of high design.

Personal museums often manage to be both absurd *and* highly effective institutions. Although they register the intra-class pecking order of extreme wealth that many of its ranks would prefer to keep veiled, and though they tend to parody rather than monumentalize their namesakes, both of these tendencies distract from how often personal museums succeed as instruments of privatized diplomacy: the Rockefellers used their dominant patronage of MoMA to mediate between the cultured classes of the United States and Europe for fifty years; the Guggenheim successfully bound post-WWII abstract painting and sculpture to a singular mythology of an earlier avant-garde; the Whitney continues to bridge between the divergent sensibilities of urban and rural America (at least in the tony pages of *Town & Country*). When they have an agenda beyond the reification of their patron, personal museums often carry out — and carry on — their missions much more emphatically than do other beneficiaries such as schools or charities.

Although personal museums were pioneered in Europe, and their future is most evident in Asia, their 20th century multiplication was led by the United States. Often founded as eccentric gifts to laborers (the Ford, Mercer, and Barnes museums, for example), personal museums in the United States quickly devolved into ornamental tax shelters, both minor and vast. The single-benefactor "architectures of hubris" that punctuate Los Angeles, anchored by the Getty campuses, illustrate the egotism and myopia that tend to drive these collections and their containment, but only hint at their current variety in the Western United States. New York's array of personal museums operate on a more rarefied plane, but pursue the same ends as they define successive waves of contemporary art and contend for global reach.[145] In a particularly American irony, we see wealth made in the *fleeing* of cities — fortunes built on suburban expansion and its appetite for fuel, transportation, housing, and services — redeployed in urban fantasies that border on private, central-city utopias. These monuments grew out of an Enlightenment ambition to not only persist in memory, but to promulgate from beyond the grave. Intrepid heirs, both familial and institutional, ensure that they do. As a senior Getty curator stood trial in Italy on suspicion of buying looted antiquities,[146] the directors of other personal museums chased the world's most bankable architects — and the collections of others — to extend their franchises.

CLUB MEDICI

Operare non meno l'ongiegno che la forza — Exercise intellect, as much as force.
COSIMO DE' MEDICI

Perhaps surprisingly, neither vanity nor guilt drove the earliest personal museums. The first private collections worthy of the name had little to do with underscoring the status of their owners and were often exclusive to the point of complete secrecy. As is the case for contemporary personal museums in general, the Mori's emphasis on spectatorship and vision is that museum's most direct link to its historical precursors. However, the orchestration of vision in earlier personal museums was intended not to entertain or condition a broader public, but to suit the passions and feed the interests of their owners. In contrast to the Mori Art Museum's monumental purview over empty space, the earliest personal museums offered intimate tableaux, chockablock with

189

relics and images. This is especially true of the "Cabinets of Curiosity," or *Wunderkammern* that were first assembled by European noblemen on the eve of the Renaissance, often strictly for their own private edification.

More furniture than buildings, the *Wunderkammern* took many forms, escalating in scale from intricately compartmentalized desks, appointed with drawers and vitrines for myriad texts and mementoes, which were common in Eastern Europe, to the *studiolos* of Italian dukes and cardinals, in which deeply coffered palace interiors were installed with formatted paintings and statuary representing religious and secular subjects, often in fantastic communion. As Eilean Hooper-Greenhill has observed, spaces such as the shrine-like *Kunstschrank* of Gustavus Adolphus, completed in 1631, served the dual role of organizing "material knowledge" into its first proto-scientific manifestations, while at the same time conferring on their owners a quasi-sacred (and in a Baconian sense, literally omniscient) legitimacy.[147] Though almost all of the early *Wunderkammern* were objects within larger architectural settings, Peter the Great imagined his as a massive building in its own right, a neoclassical colossus anchored at its center by a surgical theater under a dome to rival St. Peter's.[148]

The culmination of these early, private collections was the Medici Palace, an intergenerational personal museum that for the first time posed an entire residence — but importantly, not a seat of royalty — as a space of exhibition, display, and patronage. As Hooper-Greenhill notes: "The space and its articulations were used to position the family and to construct the position merchant/prince/patron. The structure, although based on feudal characteristics, was new in that the 'prince' was not a hereditary ruler, and he therefore had to use his persuasive power, symbol and propaganda to establish his position of authority.... Older practices included the amassing of bullion and medieval cosmology; newer practices included a new view of the past, mercantilism, and a new way of co-opting the gaze."[149]

Cosimo and then Lorenzo Medici's emphasis on aesthetic quality and competition between artists, rather than the sentimental associations or the geographical diversity of the objects displayed, would revolutionize the production of art in Florence. Though secular patronage was already well established throughout northern Europe, especially among the Dutch, the Medicis' commissions to major artists were the first major challenges to the cultural hegemony of the Catholic Church in Italy. Equal parts fortress and ideal villa, the Medici Palace also brokers between the sensibilities of the Renaissance and those of many modern collectors. In organization, many later museums including the original MoMA have followed the blank, austere, and tripartite composition of the Medici Palace exterior, its variable sequence of salons on each floor for exhibition, and its terraced internal organization around a central courtyard. More broadly, the Medici led to the common equation of the museum with all styles, and perhaps all things, Italian: witness the Roman literalism of Getty Villa, the corporate travertine of the nearby Hammer Museum, even the ill-starred neo-Venetian "lollipop" arches of the Gallery of Modern Art at 2 Columbus Circle.[150]

Adopting Michel Foucault's epistemic historical model, Hooper-Greenhill cites the micro-museological *Wunderkammern*

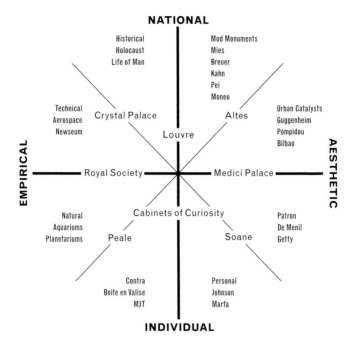

NATIONAL

Historical   Mod Monuments
Holocaust   Mies
Life of Man   Breuer
     Kahn
     Pei
     Moneo

Technical   Urban Catalysts
Aerospace   Crystal Palace   Altes   Guggenheim
Newseum   Pompidou
     Louvre   Bilbao

EMPIRICAL   — Royal Society—   —Medici Palace—   AESTHETIC

Cabinets of Curiosity

Natural   Patron
Aquariums   De Menil
Planetariums   Peale   Soane   Getty

Contra   Personal
Boite en Valise   Johnson
MJT   Marfa

INDIVIDUAL

and the Medici Palace as two counterexamples to what would quickly become the dominant Enlightenment embodiment of the museum: the Louvre. Though the Louvre too could be assessed as a personal museum, to the extent that it held the French royals' own treasure, it has come to be seen as the state museum par excellence, especially after its conversion to a national gallery organized to showcase the spoils of Napoleon's conquests, with each wing designated for a campaign. Although no doubt contributing to his imperial legacy and perhaps to a national sense of his immortality, the Louvre had the broader effect of equating state power and cultural magnanimity, a role national museums have aspired to ever since. Since the late 1700s, personal museums have developed, and occasionally flourished, in clear subordination and counterpoint to the many museums of state established during the same period.

EVERYMAN, HIS CASTLE

We have no Egyptian mummies here, nor any relics of the Battle of
Waterloo, nor do we have any curios from Pompeii, for everything
we have is strictly American.[151]

HENRY FORD

PERSONAL MUSEUMS — and private collecting in general —
usually echo and distill the preoccupations of their times. The
scientific discoveries of the 19th century, and the industrial and
cultural upheaval of the early 20th, all drove a resurgence in individual collecting and curation, as did the massive shift in economic
might from Europe to the United States in those years. In contrast to earlier aristocratic examples, personal museums in the
United States were often founded by "self-made" men. Although
the great collections of Europe were compiled over generations
and only gradually and belatedly opened to any public viewing, in
the United States it would become the rule rather than the exception that a single figure amasses a great fortune, spends much of
it on Old World plunder, and then frets over how the spoils will be
displayed for posterity.

This cliché, however true it would ring through the 20th
century, does not fully account for a rash of early American
museums that amassed eccentric, trade-based, and often native
artifacts. The Philadelphia museums of Charles Willson Peale
(completed in 1821) and Dr. Thomas Dent Mutter (founded in
1863) are perhaps the two most ambitious private attempts to
bring museology to bear on 19th century science. Peale's museum
offered the first taxonomic display of American species as a
museum of natural history; the Mutter still stands as the ultimate
collection of medical oddities and instruments. Both took the
form of exhibitions that outgrew their lodgings a few times over
before being housed in independent structures. The Peale collection was finally purchased and dispersed by P.T. Barnum in 1854
— still a profound affront to many Peale scholars, who argue that

Peale's museum was the first and last stand to be made against the sensationalizing of nature in "museums" no better than circus funhouses.[152] As a condition of Mutter's $30,000 endowment of his collection, the College of Physicians was required to build the facilities that the Mutter still occupies on its campus.[153]

For roughly the same amount — in fact, precisely $38,944.99, spent between 1913 and 1916 — Henry Mercer was able to house a vast trove of post-Revolutionary tools and products of early industry in his all-concrete, six-story museum in Doylestown, Pennsylvania.[154] Limiting his collection to instruments and goods produced before 1820, Mercer created a cornucopia of early American handiwork in order to illustrate his thesis that the great inventions of his time found their inspiration in the modest, makeshift innovations of the previous century. Henry Ford would cite the Mercer as the only museum he was even vaguely curious about (though not enough to visit) before embarking on his own museum and park of Americana in Detroit in 1929. Greenfield Village and the nearby Ford Museum act as dual venues for Ford's preservation of American historical sites — President Lincoln's log cabin and Ford's family home are given equal billing — and the vehicles that might have transited between them. Though the Peale, the Mutter, the Mercer, and the Ford museums all celebrate America's ingenuity, curiosity, and natural grandeur, most 19th century museums remained European in focus. Two more museums based on Pennsylvania fortunes, those of Henry Clay Frick and Albert C. Barnes, were more typical in this regard.

Often caricatured as the ultimate robber baron of the antebellum period, Henry Frick made his fortune in Pittsburgh overseeing the Carnegie steelworks. In 1898, he famously erected an eleven-foot-high barbed-wire fence and mustered a private army of 300 Pinkerton men to fight the unionization of the plant, thereafter nicknamed "Fort Frick."[155] Later, after surviving an anarchist's assassination attempt, Frick spent $5 million on his New York City estate on 5th Avenue, completed in 1913, and bequeathed an additional $15 million for its upkeep when he died six years later.[156] To put this in today's perspective, $5 million was close to 1% of the 1913 US federal budget of $714 million. The same share of this year's federal spending would be nearly $16 billion — enough to build more than ten Getty Centers.[157] Though a relatively small collection, the Frick's assembly of canvases by Velazquez, Rembrandt, and Vermeer is unparalleled in any private collection in the world. J. Paul Getty's estate, at the height of the Getty's buying power in the early 1990s, would have struggled to finance one or two of the "Old Master" portraits that Frick had snapped up at the turn of the century. For that matter, in their location, grandeur, and elegance, the Frick mansion and gardens shame almost any contemporary exercise in conspicuous consumption.

As Frick pillaged Europe's past, Albert Barnes snapped up its future. His collection is astounding for its prescient accumulation of modern masterworks by Picasso, Matisse, Braque, and many other avant-garde luminaries before their rise to fame, often purchased off the easel by Barnes on his annual European tour. Equally remarkable was Barnes' exhibition strategy, which

MERCER MUSEUM, Henry C. Mercer, Doylestown, Pennsylvania (1916)

stressed the congruencies between European modern and traditional African art. To this end, Barnes installed the paintings in specific combinations, salon style — that is, tiled closely up the walls — and interspersed with his extensive collection of tribal masks and statuary. In his bequest, Barnes required that the work be viewed exactly as he had displayed it, and, though this condition would be successfully disputed by his executors, only in his home gallery by appointment.[158]

In this last respect, involving conflicts between heirs, executors, and surrounding community interests, the Barnes Foundation has proven a depressingly leading-edge institution. Albert Barnes left his collection and the house it resides in to a small, historically African-American college. Over the last ten years, trustees representing variously his family, the college, and major Philadelphia art patrons, fought long battles over a plan to relocate the collection downtown to a site once used to house youth offenders. The forced urbanization of the Barnes — in a design by Williams+Tsien that replicates many of Albert Barnes' actual interiors within a network of modernist life-support — reprises a tested civic formula substituting spaces of exhibition for those of incarceration; nearby, the abandoned Eastern Penitentiary in Philadelphia now plays host to installation art.

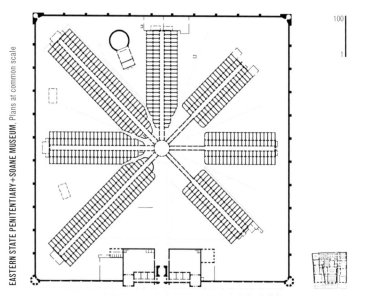

THE PLUTOCRAT-AS-ARTIST AND THE ARTIST-AS-PLUTOCRAT

Museums could bear the inscription: Entry for art lovers only. But there clearly is no need for such a sign, it all goes without saying. The game makes the illusio, sustaining itself through the informed player's investment in the game. The player, mindful of the game's meaning and having been created for the game because he was created by it, plays the game and by playing it assures its existence.[159]

PIERRE BOURDIEU

AMONG EARLY AMERICAN personal museums, the Frick and the Barnes lead more clearly into the present simply because they focused on art, which became almost the exclusive theme of single-benefactor museums for most of the 20th century.[160] However, the roles of collector and creator underwent a gradual but profound metamorphosis, leading not just to many more personal museums, but to a spectrum of institutions commemorating distinct personalities, whether benefactor, artist, or both. Personal museums now run a gamut from those founded by a "mere" and perhaps absentee collector, to those shaped by a heavily involved patron, through collaborative spaces commissioned by enlightened amateurs (often other artists or architects), out to monographic institutions devoted to exhibiting a singular talent.

Probably the least contentious of these are the last. With first the Musée Rodin and then the Musée Picasso, the French government recognized how centrally its national legacy was bound up in the legacies of specific artists, and set about preserving and propounding their work. In this, it often supported or extended a 19th century French tradition in which an artist's home-turned-studio was then preserved as a museum, as in the symbolist painter Gustave Moreau's townhouse in an outer arrondissement of Paris (which became a mandatory Surrealist pilgrimage), and Monet's Gardens at Giverny.

Ironically, the most recent and extreme shoring of French cultural patrimony in this mode was produced abroad. The Rodin Pavilion opened recently in a corporate atrium in Seoul, South Korea, to showcase just one sculptural series by the artist, *The Burghers of Calais*. The Pavilion was commissioned by Samsung and designed by an American firm, Kohn Pedersen Fox, better known for corporate towers. KPF's foray into signature architecture for art led to a Gehry-esque swoop rendered in laminated, translucent glass, held aloft by a custom space-frame of point supports. At a cost of more than $1,000 per square foot, the Rodin Pavilion may be the most expensive investment in the display of a single work of art ever, to suit a sculpture that the French government could reproduce *ad infinitum* — and thus render almost valueless — from molds the artist bequeathed to the state.

Through the 20th century, innumerable museums were established in honor of major artists, often in their historically preserved work spaces, such as the Casa Azul of Frida Kahlo in Coyoacán, Mexico; Salvador Dalí's palace in Figueres, Spain; and Isamu Noguchi's studio in Long Island City, New York. As many of these are situated in smaller towns, they often anchor a cultish local tourist economy. Many new monographic museums reside in structures designed or designated in the artist's memory. Artists as diverse as Joan Miró, Norman Rockwell, Jean Arp, and Andy Warhol have all been accorded this honor, as was Picasso, in almost every city he set foot in.

Many of the most important collections of modern art, of course, belonged to artists themselves. Manet and Picasso famously collected and supported the work of their peers, and Andy Warhol, Dennis Hopper, and many others have stockpiled the best works of their generation. Sadly, few of these are open to the public, and many are geographically remote, as is Donald Judd's installation of his own work and those of a few contemporaries in a defunct military barracks in Marfa, Texas. When artists showcase other artists, as Judd did Dan Flavin and John Chamberlain at Marfa, it is often challenging to sort out the creative labor of the artist from the "creative" capital that supports and preserves his or her work.

This increasingly incestuous ambiguity between author and steward of the work, and the *frisson* it confers on all parties involved in the traffic of contemporary art, has had the net effect of glorifying the buyer, and drawing more and more collectors into the fray of collecting and exhibiting new art. Many collectors now purchase the art of living artists with an eye to those who might someday merit specific museums of their own, while other collectors have become much more active patrons — commissioning and sometimes collaborating in the work they purchase to shape a museum-worthy inventory. The über-galleries of impresarios like Larry Gagosian (who now has eleven locations) and "foundations" of career-making collectors such as Charles Saatchi are private fiefdoms, personal museums in all but name.[161]

LA APOTHEOSIS

And I liked the way history did not run loose here. They segregated visible history. They caged it, funded and bronzed it, they enshrined it carefully in museums and plazas and memorial parks. The rest was geography, all space and light and shadow and unspeakable hanging heat.[162]
DON DELILLO

WITH SOME NOTEWORTHY exceptions, the building of personal museums during the Cold War devolved into its own arms race, between New York and Los Angeles — with Los Angeles usually in the more pyrrhic, Soviet role.[163] In New York, many of the single-name institutions matured in the last quarter century into truly public polities, with multiple major donors, depersonalized but increasingly politicized in their scope. In the last twenty years, the Guggenheim has received at least two major transfusions of cash from nonfamilial trustees, and the Metropolitan Museum of

Art and MoMA, linked for much of their histories to the Vanderbilt and Rockefeller fortunes respectively, have built extensive, named, and often stand-alone gallery space to house the work of other collectors. In Los Angeles, by contrast, the funding of personal museums stayed "centralized," rarely expanding beyond their namesakes, and as a result their appearances remain more stolidly bound to the dictates of those benefactors. Less abridged by art world consultation or pressure from their peers than they would be in New York, LA patrons' architectural tastes run to the late, safe, and overbuilt.

Although the Getty overshadows the rest, the Armand Hammer and Norton Simon museums are formidable vaults in their own right. The low arches and high blank facades of the Hammer Museum are a misreading of Kahn's austere arcades and unadorned end-walls at the Kimbell, somehow with the urban mass of his Yale Center for British Art.[164] The Norton Simon hides behind a Kahn-like blank wall as well, though it benefits hugely from a recent remodeling by Frank Gehry, spearheaded by FOG partner Greg Walsh.[165] Both share with the Getty Center a corporate travertine monumentality, a fixation on stone for stone's sake, borrowed from LACMA and continued in terracotta at MoCA. If the ramparts of the Getty take this lapidary impulse to an absurd extreme, then the rest of LA's major museums — and here one should also add the Petersen Automotive Museum, as well as the nearby institutions dedicated to tolerance and television — offer little but novel veneers to compete with the anchortenant on high.

Two of the most inspiring but least heralded personal collections in Los Angeles grapple with conceptual art and pose new models for the museum as "anti-edifice": not bunkers for high cultural storage but rather flexible, contingent spaces that artists might appropriate for their own ends. Though now based in Santa Fe, the Lannan Foundation resided in Los Angeles for eleven years as a lending museum with a small exhibition space in Mar Vista. The vast majority of its contemporary art collection was on constant loan, with just a few pieces — often difficult and incendiary work like Chris Burden's monument to the Vietnamese losses in the Vietnam War, a ten-foot-high bronze rolodex with hundreds of thousands of Vietnamese names, some generated by random syllabic combination for lack of actual records — shown in its base gallery. With a mission to bring as much contemporary art to as broad an audience as possible through all available venues, the Lannan poses one of the few easily defensible models for personal collecting made public.[166]

David Wilson's Museum of Jurassic Technology takes a very different though equally self-effacing tack to initiate visitors in the elliptical potential of conceptual art. As Lawrence Weschler has exhaustively explored in his monograph on the MJT, "Mr. Wilson's Cabinet of Wonder," the Museum of Jurassic Technology inhabits a Culver City storefront only to pose a multitude of sometimes mundane, often paradoxical exhibits.[167] Armenian micro-miniatures that may or may not be to scale compete for one's attention with an elaborate installation documenting the complicated love triangle of Iguazu Falls whose incommensurable plotlines, tortured geography, and pseudo-science are on par with the internal complexities of Marcel Duchamp's *Large Glass* or Matthew Barney's *Cremaster Cycle*. Robert Mangurian and Mary-Ann Ray's multiple proposals for revamping the MJT, parts of which may or may not have been realized surreptitiously, only compound the institution's occult allure. Matt Coolidge's nearby storefront, the Center for Land Use Interpretation extends the MJT's charms as well.

In addition to the examples above, the massive personal collections of contemporary art currently held in private homes such as those of Michael Ovitz, Stanley and Elyse Grinstein, and Edythe and Eli Broad — to list only those on O.J. Simpson's former street in Brentwood — will provide ample fodder for new experiments in personal museology in Los Angeles over the coming decades. The soon-to-be completed Broad museum downtown, by Diller Scofidio + Renfro, is a far more daring proposal than the Broad

museum at LACMA, with a translucent coral sponge-like exterior shell that should cast the remainder of the Broad collection in a distinctly new light.

DOUBLE DUTCH

If Los Angeles extends the tradition of the personal museum both to new extremes of ostentation and, at the Lannan and MJT, to more modest and promising possibilities for the future, all coexist with a comfortable degree of civic isolation from one another. New York's personal museums operate in a radically different context, given that city's density and century-long role as the clearinghouse of the avant-garde. Although art culture is less funereal in New York than elsewhere, it is also more socially competitive. Among patron-class New Yorkers, board seats for the living matter more than gallery real estate for the dead, and an attunement to the quality of works on display is still required. In

DIA CHELSEA, Bridget Riley: Reconnaissance Exhibition, Roger Duffy, New York, New York (2000)
Opposite: **THE GEFFEN CONTEMPORARY AT MOCA**, Frank Gehry, Los Angeles, California (1983)

all of these respects (and in at least their initial taste in archi-tects), New Yorkers remain rather Dutch.

New York's dominance of the 20th century art market has resulted in a network of vast, proactive galleries that often leaves the experience of art in its museums feeling late and warmed-over. Many of the most compelling personal museums in New York, as well as some of its most dubious, follow a gallery model, and many New York galleries could plausibly call themselves museums.

The most important of these not-quite-for-profit experi-ments was Peggy Guggenheim's Art of This Century exhibition space, an intestinal circuit of curved display spaces designed by Fredrick Kiesler and opened in 1942. A niece of Solomon Guggen-heim, whose museum was under discussion when she opened her own space, Peggy Guggenheim set a far more progressive agenda for Art of This Century, showcasing the latest work of the Surrealist émigrés during WWII and championing Jackson Pollock and other first-wave Abstract Expressionists. Though Art of This Century showed for only a few years before being absorbed into the larger Guggenheim "mothership" uptown, it set a precedent for independent art exhibition that gallery owners, many of them also women such as Ileana Sonnabend, Mary Boone, and Barbara Gladstone, would emulate in their retail spaces and extend quickly to installation and performance art.

Philippa de Menil, another art dynasty "black sheep" (she is the renegade daughter of Dominique de Menil, who commissioned Piano's Houston pavilion), converted to the Sufi faith and founded the Dia Art Foundation with curator Heiner Friedrich in the mid-1970s. Dia may be to the art of the 1960s and 1970s what Art of This Century was to the 1940s and 1950s.[168] Concentrating on a small stable of major artists, many "post-gallery" in the siting and scale of their work, such as Walter De Maria and Michael Heizer, the Dia has enabled or preserved more Land Art and large-scale Minimalist and post-Minimalist work than any other organization to date. In addition to the specific sites of works across the Western US, Dia showed a wide array of contemporary art in an eight-story Chelsea warehouse (a brilliantly understated — and thus, for many, architecturally inconsequential — conversion by Richard Gluckman) and now at Dia:Beacon, a half-million-square-foot Nabisco factory in upstate New York refurbished by Robert Irwin and OpenOffice.[169]

Finally, the three major New York museums of 20th century art, however singular their origins, can only distantly be understood now as personal museums. The Museum of Modern Art, the Guggenheim, and the Whitney were all founded on a single collector's body of work, but have grown and diversified more in the manner of private universities than other museums.[170]

All three are in the throes of major expansion plans, and those plans say a great deal about the futures of both art and architecture in the United States. Tellingly, Rem Koolhaas was in contention in every case, with schemes that either fell short in competition (the invitational MoMA charette), were, like LACMA's, judged to be too expensive and abandoned (the NeWhitney), or were realized, only to be quickly shuttered (the

Guggenheim Las Vegas). Koolhaas' common involvement, and his commitment to a "Metropolitanism" he coined in *Delirious New York* more than thirty years ago, suggests that as much as the current stewards of these institutions might like to raise (or raze) them to a uniform, if progressive urbanity, the eccentricities of their founders persist, at least as obstacles to their homogenization by a single architect. For his part, Koolhaas blames philistinism and cowardice on the part of museum trustees for not following through.[171]

MoMA and the Guggenheim have developed beyond the confines of personal museums, and have been discussed previously here, but the Whitney remains both the most mission-specific, concentrating on American art, and, largely for that reason, the most parochial. The Whitney's biennial survey of American art has become a regular excuse, at all points of the cultural spectrum, to grouse on the paltry offerings and/or offensive new directions of domestic art. Whether these cycles of hand-wringing improve US artists' prospects — and for politically savvy artists of the "NEA 5" generation, they almost certainly did — they underscore a distinctly American friction between private taste and public edification. Expansion plans for the Whitney deserve a book of their own at this point, as does Breuer's original building. The Whitney's stepped facade and cyclopean window facing Madison Avenue are enjoying a fashion revival, as was evident in Koolhaas' NeWhitney addition, a similarly faceted form that extended up from behind the original like a phantom of its host. A famously antithetical addition proposal by Michael Graves in the '80s posed a collection of buildings like postmodern trinkets over and around Breuer's, reducing his to a scaleless toy. Less a response to Koolhaas' scheme, which it replaces, and more a diametric understatement of Graves', the current plans for a Whitney expansion by Renzo Piano are virtually invisible, with all design controversy reduced to whether one or two neighboring brownstones will be sacrificed to reach a characterless new entry.[172]

WE SHOULD ALL BE SO LUCKY

As James N. Wood, Director of the Art Institute of Chicago put it, "the authority of the American art museum is derived ultimately from our Constitution, which assured the climate in which private individuals could create museums for the public good." Mighty white of them, eh?[173]

PAUL WERNER

The globally ranked museums, whether named for individuals or otherwise, now expand as brands rather than as sensibilities. Two of the biggest US museum donors of the '90s, Paul Allen and Paul Lewis, avoided one-off structures in favor of influence and naming opportunities elsewhere.[174] Though he too serves on many museum boards, New York City Mayor Michael Bloomberg learned from Nelson Rockefeller (who claimed all of his political skills were honed dealing with MoMA curators) that it's faster, cheaper, and less complicated to buy an office than an edifice. On this logic, we will likely see fewer new tombs for art, and more museums of celebrity and calamity. But as has often been the case in museum patronage, a woman of means (and like Peggy Guggenheim, one whose fortune relied on suburban expansion) has proven the exception. Crystal Bridges Museum, the brain-child of Walmart heiress Alice Walton and architect Moshe Safdie, opened last year in remote western Arkansas. Though Safdie's design looks like big-box Bruce Goff, and the curatorial emphasis on American art runs the risk of the Whitney's limitations (or worse), Crystal Bridges will almost certainly redirect an eddy in the tide of US tourism from coast to center.[175]

Single-benefactor museums are effectively churches of one, and architectures of faith, however dubious and egocentric, persist better than most. Though ostensibly "about" whatever is on view, personal museums are at all times exhibits of their patrons' power, wealth, and generosity — their transcendence over worldly limitations and selfless return of treasure to the general good. Most of us accord personal museums (if not all museums) the basic mute respect and curiosity we grant houses of worship serving faiths other than our own. We may roll our eyes at their pomp and snicker at their self-serving credos, but both cults and art collections maintain their exclusive auras against formidable odds. Personal museums display an almost Catholic resilience to scandal. They have weathered all variety of threats to the legitimacy of self-deification, including failures of mission,

WHITNEY MUSEUM OF AMERICAN ART, Marcel Breuer, New York, NY

Opposite: WHITNEY MUSEUM EXTENSION CONCEPT DESIGN, OMA, New York, New York (2001)

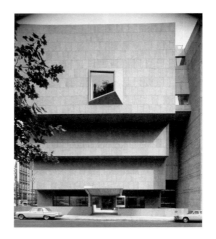

funding, and the shaming of their leadership (to take only the example of the Getty).

And, as personal museums are at pains to remind us, their namesakes could have made far worse use of their largess. On a recent and badly jet-lagged visit to the Mori Museum atop the Mori Tower, I found most of J.G. Ballard's *High Rise* predictions realized in what he termed elsewhere "a surrealism without dreams." In addition to truly epic views of Tokyo and a broad and compelling survey of contemporary African art, I took in some less refined fare: an extensive diorama entitled the *Da Vinci Code Museum*, courtesy of that movie's producers, and a special exhibit room devoted to the diamonds of Botswana, courtesy of that nation's government. I recovered the following day at another of Tokyo's 124 museums, the discreet Hara Museum, in a converted Deco mansion on the western edge of the city. Built in the 1930s, the Hara's fanning, streamlined architecture suggests a lost world, a Japanese version of Weimar-era decadence and sophistication that, although no less self-serving than the brute scale of the Mori, feels far less naive. Tabaimo, a thirty-one-year-old artist working in anime-style stills and animation, had installed her work throughout the Hara, customizing each space to reveal the evolution of her ideas. Weeks later, I remember hers as the only art I really saw and thought about in a week of whirlwind travel.

The Hara, much like the earlier house-studios of John Soane and Gustave Moreau, preserves a sensibility, more than it does artifacts or memories. It showcases a unique way of coming to terms with the world, not a vain attempt to transcend it.[176] These personal museums are in fact intensely *personal*, organized according to their authors' curiosities, biased toward their passions (however misdirected), and run for posterity to share those enthusiasms with the like-minded. The hubris of most contemporary personal museums builds not only in direct proportion to their scale, but also in proportion to their patrons' distance from lives unlike their own, and their often Pharaoh-like preoccupation with securing that distance in this life as well as the next.

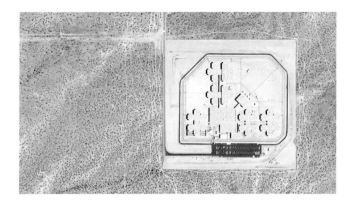

PRIVATE IDAHOS

It will help us get a theater, a shoe store, a supermarket, all the commercial shops you get in most small towns....It will help us get a new high school and a new hotel.[177]

JACK STEWART, CITY MANAGER, CALIFORNIA CITY

I know it all sounds like Alice in Wonderland. But I promise you, we did work. It wasn't all serendipity.[178]

DOCTOR R. CRANTS, PRESIDENT, CORRECTIONS CORPORATION
OF AMERICA, 1983–2009

CALIFORNIA CITY is a hamlet of 9,000 residents and 205 square miles in the Mojave Desert, where Corrections Corporation of America completed a $100-million, 2,300-bed maximum security prison in 1999 *on spec* — without a contract from any government agency to fill its beds.

Incarceration for profit has at least as long a history as the one above tracing personal museums. Poorhouses and debtors' prisons, like orphanages, were often outsourced to independent jailers, and prison ships were almost always under the helm of freelance captains. In fact, more early prisons were likely privately run than state-run, and again, like museums, their early variety

CALIFORNIA CITY CORRECTIONAL CENTER. California City, CA, USA (1999)

reflected the eccentricities of their founders. However, with the exception perhaps of the theatrical dungeons of the Marquis de Sade, private prisons were run less to entertain their owners than to exploit both their charges and the governments that forfeited their custody. Contemporary private prison operators are at pains to shed a mercenary, profiteering past — while still guaranteeing healthy returns for their investors.

In the United States, large-scale private prison corporations are a recent phenomenon dating from the early 1980s, with origins in the South but increasing penetration north and west. The two largest, Corrections Corporation of America and the Geo Group (formerly Wackenhut), are based in Tennessee and Florida, respectively, and between them account for the vast majority of private prison beds in the United States. CCA boasts more than sixty facilities under management holding more than 80,000 inmates, and Geo Group can house 66,000 inmates in sixty-five facilities, making them the fifth and sixth largest prison systems in the country, respectively, behind the Federal Bureau of Prisons, and the state systems of Texas, California, and Florida.[179]

If the first US prison boom was driven largely by the unionized lobbying of the CCPOA, the last bears the stamp of the corporate free market. Like a white-shoe Don Novey, with a degree from West Point and profitable cable TV empire, Doctor R. Crants founded Corrections Corporation of America in 1983 at the age of thirty-eight with more interest in the privatization of services in general — hospitals, schools, etc. — than in operating prisons. But like Novey, Crants saw a promising monopoly: As his CCA partner Tom Beasley explained in 1998, "I was not very worried about the competition. I thought we should let everybody develop the concept. He thought it was much more important to pare the expense and the burden to become the clear front-runner."[180] In the end, there was room for two industry leaders — investors who would eventually include Dick Cheney, via the Vanguard Group, have profited handsomely from Crants' decision to specialize, as have those who held onto Wackenhut/Geo stock.[181]

In the Deep South, particularly Louisiana, and in Missouri, there are large and small private prison operators — often the side businesses of county sheriffs — that echo pre-civil rights era racial dynamics. Many recent stories have focused on "mom and pop" incarcerators running halfway houses for parolees, recovering addicts, or the mentally ill, many of these in the Northeast. The major story of the last decade, however, has been the massive shift to private contractors at the federal level, both by the Bureau of Prisons, which doubled its private beds from 15,524 in 2000 to 32,712 in 2008,[182] for a total of 16% of federal prisoners, and by the Bureau of Immigration and Customs Enforcement (ICE), which held almost 16,000 detainees in private facilities in 2009, 49% of its total count.[183] (It was ICE that saved CCA in California City with a 2000 contract for foreign-born detainees.)[184]

Private prisons take advantage of new building technologies and odd existing structures far more readily than their state-run rivals. Prefab cell construction, by companies such as Rotondo Weirich, has been particularly embraced by private facilities, as have more elaborate kit building systems. Still another, and a more architecturally compelling, direction in recent private prison contracting has been broad-span temporary holding tents by Sprung and other manufacturers and other fast, light, and nominally "family-friendly" designs for immigration detention. Private corrections managers have also suggested more adventuresome conversions of other building types into holding facilities, including schools, hotels, and hospitals. Perhaps a more salient feature of their recent boom is temporal rather than spatial. As private prison watchdogs lament, the major companies profit both by passive and unruly inmates:

> The CCA has an ultra-modern prison in Lawrenceville, Virginia, where five guards on dayshift and two at night watch over 750 prisoners. In these prisons, inmates may get their sentences reduced for "good behavior," but for any infraction, they get 30 days added — which means more profits for CCA. According to a study of New Mexico prisons, it was

WEST VALLEY DETENTION CENTER

Justice Systems Corporation, Rancho Cucomonga, California (1991)

found that CCA inmates lost "good behavior time" at a rate eight times higher than those in state prisons.[185]

Private prisons have a litany of shortcomings, first among them that they don't appear to save money, according to recent cost studies in Arizona and Louisiana.[186] Beyond that bottom-line irony, there are other issues: they operate with, at most, limited government oversight; their staffers, who are not law-enforcement personnel, may not use force to quell disturbances; they are incentivized not to improve lives but to provide the cheapest care and feeding of their populations as possible. In almost all cases of inmate misconduct and violence in for-profit prisons, the private operator argues that the inmate was misplaced in its facility, because it is not in fact qualified to deal with aggressive, high security inmates.

Charges of mismanagement and unprofessional conduct are harder to duck, but private prisons still enjoy a few major advantages over state and federal ones: no governmental compensation requirements, little unionization, and far more flexible rules for housing and "programming" inmates' time. Think of them as the charter schools of the correctional system, and one can quickly gauge their promise, limitations, and political allure.

Opposition to privatization is strongest among organized labor — and here, for once, guards had to learn from the teachers they usually mock. Unlike other states where corporatized corrections have reengineered or replaced ailing government-operated prisons, California's state-run prison system, like its higher education system thirty years ago, poses a serious challenge to outside competitors. Entrenched correctional officers unions and building industry lobbyists have led California through the fastest and largest building boom in penal history, not only ensuring the financing of new prisons and staff, but also shaping the law-and-order measures to keep them filled. (It didn't help the cause of privatization that 150 inmates rioted in 2003 at a trial private facility for state convicts in Riverside County, outside Los Angeles. Two inmates died before an off-duty state correctional officer was summoned to fire warning shots that the private staffers could not deploy.)[187]

However, even in California, stymied at the state level, private prison operators found ample opportunities in federal, county, and municipal detention. Geo Group supplies more than 2,000 beds to federal agencies in California, especially ICE or immigration-related custody, and runs eight municipal jails there (including the forty-one-bed Fontana City Jail in Mike Davis' hometown). Though federal agencies are the biggest clients for new facilities, county and municipal jails and youth authorities are the ripest targets for privatization, especially as the increased pressure put on state prisons by consent decrees keeps county jails, detention centers, and "honor ranchos" near urban centers at a perpetual boiling point. Private prisons have

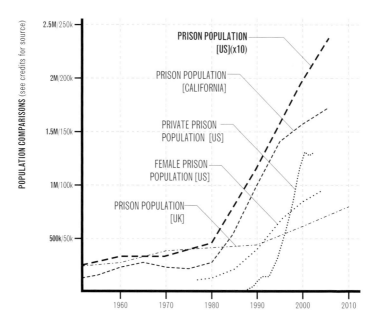

POPULATION COMPARISONS (see credits for source)

PRISON POPULATION
[US](x10)

PRISON POPULATION
[CALIFORNIA]

PRIVATE PRISON
POPULATION [US]

FEMALE PRISON
POPULATION [US]

PRISON POPULATION
[UK]

also been tailored to the least contested niche "markets" under-
served by larger systems: inmates with medical needs, psychological issues, or other vulnerabilities. Here, privatization is
no guarantee of quality: a center for sex offenders in Arcadia,
Florida, run by the Liberty Behavioral Health Corporation was
described in a company memo quoted in *The New York Times* as a
predatory "war zone."[188] One can also imagine private incarcerators catering to the increasing segregation of male offenders
by age and life interests — devotees of disparate belief systems
or twelve-step adherents. (The constitutionally protected tribal
rites of Native American inmates, for example, require many state
prisons to cordon off sweat lodges in yards accessible only to
those inmates.)

The incarceration of women is another specialization. With
112,822 women behind bars in 2010, up *twentyfold* from the 5,600
held nationally in 1970, female inmates now form 6.9% of the total
US inmate population.[189] As Angela Davis has pointed out, the

rising number of women behind bars correlates with a decline in criminal paternalism — women are now sentenced more like men, rather than being left to the discipline of the men in their lives.[190] However, the surge in across-the-board numbers also reflects the draconian, gender-blind effects of mandatory drug sentencing.

As all the correctional "players" already know, women are cheaper to incarcerate. Unlike men who must be classified by levels of security risk — and housed accordingly — women are generally held together without regard to offense, in facilities built to withstand only the lowest levels of male prisoner aggression (with standard, non-correctional fixtures and drywall, much less expensive to build).[191] Though the women's prison in Frontera, California, is the largest such facility in the world, the state system is showing signs of frustration with the specific, well-articulated medical demands of female prisoners and the societally thankless and complicated work of locking up mothers caring for young children.[192] Politically and financially, this is where corporatized incarceration will find its easiest foothold.

Sadly, incarcerating women will also be the fastest solution to a problem now plaguing private prisons across the country: the failure of government-run corrections to adequately classify and remove predatory male inmates from the low- and medium-risk inmates generally contracted out to private facilities.[193] Neither state-run nor private prisons want more violent offenders: they endanger guards and other inmates, and they cost more to house, move, and police. But state-run prison systems have a mandate to deal with all wards of the state, no matter how dangerous. By contrast, private prison corporations, which depend on docile low-end offenders for cost savings in facility construction and management, cannot absorb inmates for whom they have no security provision. By downgrading the security profile of convicts and then shuffling them to private prisons, state prison wardens play a game of "inmate arbitrage" where violence is the currency sold short. Though it's unlikely that either the state or private contractors will be held accountable by prisoners, the companies at the "buying" end of this predicament will take what precautions they can. For increasing risk-adverse private prison managers, any busload of men may contain an unmarked explosive. Equally capable of mayhem, but statistically less inclined, women will be a safer bet for corporate incarcerators.

CAVEAT EMPTOR

Although a common and growing issue in both museum and prison design, privatization actually points in opposite directions in the two fields. A surge in private and personal museums in the 1970s presaged the explosion in public museum establishments and expansions between 1980 and 2000. By contrast, the heyday of private prisons is now: an echo-boom of niche and overflow facilities tending to the margins, both demographic and geographic, of overtaxed state and federal networks. In fact, private prison growth is the fourth wave of mass incarceration in the United States, with California's ramp-up to more than 150,000 inmates beginning and peaking first in the 1980s and '90s, Texas and the federal system reaching that figure in about 2000, and private prison populations approaching it a few years later.

Private prisons and museums also operate at the cusp of politics in ways that few institutions do. Getty curators have stood trial for misappropriations in Italy when those from national museums do not. On the other hand, as Governor Chris Christie of New Jersey learned to his chagrin, the buck stops pretty far up the governmental food chain when private oversight of wards of the state goes astray. In 2011, parolees assigned to a priavtely managed Newark halfway house went missing, and committed new and occasionally heinous felonies, without their absence noted.[194] Although state correctional officers could have made the same blunders and supported Christie's last campaign at the same order of magnitude, he would have enjoyed far more political insulation from the fallout.

Both are more "nimble" architecturally than their more stolid state-run counterparts, but their innovations serve opposite ends. Although personal museums often begin as eccentric tax shelters, they remain optimistic ventures, often evolving to become beloved, defining cultural touchstones for their communities. Private prisons, even at their best, exist to maximize a return on human subjugation. Nowhere is "realism" about human nature more easily seen for the cynicism that in fact it often is.

WILLACY DETENTION CENTER. Hele-Mills Construction, Raymondville, Texas (2006)

POST-MILLENNIAL

Since 2000, institutions of display and discipline have taken on transnational dimensions, many of them unanticipated and controversial. In the most literal of convergences, yesteryear's prisons have simply been reopened as today's museums. Chapter 07, Collide, explores the confluence of art and crime in prisons-turned-museums, museums as crime scenes, and in the work of artists and inmates that no longer observe clear distinctions between curatorial and custodial agendas. These post-Millennial demands were anticipated by Rem Koolhaas in his early schemes for Arnhem prison, which proposed a panoptic display of failed architectures of reformation, and in his many museum proposals, an encyclopedic, and in some senses captive, catalog of exhibitionary strategies. New, often paradoxical, architectures of exhibition and incarceration reflect a state of constant global flux. Chapter 08, Disperse, surveys the transient art events that now surpass museums in ratifying any emergent avant-garde, with spectacular installations setting the terms for future art practices. These celebrations of world citizenship contrast with a silent surge in the detention of foreign nationals within and beyond US borders. Both the internationalization of incarceration and the annual city-to-city migration of vanguard art culture reflect new and complex cosmopolitan realities.

07.COLLIDE

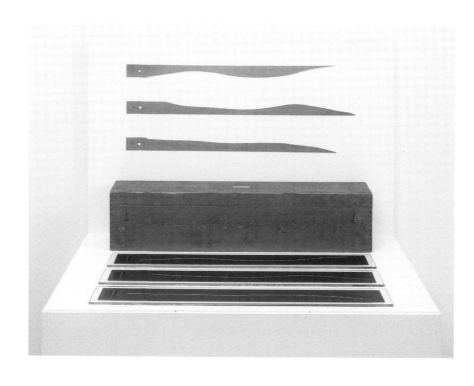

PRI/MUS

Dada affirmed what culture denied: that a gratuitous gesture, a vulgar expression, an obscene act, even an act of violence might be more creative in liberating man's poetic energies than the entire stock of works of art incarcerated in the cemeteries known as museums.[195]

HILTON KRAMER

IN 2006, A TWENTY-YEAR-OLD American artist named Seth Wulsin selectively broke windowpanes in the abandoned Cárcel de Caseros in Buenos Aires, creating pixilated portraits of forty-eight political activists. Though built only twenty-five years earlier, the high-rise prison was demolished floor by floor in 2008, in part because of its role in political "disappearances" in the

THREE STANDARD STOPPAGES, Marcel Duchamp (1914)

Previous image: **MICHAEL ASHER**. Santa Monica Museum of Art, photograph by Grant Mudford (2008)

late 1980s. In a likely homage to Gordon Matta-Clark's *Blow Out*, in which Matta-Clark shot out the windowpanes of Manhattan's Institute for Architecture and Urban Studies in 1976 and replaced them with images of failing South Bronx housing towers, Wulsin's project was also motivated by a macabre design flaw in the prison. The glass block facade of Cárcel de Caseros limited the sunlight reaching the interior so completely that most inmates developed a vitamin D deficiency, *turning their skin green*. Wulsin's "vandalism" followed a series of punctures in the walls that prisoners had made to emit light and communicate with their families.[196]

The last decade in corrections and in collecting has been typified by collision and dispersal. Prisons "collide" with museums in the many conversions of the former into the latter, but also in the carceral role both often play vis-à-vis contemporary art. More than three-dozen US prisons have been closed and reopened as museums, almost all in the last decade, while other art institutions find themselves defending renegade curators, or hosting artists that simulate their own incarceration. More

CASEROS PRISON DEMOLITION PROJECT — 16 TONS
Seth Wulsin, Buenos Aires, Argentina (2006)

broadly, there has been a sharp rise in the behavior associated with one becoming commonplace in the other: art that mimics criminal activity or prison life (for example, Marina Abramovic's and Darren Almond's recent self-incarcerations), crimes against museums (high-profile heists, looting), curatorial crime, and the rise of jailhouse "outsider" art. The multi-mediation of art and crime via cinema, television, and the Internet has exploded: prison interiors are now ubiquitous in major motion pictures, TV dramas and sitcoms, and, often catastrophically, in webcam footage.

In parallel with these collisions of typology, intention, and behavior, institutions for exhibition and incarceration have also become markedly more dispersed and transient, taking the forms of art fairs and festivals on one hand, and of transnational detention on the other. Post-Millennial prisons and museums share a cluster of tendencies in terms of their thematics and site selection. Many of the radical innovations in both sorts of "holding" have moved sub rosa, off-radar, beyond reach.

Instances of *collision*, discussed in this chapter, include prisons-turned-museums, the advent of art-as-crime, as well as a rise in crimes against art, and the proliferation of multimedia portrayals of both environments in film, television, and gaming. Tendencies toward *dispersal*, discussed in the next chapter, include transient art (fairs, festivals, biennales), transnational detention and rendition, containerization, and subterranean holding spaces.

"PRESENT DAY INSIGHTS"

REM KOOLHAAS anticipated many of these post-millennial currents in a pair of early projects that examine one institution in terms of the other. OMA's 1980 proposal for staging the history of prison reform architectures through the Koepel Panopticon, at Arnhem in the Netherlands, both acknowledges the predominant cycle of failure in penitential design and attempts

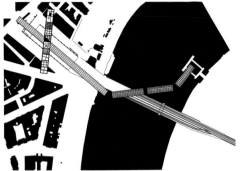

to salvage, rather than replace, an institution born of a flawed diagram. Slicing two new "streets" through the enormous Pantheon-like void of Arnhem, OMA replaced the central tower with a new subterranean intersection, eliminating the "all-seeing eye" above as it opened a new penal archeology below. In response to what Koolhaas cites, repeatedly and ironically, in the project brief as "present day insights," the Arnhem renovation suggests that each wave of "insight" into penal reform obscures as much as it reveals about human nature and architecture's potential to reshape its charges. Tellingly, his proposal for curating Arnhem followed another early OMA project (co-authored by Elia Zenghelis and Zaha Hadid in 1977) for a "Museum of 19th-Century London," in which a similarly linear intervention, a space-frame, bridges the Thames and connects fragments of the premodern city. In both cases, curation and linkage are understood not just as means of organization, but as defining architectural ambitions. Nowhere was that more evident than in his winning but unbuilt scheme for the encyclopedic LACMA. There, OMA proposed an open-span structure with holdings arrayed in the lateral X-axis by nationality, in the longitudinal Y-axis by time period, and in the vertical Z-axis by object type. Such a Cartesian sorting of holdings — usually by inmates' age, term of confinement, and security risk — is common in linear, multistory prisons.

The museums that OMA has realized — the Kunsthal in Rotterdam, as well as the Seoul National University Museum of Art and Leeum Museum in Seoul, for example — often resolve in a 'leaking" Corbusian spiral, rather than in the linear extrusions governing earlier speculative proposals. (That leakage took an all too literal form in Rotterdam on October 16th, 2012, when two thieves, capitalizing on a panoptic but unmanned electronic security system, stole between €50–200 worth of paintings from the Kunsthal in just two minutes.) Koolhaas' bifurcation of the spiral parti in the Kunsthal — so that visitors may scissor up into art, or turn down, to pass from city to park — introduced the multi-spiral and braided strategies governing Herzog & de Meuron's de Young Museum, UNStudio's Mercedes-Benz Museum and Preston Scott Cohen's Tel Aviv Museum of Art, among many others. Though Koolhaas can claim many breakthroughs, this "snakes-in-a-box" play on Le Corbusier's Musée Mondial has become the default diagram for 21st century art space. OMA hasn't revisited the prison since Arnhem, but Koolhaas' fruitful "misapprehension" of that structure's promise, and the circuitry he devised to renavigate the project from within, inform many of his buildings for art.

KUNSTHAL ROTTERDAM, OMA (1992)
Opposite, left: KOEPEL PANOPTICON PRISON, OMA, Arnhem, Netherlands (1980)
Opposite, right: MUSEUM OF 19TH CENTURY LONDON, OMA+ZAHA HADID (1977)

ONCE PRISONS, NOW MUSEUMS

MANY COMMENTATORS have equated prisons and museums over the years, but few anticipated how many prisons would simply *become* museums after 2000. Until recently, museums could replace prisons, as the neoclassical Tate Gallery was built on the former site of Millbank Penitentiary 115 years ago, or run in parallel with them, as the Folsom Prison Museum adjoins the entrance to that state prison, but actual one-for-one reoccupations were rare. If Rosalind Krauss once mapped an "Expanded Field" in the production of contemporary art, the arrival of the prison-turned-museum marks an important turning point in an expanded field of curatorial engagement, and an extreme example of nominalist museology.

Though we've built many new prisons, we've also decommissioned quite a few. A recent *New York Times* Travel section identified three-dozen prisons-turned-museums in the United States alone, and discussed their unexpected allure. As Paul Williams notes in his sharply observed *Memorial Museums: The Global Rush to Commemorate Atrocities*, "Of the institutional spaces converted into memorial museums, the most common is the former prison.... There is something about the aestheticization of the prison-museum space that, in an uncanny way, relates to the psychic disturbance associated with incarceration itself."[197]

The "disturbance" that Williams identifies tends to vary according to a former prison's notoriety, or that of its inmates. Many defunct prisons were deemed museologically remarkable for the evident cruelty or deprivation they imposed on those held. Dungeons, pits, death chambers, as well as the macabre chairs, gurneys, and stockades furnishing them, all are pungent reminders of our species' sadistic potential. Many prisons become museums, however, simply because they are spatially or structurally compelling (and, in any case, very hard to demolish). Alcatraz, Eastern Penitentiary, and the Bastille in Paris (which housed studios of the École Nationale Supérieure des Beaux-Arts for

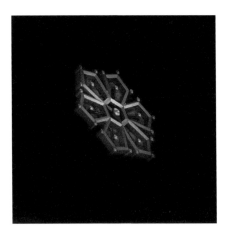

MILLBANK PENITENTIARY / TATE GALLERY MILLBANK, Langlands & Bell, London, England (1994)

much of the 20th century) all partake of the same quasi-infrastructural sublime. Just as Joan Didion found herself liking Alcatraz, many architects fall prey to a certain suspect romantic revelry in abandoned prisons: at least in these spaces, all were once captive to design.

Though many prisons-turned-museums are akin to generic theme parks of incarceration — with open cells, defunct restraint hardware, and plaques commemorating their most infamous charges — the most successful of them, in terms of tourist draw, are sites of political trauma, such as Tuol Sleng Genocide Museum in Phnom Penh, Cambodia, and Nelson Mandela's cell at the Robben Island Prison Museum.

At the 798 Art Zone in Beijing and in a MOCA for Perm, Russia, major sites of forced industry, if not outright incarceration, have been converted into vast arts campuses along the lines of MassMoCA. In these examples, as with earlier openings of concentration camps and gulags in the former Soviet Union, 20th century sites of catastrophic folly and cruelty have, in only a generation's time, become nodal points in 21st century tourism.[198]

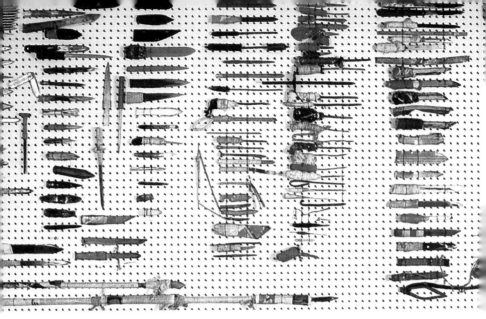

ART AS CRIME AND CRIMES AGAINST ART

Artists have long posed as outlaws and revolutionaries, even if they rarely broke the law. By the same token, the incarcerated often style themselves artists, devoting their hours and limited resources to muralism, tattoo art, etc.[199] Detective novels often explore artistry in crime (and the role of chance, coincidence, and accident in both). But more pervasive alignments between spaces of exhibition and detention reflect a now spectral notion of what constitutes cultural and societal transgression. Trends include: the commonplace violation of museums; escalating incidences of looting, art theft, and defacement; performance and video art that depict various states of incarceration, self-confinement, and staged punishment; and the mass marketing of both connoisseurship and disciplinary restrictions.

Though the recent, well-publicized incarcerations of artist Ai Weiwei in China and members of the female punk rock band Pussy Riot in Russia renew long-dormant controversies regarding art, protest, and free speech, a wider array of artists has taken up residence in museums and galleries willingly. The self-imposed "sentences" of performance artists, from Chris Burden's notorious *Five Day Locker Piece* (1971) through Marina Abramovic's recent gallery occupation, retrospective, and ninety-day furlough at MoMA, underscore the fundamentally temporal, rather than spatial or interpersonal, stasis of imprisonment.[200]

The early 2000s were banner years for art thievery and cultural misappropriation in general. The Taliban's demolition of two mega-scale Bamiyan Buddhas in Afghanistan in March 2001 presaged a dire decade of looting, heists, and pilferage throughout the Middle East and Europe, many acts driven by nativist or anti-secular sentiment. The 2003 looting of Baghdad's National Museum of Iraq is an even more extreme example of patrimonial violence. The gutting of the museum, mitigated only by the return of a few works spurred by a plea from senior Shia Mullah Sistani, leaves Iraq utterly bereft of its Babylonian heritage.

As unthinkable as either of these official UN "Crimes Against Culture" was in a pre-9/11 context, the recent onslaught of art thievery and vandalism across Europe was equally inconceivable. The much-publicized theft of Edvard Munch's *Scream* from a Norwegian museum in 2004 has been followed by a series of brazen museum invasions.[201] In 2007, a Zurich museum, the E.G. Bührle Collection, was robbed of canvases by Monet, Cezanne, Van Gogh, and Degas at gunpoint, after a nearby theft of two Picassos two weeks earlier. These crimes are remarkable for their constancy as much as their take — a 1990 heist at the Isabella Stewart Gardner Museum in Boston set the record of $200 million for a single burglary, but combined, these recent thefts likely exceed $400 million. Perhaps more disturbing, though less costly, was a series of attacks on artworks. In October 2007, a Monet was punctured at the Musée d'Orsay by rampaging vandals, just months after Christian-right skinheads destroyed a number of Andres Serrano photographs in Sweden. Far from remorseful, the latter individuals were detained after they broadcast footage of their exploits, complete with a death-metal soundtrack, on YouTube.

229

Heist coverage usually focuses on the virtuosity of the criminal enterprise — the cat-like break-in, the connoisseur's judgment in works stolen, the attunement to the schedule and security vulnerabilities of the violated institution — but some gleam in their incompetence. In 2003, four guards at Rikers Island sought a windfall in forging and replacing an original Salvador Dalí drawing that had hung in the prison mess hall for half a century. (The Surrealist painter had sent the work to the prison after touring the facility in the 1950s.) Giving a whole new meaning to the phrase "my kid could have done that," the correctional officers took turns imitating the cruciform design of the Dalí original, picked their best effort, splattered it with ketchup (not for blood, but because of actual ketchup stains from plates scraped clean below where the piece hung) and pinned their forgery in the place of the original without bothering to reframe it.[202]

TELE-CARCERATION: TRAGEDY, PLUS TIME[203]

It looks like the 1990s are the golden age of the art museum....Image began to reign supreme over the written and spoken word once television started to dominate the national consciousness, beginning in the 1950s.[204]
JUDITH H. DOBRZYNSKI

CINEMA, TELEVISION, AND THE INTERNET have made all of us far more subtle arbiters of both artistic and custodial technique than any generation in the 20th century. Though surveillance technologies and neo-panoptic cellblock design facilitated the incarceration boom of the 1980s and '90s, digital panopticism has cut against the keepers since 2000, when handy digital video and ubiquitous security cameras captured far more iconic scenes of inmate abuse than of their misbehavior.

As the Abu Ghraib images attest, this is an arena where fact often beggars fiction, and where life imitates art at its peril.

Scenes of torture enacted by sympathetic characters on *Battlestar Galactica* appear far more nuanced and "realistic" in their moral ambiguity, for example, than do recent allegations against Theo Lacy Jail in Orange, California. In 2007, deputies there watched the television show *Cops* and sent text messages to one another from a control room as inmates raped and killed a forty-one-year-old man, a pretrial detainee who deputies had mistakenly led cellblock gang captains to believe was accused of molesting children. Then, descending from the fearmongering of *Cops* to the utter, satirical incompetence of *Reno 911!*, the deputies summoned to testify on the incident lied to a grand jury and illegally shared testimony among themselves to stonewall the inquiry.[205]

The collision of disciplinary and exhibitionary complexes reverberates in shifting mass-media coverage. Running in a lurid arc from "biker-chicks-behind-bars" grind house films to the *Escape From New York* franchise, prison are also sites of on-screen redemption, as in *The Public Enemy* (1931), *American Me* (1992), and *Dead Man Walking* (1995). Similarly, if less sensationally, museums often provide a crucial pivot in dramas and comedies, from John Cassavetes' stroll through the garden at MoMA in *Shadows* (1959), and the turn Kim Novak takes through galleries in *Vertigo* (1958), through *Ferris Bueller's Day Off* at the ICA in Chicago in 1986, and Jonathan Rhys Meyers and Scarlett Johansson's visit to the Tate Turbine Hall in Woody Allen's *Match Point* (2005).

But backdrop has become foreground recently. Two big-budget films, *Night at the Museum* and *Let's Go to Prison* both opened in theaters in December 2006. Neither was a masterpiece, but both films were remarkable for their self-consciousness about genre. Far from innocent wonder, the young protagonists of *Night at the Museum* mock the self-importance of come-to-life dioramas at the Museum of Natural History, and every homophobic trope of prison life in movies — the intimidating cell mate, the soap-dropped-in-the-shower scene — fade into "bromance" in *Let's Go to Prison*. By the time Harold and Kumar managed their escape from Guantanamo in 2008, of course, US policies and techniques of confinement were ridiculed globally. But perhaps at least we laugh together, more than we cry: the $40 million gross of Harold and Kumar's recent exploits, with more than $10 million coming from overseas, likely outstripped the combined earnings of a dozen recent dramas and documentaries about the Iraq War.[206]

As common as they were in film, prisons rarely appeared on US television before the 1990s — many a *Law & Order* interrogation room, but little of life in confinement after Stalag 13 on *Hogan's Heroes*. Now one finds a vast array of detention-related prime-time offerings, in the form of dramas, comedies, documentaries, and game shows. The series *Prison Break* and *Big Brother* now vie for viewers around the world, but a more telling arc runs from HBO's *Oz* (1997–2003) — a visceral, full-frontal soap opera set in an imaginary but well-observed lockdown wing of Emerald City Penitentiary — to Fox's *Arrested Development* (2003–06), a farce in which the family patriarch is doing low-security time for fraud (and possible real estate dealings with Saddam Hussein) while his family runs amok.[207] As Michel Foucault observed of gallows humor and the demise of the debtors' prison, public perceptions of incarceration often soften when punishment is perceived to be too widespread or arbitrary.[208]

These examples of detention-themed but fictional programming pale in documentary value and in sheer volume when com-

FTC OKLAHOMA CITY, Federal Bureau of Prisons (2010) | Opposite: **MUSEUM, MODEL 1:10,** Katerina Frisch (1995)

pared to facility-specific half-hour reality shows like *Lockup* on MSNBC and *Lockdown* and *Inside the World's Hardest Prisons* on the National Geographic Channel. All provide remarkable, if often airbrushed, entree into new carceral spaces, and all have turned out to be money-spinners.[209] In the early '90s, when the ride-along mayhem of *Cops* established the law-enforcement reality genre, one could quickly foresee the exhaustion of the format in the forced "busts" and minor infractions that became the driving plot points of the show. In a telling shift of perspective, however, the new shows centered on prisons and jails opt instead for the inmates' point of view — and they make for dramatic narrators. After catching up with news anchor Rachel Maddow on MSNBC, viewers may now join the women currently doing time at Theo Lacy Jail (the same California facility scandalized in 2008). Not unlike Maddow, the inmates are surprisingly young, white, and well-spoken, though their enthusiasms for men and methamphetamines have led them to a very different soundstage.

The secret of these shows, however, is aesthetic — today's prisons turn out to be oddly camera friendly. If the default view

in *Cops* was a night shot from the passenger seat of a cruiser rolling through downtrodden, vacant neighborhoods, the new prison reality hours capture an over-lit world of geometrically exacting prison yards and spic-and-span interiors. More generally, these shows feature landscapes and dress codes that quickly resolve into winningly abstract compositions. The crisp orange jumpsuits and well-cordoned and banded interiors of the Hillsborough County Jail featured on MSNBC's *Lockup: Extended Stay Miami* caught my eye while channel surfing on a recent JetBlue flight for their similarity to scenes in Matthew Barney's early films.[210] As in Barney's work, the new depiction of incarceration on television and in video games foregrounds the intersection of discipline, gamesmanship, and environmental control. Both the *Prison Break* franchise and *Behind These Walls* (2011), a documentary on the odd popularity of tennis at San Quentin, hinge on athleticism — not as a pastime, but as spatial choreography.

FELONS AND FAUNA

San Diego Zoo and Ironwood State Prison were combined earlier this week, bringing local inmates and wildlife together for the first time under the same roof….San Diego Zoological & Convict Reserve.[211]

THE ONION

THE "NEW NORMAL" of mass incarceration was the theme of *YouPrison*, an exhibition mounted in Turin, Italy, in 2008. Curator Francesco Bonami asked eleven design practices and an equal number of theorists to reflect on the "Limitation of Freedom and Space" that now pervades the neoliberal West, and to suggest alternatives to or illustrations of that situation. Many designers responded with variations on their previous work in encapsulated miniature (Atelier Bow-Wow, for example) or evasive if telling riffs on the theme (Jeffrey Inaba: "I thought you said Prisms…."), but a few delved into carceral specifics. Diller Scofidio + Renfro designed a variable cell interior that seemed to pull one of its museological soft-scapes inside out, and Ines and Eyal Weizman offered CELLTEXTS, a library of prison-generated literature with special resonance in a country that only recently incarcerated two of its most influential political theorists, Antonio Gramsci and Antonio Negri.

The multinational reach of *YouPrison*, as well as many of its projected installations, find a mainstream and more museological complement in the film *The International*, released the next year. A political thriller spanning three continents and five color-coded cities, *The International* features a series of actual museums collaged as sets for other buildings, and a shoot-out in a reconstructed Guggenheim in which Wright's smooth, spinning interior is pocked with bullets and desecrated by a falling chandelier of projection screens. Architects trying to develop new approaches to environments for art should closely follow the dialogue between Clive Owen and an unfortunate assassin as they make their escape. Trapped in the rotunda with fast-diminishing rounds, the two duck into one of Gwathmey's side galleries, only to realize they have no option but "the ramp." Staggering their descent, they discover a number of ways to capitalize on the spiral, by firing across it, ducking behind its balustrades and finally by bringing down the roof.

Many of today's museum architects are still escaping the Guggenheim, often less resourcefully than the duo in *The International*. Some try to rival it as a vacant icon; others try, as Koolhaas did in Rotterdam and since, to sample and transform its logic, rather than its form.

08.DISPERSE

HOLDING PATTERNS

Retail brand, tourism generator or Junkspace: the terms that
describe the new museum sound bleak and jaded, like economic
perversions. Rolling off the tongues of industry insiders, they
take on democratic overtones.[212]
MIMI ZEIGER

IN 2005, I thought two friends of mine wrote the same book. Raul
Barreneche and Mimi Zeiger each produced a survey titled *New
Museums* — for Phaidon and Universe, respectively. Barreneche's
is without subtitle, large-format, and hardbound; Zeiger's *New*

Museums: Contemporary Museum Architecture Around the World is a more travel-friendly 6'x9' softcover. Both tomes are brilliant, in their way, and each includes a staggering spectrum of new museum architecture, almost all of it completed since the turn of the millennium. They feature roughly thirty museums apiece, of which thirteen projects are repeated in both. An additional half-dozen projects in each book are different buildings by architects included in both collections. Tellingly, both feature views of Zaha Hadid's Contemporary Arts Center in Cincinnati on their cover.

Both authors are in their mid-thirties, and could be said to be slumming upward in *New Museums*. Barreneche and Zeiger are magazine people: Raul is hyper-refined, as close as American architecture is going to get to the United Kingdom's Tyler Brûlé, the founding editor of *Wallpaper**; Mimi is more alt-rock, having founded *Loud Paper*, an architecture 'zine dedicated to the intersection of dissident design cultures in music, filmmaking, and the building arts.[213]

Museums are very staid territory for both of them, and both books benefit perversely from the candor and occasional condescension of their authors. Because, as they both point out, there are simply too many new museums, and to take them all as seriously as the museums take themselves would be ludicrous. Both *New Museums* will serve as guidebooks for some, and in-jokes for others. Journalists as much as they are theorists, Zeiger and Barreneche write ambitiously about ambitious architecture, but with the precision and currency of *Time Out* or *Zagat*. Though their appetites differ profoundly, both would likely subscribe to the idea that there can be no criticality without first connoisseurship.

Although, as their overlapping projects suggest, they do cover much of the same ground, the authors survey and assess their territory uniquely. Barreneche's *New Museums* features beautifully built buildings; Zeiger favors innovative exhibitionary solutions. The illustrations in both are generally free of people, but Zeiger focuses more on the sequencing of interior spaces, Barreneche on exterior details and disposition. Barreneche includes drawings, plans, and sections, but sparingly. Zeiger omits them.

Though neither collection includes new work by Gehry (nor Meier, nor Eisenman), the term "post-Bilbao" haunts both introductory essays, as it does most museum discussion of the last five years. Barreneche cites Victoria Newhouse's *Towards a New Museum* extensively, but perhaps a more salient earlier study is *The Museum Transformed: Design and Culture in the Post-Pompidou Age* by Douglas Davis. Truly a relic of another era, *The Museum Transformed* was published in 1991 with an introduction by French Minister of Culture Jack Lang, and highlights European and Japanese cross pollination in the 1980s.

More than most building types, urban museums are understood by architects to have developed from one watershed precedent to the next. Gehry's Guggenheim Bilbao is thus one in a series of typological breakthroughs that would doubtlessly include the Centre Pompidou and the first Guggenheim as immediate precursors, and a more variable list before those receding back to the Altes Museum by Schinkel. Zaha Hadid's CAC may be next. All of these buildings "reframe the city" in unforeseen ways: the Altes, Pompidou, and CAC by running their entry stairs/escalators parallel to, rather than away from the surrounding cityscape; the two Guggenheims by spiraling up from contextual attunement at grade into architectures of sharp contrast above.

CULTURAL BAGGAGE

Too reverent to scoff and too dizzy to judge, my unexpected companion and I dutifully unwound our way down the exitless ramp, locked in a wizard's spell.[214]

JOHN UPDIKE, "MUSEUMS AND WOMEN"

IT'S OFTEN TEMPTING to ridicule the "Starchitects" of Signature museums, but designers who do so too reflexively risk missing the fruits of an accelerated evolution in our discipline. Enough architects have built multiple museums that the study of individual buildings should perhaps give way to charting trajectories, gambles, and discoveries across a firm's portfolio of architecture for art.

By this standard, prolific museum architects often fall into a few habits of design, some more promising than others. If Gehry and Koolhaas are clear revolutionaries here — protagonists that reframed the basic terms of exhibitionary architecture a few times over — then Daniel Libeskind, Santiago Calatrava, and (with greater success) Zaha Hadid form a more mannerist generation. By contrast, Richard Meier and Renzo Piano developed in retrograde, with startling early projects (the Atheneum and the Pompidou, respectively) followed by stolid, increasingly predictable work. Artist-architects plying more phenomenological or materialist approaches, such as Hans Hollein, Williams+Tsien, and Peter Zumthor, are still much in demand, but remain, perhaps intentionally, ineffable in terms of typological or disciplinary advance. Perhaps the most succinct and incendiary trajectories are those of Peter Eisenman and Wolf Prix, both of whom managed to subvert quite a few museological expectations in just a few uncompromising structures: Eisenman mines an ever-more complex rapport between field and ground in the Wexner Center, Berlin Memorial, and now Santiago; Prix's Coop Himmel-b(l)au imagines super-structural "thought bubbles" exploding in

a pavilion for Old Visual Art at the Groninger Museum (1994) and as a cloud/carrier hovering over the Akron Art Museum (2007).

The most compelling museums by the current, baby boom generation have been brokered by partnerships, and have in turn redefined those practices as their stance toward contemporary art grew more evidently sophisticated in subsequent projects. Though geographically and culturally disparate, the collaborative practices of Herzog & de Meuron, Diller Scofidio + Renfro, UNStudio, and SANAA have each made sequential breakthroughs in architecture for art. Each of these partnerships has produced a series of museums that modulate architectural scale, orientation, medium emphasis, and urban disposition to diverse ends, ends that become more specific and resonant in later work. The most prolific of these, Herzog & de Meuron, move from Kahnian reflections in Munich's Goetz Gallery, through mega-scaling in the Tate Turbine Hall, the urban/bucolic negotiations of the de Young, on to their recent floating addition in Spain, with many galleries and much retrospective self-curation along the way. Diller Scofidio + Renfro began in performance and installation art; then

Architecture as/for Art: 300 Museums in 30 Years

AUTONOMOUS

< ABSTRACTION >

Music Video Pavilion
Carnuntum Museum
Museum of Islamic Arts
Reina Sofia

GREG LYNN
Eyebeam Museum
St. Gallen Kunstmuseum

PETER EISENMAN
Wexner Center
Castelvecchio Museum
Holocaust Memorial
City of Culture of Galicia

PETER COOK
Kunsthaus Graz

MORPHOSIS
Nature and Science

FUTURE SYSTEMS
Museo Casa Enzo Ferrari

ZAHA HADID
Royal Collection
Art Museum in Graz
Science Centre Wolfsburg
Plaza des les Arts
Cincinati Contemporary
MAXXI
Riverside Museum

Jewish Berlin
Imperial War
SF Jewish Museum

DANIEL LIBESKIND
Denver Art
Danish Jewish
Royal Ontario
Military History

Temporary Contemporary
LA Science Museum
Vitra Design Museum
Frederick Weisman Museum
Guggenheim Bilbao

FRANK GEHRY
Experience Music Project
MARTa Museum
Art Gallery of Ontario
Serpentine Gallery
Ohr-O'Keefe Museum
Guggenheim Abu Dhabi

PATTERNS
Prism Gallery

ITERATIVE

ANDREW ZAGO
Museum of Polish History
MoCAD

REISER+UMEMOTO
Eyebeam
New Museum

TOYO ITO
Yatsushiro Museum
Serpentine Gallery
Museum of Architecture

MICHAEL MALTZAN
MoMA QNS
Sonoma County
Fresno Metropolitan
Victoria & Albert

OPEN OFFICE
Dia Beacon
Dia Center
Andy Warhol
Whitney Museum
Georgia O'Keeffe

GLUCKMAN MAYNER
Mori Arts Center
Museo Picasso Malaga
San Diego MoCA
Perelman Building
Georgia

DALY GENIK
HUAM Art Center

Zero

Kirchner Museum
Museum Liner Appenzell
Museum Kalkriese
GIGON/GUYER
Ketterer Gallery
Kunstmuseum Basel
Swiss Transport
Löwenbräu Art Complex
SANAA

HITOSHI ABE
Kanno Museum

N Museum
O Museum
MCA Sydney
21st Century Museum
Glass Pavilion Toledo

White Cube

PETER ZELLNER
Matthew Marks

Mercedes Benz
Rietberg Museum
Valencia Modern Art
New Museum
Louvre-Lens
Serpentine Gallery

ATMOSPHERE

Akron Museum
Ciudad Del Motor
Het Valkhof Museum
Wadsworth Atheneum

JOHNSTONE MARKLEE
Menil Drawing Institute

Blur Building
Eyebeam Museum
ICA
Berkeley Museum
DS+R
Image and Sound
Broad Museum
Hirshhorn Museum

NEIL DENARI
Umetnostna Galerija
Dallas MoCA Extension

UN STUDIO
Jewish Historical
Mercedes-Benz
New Amsterdam Plein
Te Papa Museum
Middle Eastern Modern
National Museum China

STUDIO SUMO
Mizuta Museum

PRESTON SCOTT COHEN
Tel Aviv Museum
Taiyuan Museum

BENTHEM CROUWEL
Stedelijk Museum

TREY TRAHAN
Louisianna Sports

DIAGRAMMATIC

Kunsthal
Guggenheim Las Vegas
LACMA Extension
Whitney Extension
Leeum Museum

DELUGAN MEISSL
Porsche Museum

Tate Modern
Küppersmühle
Fünf Höfen
Kunsthaus Aarau
Schaulager

HERZOG & DE MEURON
Walker Art Center
De Young
TEA
VitraHaus

Nice CAC
Guangdong
ERIC OWEN MOSS
QUEENS MUSEUM
Perm Museum XXI

MAD
Ordos Museum
China Wood Sculpture
KBH Kunsthal

OMA
Seoul University Museum
Kohlenwäsche
Hermitage 2014
Des Beaux-Arts Quebec
National Museum China
24-Hour Museum

FERNANDO ROMERO
Soumaya museum

Groninger Museum
Akron Art Museum
COOP HIMMELB(L)AU
Musée des Confluences

ROJKIND
Nestlé Chocolate Museum
Tamayo Museum

MOCAPE
Museum Strongoli

R&SIE(N)
Dustyrelief / B_mu

CONCEPTUAL

won the Eyebeam Museum competition with an entry redolent of many Deleuzian practices; retrenched to their de-materialist strengths in the vanishing Blur Building; set a viewfinder over the Charles River with the ICA Boston; turned amorphous again in their sponge for the Broad Museum in LA; and now plan to blow a balloon through the solid ring of the Hirshhorn. In the museological trajectories of both H+dM and DS+R, one can trace specific, progressive inquiries into the nature of architecture as object, atmosphere, figure, and ground, and genuine curiosity about how those variables alter the experience of art, as well as the purview of artists working with(in) those spaces. In all, *dialogue* seems key.

TRANSIENT ART: FROM BILBAO TO FRIEZE EFFECT

Gone are the easy-money days of the millennium's turning, and with them (for the moment) the museum world's struggle to secure a place in the spectacular firmament of popular culture.[215]
KEVIN PRATT

IF NEW MUSEUMS were the 20th century stage sets for the art world, art fairs and festivals are its principal backdrop now. Though museum construction continues apace, especially in the East and Middle East, the choreography of the art market is based

on a schedule of destinations — Basel, Miami, Venice, Cologne, etc. — rather than a constellation of exhibition spaces.[216] The traditional high season for galleries and museums, October through December, has been displaced by a year-round circuit of art tourism. Though art fairs are hardly new — Documenta in Kassel, Germany, has been running for more than fifty years, since its first "Museum of 100 Days" in 1955 — their rise and their swing from local and societal concerns to global and popular embrace in the last decade have been extreme. As cultural critic Jan Dalley noted recently, "The once cast-iron divide between shows where you bought things and shows where you only looked at them has continued to dissolve."[217]

The Venice Biennale, which alternates between art one year and architecture the next, is the best-known in architectural circles, but no longer the most influential for artists. It is, however, still the most complete, cyclical conversion of a city into a single, vast space of common faith one is likely to experience outside of Mecca. Combining every imaginable venue — palaces, churches, galleries, museums, and national pavilions in the Giardini gardens and the 316-meter-long Arsenale, as well as innumerable piazzas, rooftops, and cafes — each Biennale consumes Venice anew, converting the island city into an alternative magical kingdom of the visual arts and design. Like Documenta, each Venice Biennale adheres to a theme devised to vex or bemuse those who make the hajj in a particular year. In 2008, Aaron Betsky organized the Biennale in terms of "Architecture Beyond Building," and lined the Arsenale with architects' full-scale spatial alternatives, often micro-galleries in their own right. Telescoping exhibition within exhibition in a long series of white-cube Russian dolls, each installation in a sense depicted its own architect, even as it looked ready to nest in or envelop the one following. (We'll likely see more Russian doll schemes, given the shifting geography of art patronage.)

Artists who once envied rock stars now live like them, touring much of the year to produce *in situ* works, scrambling between homes and gallery representation in various countries to meet the appetites of the new global patron class. Rirkrit Tiravanija typifies this new stage in transnational art production, even as he tries to transcend its limitations. His recent retrospective at the Serpentine Gallery was composed of 1:1 plywood reconstructions of each of the gallery spaces that had previously hosted his exhibits, to be occupied through the retrospective in the manner of the original performances. His longer term, more utopian project, The Land Foundation in Thailand, involves the collaboration of many friends of Tiravanija in the construction and occupation of a tract of land that he has offered as a latter-day commune for artists exhausted by their travels.

TRANSWORLD DETENTION

Incarceration has also grown more cosmopolitan, though more as a result of warfare than tourism. Singapore is more arbitrary and draconian with the citizens of other countries, but the United States holds the most foreigners, with the least legal recourse. As was mentioned in Chapter 01, the most infamous of our Revolutionary prisons was a dungeon in a mine shaft in central Connecticut enlarged to hold British prisoners of war. America's treatment of POWs has recently hit new lows, but US misadventures distract from a larger shift: international detention has become a Tower of Babel in which consortia of nations hold similarly diversified prisoner populations, with little or no communication possible between keepers and kept, nor indeed among either group.

On June 13, 2008, 1,200 Afghan prisoners escaped Kandahar's central jail, freed by thirty rocket-armed insurgents and two suicide bombers who detonated themselves at the main gates of the facility. Of the 1,200 freed inmates, 350 were known Taliban fighters, and many of those senior commanders — 100 more fugitives than we now hold in total at Guantanamo Bay. Fifteen guards

○ MAJOR ART FAIRS
● BLACK SITES

MAJOR ART FAIRS+CIA BLACK SITES. ddd llc (2012)

were killed in the fighting, according to Kandahar's governor, Ahmed Karzai (who soon after the jailbreak fell prey to assassination himself — he was also the brother of Hamid Karzai, Afghanistan's embattled president).[218]

There have been so many astounding failures in international incarceration that the above story was buried on page 9 of the following day's *New York Times*. As the Kandahar central jail was technically under local control, it might appear more a case of local ineptitude or corruption, but Canadian peacekeepers under NATO command in that part of the country arrived like the Keystone Kops after every inmate and their Taliban liberators had fled the facility.

Though later events in Afghanistan — including the subsequent bombing of the Indian Embassy and the Karzai assassination — suggest that the Kandahar jailbreak was a pivotal event in the "war on terror," at least it didn't again showcase US disregard for the Geneva Conventions. The trial-less detentions at Guantanamo Bay, the Abu Ghraib debacle, renditions to torture-friendly Egypt and Kazakhstan, even the twenty-year sentence in solitary

for Public Enemy fan and "American Taliban" John Walker Lindh, all suggest that for the John Ashcroft and Alberto Gonzalez Justice Departments, freedom was just another name for whatever we chose to do with those in our custody. This perceived latitude in the treatment of prisoners paralleled equally laissez-faire guidelines about where to hold them. As mounting reports of CIA rendition suggest, we shopped for safe-harbor countries with easy attitudes toward coercion and abuse the way sophomores pick spring break destinations, and when we couldn't find one amoral enough for our plans, we invented extrajudicial zones such as Guantanamo and other clandestine facilities. Two presidential election cycles later, the hangover persists.

Similarly, and even less happily, we have exported our techniques of incarceration to these black sites, schooling the world in the new lowest common denominations of prisoner treatment. It's precisely because we incarcerate so many in the United States that the guardsmen implicated at Abu Ghraib, led by an off-duty correctional officer from West Virginia, were able to develop such a stunning array of humiliations for their charges, and enact them so shamelessly. The nudity and leashes seen at Abu Ghraib were in no way accidental or exceptional, but simply illustrative of the nonlethal trauma that is part and parcel of prisoner management in contemporary US maximum security environments. In fact, the restraints were probably laughable to military personnel familiar with the wrist and ankle shackles and triple-guarding that are regulation for high-security inmates throughout the United States.

It's possible that the Abu Ghraib images were first circulated as further proof of how under-equipped our forces were, and how they were forced to make do. The smirks and grandstanding of the soldiers reflects not their inexperience, but their utter confidence in proven methods applied under trying conditions. (Granted, the human pyramid was an innovation, and Pfc. Lynndie England would not have been smoking in a US facility.) As Susan Sontag pointed out to much protest, those images show not an aberration from, but a caricature of, standard practice.

Top: SEGREGATION CELLS, CAMP REMEMBERANCE, NEW ABU GHRAIB PRISON, Abu Ghraib, Iraq, Richard Ross (2006)
Bottom: HOLDING CELLS, JOINT TASK FORCE, Guantánamo, Cuba, Richard Ross (2006)

NEW MUSEUM OF CONTEMPORARY ART, SANAA, New York, New York (2007)

CONTAINERIZATION

Seen from above, the 20-odd compounds of the Bucca camp have a clinical stillness that befits what goes on below: what Stone calls his 'massive experiment' and what his critics call the world's largest religious education camp.[219]

ANDREW K. WOODS

A NEW SOBRIETY, however, has emerged in a host of "show prisons" in Iraq. A week after the Kandahar liberation, the *Financial Times* profiled Maj. Gen. Douglas Stone, a Marine reservist charged with overhauling the American detention facilities and procedures in Iraq in the wake of Abu Ghraib. His primary responsibility was Camp Bucca, a sprawling city penitentiary holding 19,000 detainees (a 3,000-inmate facility, Camp Cropper near Baghdad, also fell under Stone's command). Three hundred miles from Baghdad, Camp Bucca is assembled from tents, containers, and miles of razor wire.

Following recommendations made by Rand Corporation, Stone commissioned a revisionist translation of the Koran for his charges and instated a guidebook featuring "Ahmed," an unfortunate Iraqi detained because of his dangerous friends and their ideas. Cartoons depict Ahmed interacting with other Iraqis and politely declining the bad influence of jihadis and Sadrists trying to destabilize the country. (To reach a similar level of paternalism in US prisons, jailers could require our many new converts to the Nation of Islam to watch an endless loop of *Good Times* and *The Cosby Show*, or sharply redact *The Autobiography of Malcolm X*.)

Although many prefab military prisons look like gargantuan Quonset huts, some of the inmates at Bucca may occupy made-to-order prison cells by Maximum Security Systems in Penrose, Colorado. Available in multiple layouts for double occupancy and welded entirely from structural steel, these cells weigh roughly six tons and may be plugged into the sides of conventional steel buildings. Perhaps most efficient of all, the cells are constructed with the help of inmate labor.[220] The systems of flexible detention devised for holding prisoners of war have more recently proved useful for immigration and INS detention at the US border.

Prefab turns out to be a trickier proposition for art space, but quite a few of the pavilions and installations punctuating art fairs aspire to standardization, and many new museums make a fetish of shipping containers, and of globalized freight more generally. The New Museum on the Lower East Side of Manhattan stacks box upon box; the Institute for Contemporary Art, Boston, resembles neighboring cargo facilities along the Charles River, almost a magnification and merger of container and crane; the Nomadic Museum, by Shigeru Ban, was assembled at each of its four ports of call from locally sourced containers.

CAVES AND VAULTS

Prisoners beyond borders, art below grade, and both in unmarked containers — these would appear the first habits of extreme, post-millennial "content management." Bunkers are an underappreciated tendency in both contemporary art space and detention facilities. Galleries and cellblocks have a long subterranean pedigree, and their not-so-distant affiliation with entombment — and archeological plundering of burial sites — have been at issue since John Soane's time. Saddam Hussein's last months in a spider hole offered a lesson in functional ascetics. However, the new art vaults take excavation and fortification to new depths. Larger and larger art venues of course demand larger basements, but new media art, and the darkness required by projection, also drive the expansion below grade. Once considered ancillary service spaces, underground art storage is now often the culmination of a tour.

In the 1960s and '70s, underground gallery space usually "solved" an urban dilemma, as Mies did by packing two-thirds of the exhibition space in the Neue Nationalgallerie in Berlin in an underground plinth, thus allowing for the radical transparency of the upper entry gallery, and leaving a much larger plaza to frame it. In the '80s and '90s, however, museums often made a show of burying themselves because they could. Ando's Naoshima Art Complex, Herzog & de Meuron's Goetz Gallery in Munich, and Rem Koolhaas' Guggenheim Las Vegas are all self-consciously embedded in their settings. Naoshima is bored into its island setting as a series of Turrell-like light wells, preserving, but critically disciplining the nature of its site. Both the Goetz and the Guggenheim Las Vegas treat bunkered gallery space as an architectural sleight of hand, deceptively doubling the gallery space in the former, and concealing it like a safe in a casino in the latter.

Suppressed, super-privatized and/or secreted art spaces are again in vogue. Eli and Edye Broad keep a dozen late Stellas — assemblages made from aluminum shards of fuselage — in a bunker under their driveway. A recent reflection on Philip John-son's campus in New Canaan in *BookForum* showed only the sub-terranean gallery interiors and a long view from below of his Glass House. If the container museum is a latter-day recuper-ation of Gordon Matta-Clark's "Non-ument," then the many new subterranean galleries are akin to Robert Smithson's notion of the "Non-Site." Museums now take forms described by the most doctrinaire of post-gallery artists, who compared museums to graves better left unmarked. All recall extraterritorial holding spaces that are similarly elided, or elisional, in terms of space, law, cost, and time.

If the 1990s saw huge consolidations of cultural product in new and expanded historical and encyclopedic museums, the new century has tended more toward specialization. In new buildings for art, exhibition and storage are often divorced. Although the best-publicized new buildings are Kunsthals and Contemporary Art Centers without permanent collections, a host of new and less heralded art vaults have been designed for storage, repairs, and limited exhibition. Though most of these are simply the private galleries of collectors, many have amplified the requirements of art storage and handling to a point of radical dif-ference — and then found themselves subject to much uninvited, but not completely unwelcome, art world attention. As a recent *New York Times* feature on the extraterritorial Freeport in Geneva made clear, this is a market of secrecy and security dominated by the Swiss, but now global in scope.[221]

Vaults come in Signature and Ready-Made variations. Imagine a safety-deposit box withdrawn from a Swiss bank, mag-nified a thousandfold in size, and then struck by a battering ram. The Schaulager, outside Basel, Switzerland, holds the collection of the Emanuel Hoffmann Foundation, founded in 1933. Designed by Herzog & de Meuron and completed in 2003, the Schaulager is a warehouse for works by roughly 150 artists, where all "other activities and projects are byproducts of the handling of stored art." Even given the concentration of art storage, rather than

SCHAULAGER, Herzog & de Meuron, Newmünchenstein, Switzerland (2003)

exhibition, the Schaulager is a vast holding facility, with 73,000sf of art storage on three upper levels, and 37,000sf of exhibition space, including permanent installations by Robert Gober and Katharina Fritsch, at grade and below. The remaining third of the 170,000sf institution is given over to art handling, conservation and auditoria, with all transitional processes and outreach activities revealed, to an unusual degree, to visitors.[222]

If the Schaulager is a bespoke safe, the "Fortress" network in the United States offers more standardized, though still full-service, art storage. Fortress has three branches, in New York, Boston, and Miami, reflecting the concentration of US collectors in the first two cities, and the "snowbird" aspect of Miami — as well as its rise in the international art market. As collector and graphic designer Richard Massey explains, "Miami has a distinct warehouse culture, as much of the town packs up and heads north for the summer. The Wolfsonian Museum, for instance, is in an old storage building on Miami Beach, where winter residents parked their furs and Rolls-Royces when they left town. Miami has a very high water table — most of the place is only four to eight feet above sea level, so there are very few basements for storage in the city — and probably none on Miami Beach, which is mostly landfill. So storage facilities are always in demand. There's usually a wait for Fortress units of at least a month."[223]

Both the Schaulager and the Fortress vaults land in their low-rise suburban settings like exotic, meteoric boulders (as does Farshid Moussavi's new MoCA in Cleveland), but in a sense all the most compelling new museums and prisons appear to be airborne, subsumed, or, like these, in transition between. This points to a utopian polarization: new holding spaces appear *either* aloft, ethereal, and light-infused, *or* solid-state, infrastructural, and subterranean. The current mechanizations of transcendence and transformation seem to beg one sublime extreme or the other.

BORROWED LIGHT — AND, THUS, NO BLIGHT FOR WRIGHT

The color is thin brick cast into the panels organizing the security sized fenestration into a hieroglyph of human intention. Flat as Judd, abstract as Albers....In my mind, the key is the window.[224]

JAMES KESSLER

WHETHER ABOVE or below grade, both museums and prisons are more and more frequently imagined as fortified redoubts against uncertain times and circumstances. If the Schaulager and Fortress suggest that contemporary art is best held in isolation from a greater public — even as that isolation might be variously tailored — two recent jails, in Marin County, California, and in Richmond, Virginia, debate that premise for the storage of malefactors, with a parallel bifurcation in their architectural resolution. The two jails illustrate the subterranean and prefab states of the art in detention, and set some contemporary correctional issues in high relief.

A "cave" in all but actual burial, the new Marin jail addition by DMJM is located immediately to the north of Frank Lloyd Wright's Civic Center, almost touching its northernmost wing. One enters the facility, a hexagon in plan, through a cleft in a berm that surrounds the addition, masking it completely from surrounding access roads and from Wright's building. The visual foreclosure is even more profound within the building, where in an innovation termed "borrowed light," individual cells are lit indirectly by large common skylights over common rooms at the hexagon's corners, but are not provided individual windows. Though inmates receive guaranteed minimum lumens of daylight based on Marin's climate, they enjoy no view of their surroundings, nor any private sliver of daylight from their cells. Suppressing the legibility and presence of the jail was paramount, both because of its monumental neighbor, and because local residents were by no means enthusiastic about a new jail in general.[225] A wealthy, white, and liberal county, Marin reaches more often to San Francisco via the Golden Gate Bridge than east, past San Quentin, to Contra Costa, in its politics and culture. Like the "Glamour Slammer" but even more virtual to passersby, Marin's discreet, geometrically exacting, and expensively landscaped facility has the chief virtue of adding no recognizably penal architecture to threaten surrounding property values. Marin has designed away its jail.

By contrast, the new Richmond Justice Center by HOK is seen as a major and much anticipated new institution in that city, and a boon to local politicians and businesses. Though many of the US prisons and jails included here are the overt symbols of racial inequity and persecution, Richmond's has a more nuanced backstory. The population of Richmond, once a colonial hub of the transatlantic slave trade, is 53% African-American. The city has a black mayor, police chief, and majority on the city council, and more than 50% of the contracting for the new jail's construction was awarded to minority-owned businesses.[226] The new jail replaces a failing old one, and will provide more room not only

MARIN COUNTY JAIL ADDITION, DMJM (2011) at north end of Wright's Marin Civic Center, San Rafael, CA

for law enforcement, but also for drug treatment facilities, community outreach, etc. For better or worse, this will be a major, architecturally distinguished presence "across the tracks" of the major interstate bordering Richmond, and a likely anchor of future development in that part of the city.

The 1,680-bed facility is composed of prefabricated cellular modules designed by James Kessler, director of HOK's justice practice in Washington, DC. A pioneer in precast concrete podular housing units, Kessler began his career in tandem with the first Metropolitan Correctional Centers in the 1980s, and his earlier designs for jails in Mecklenburg County, North Carolina, and Fairfax, Virginia, are precisely the kinds of county and municipal reinterpretations of MCC principles the Federal Bureau of Prisons hoped would result from its early urban towers. Kessler's faith in podular housing, and especially Direct Supervision, remains unwavering. The Richmond design calls for four stacked, triangular wings of housing behind a more anodyne, terraced collection of office and intake spaces. Though they've been turned to the rear, the cellblocks break far more ground architecturally than the rest. Composed of four-cell modules stacked six high in offset bars, the wings of the jail are monuments to precast ingenuity,

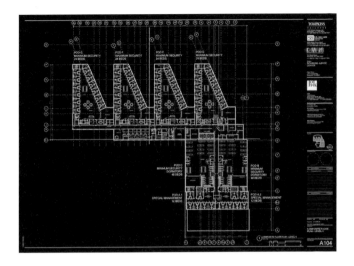

with fully integrated plumbing and electrical services, security systems, and even exterior, embossed brick coursework to reduce the apparent scale of the fully assembled facility.[227]

HOK's command of poured concrete is hardly incidental here. Kessler, it turns out, earned a BFA and an MArch from the Yale School of Art and Architecture in the late 1970s, as the Center for British Art (the "Mellon Center," as he remembers it) was under construction. If many of the museums of the last fifty years are indebted to prisons, the prisons designed by Kessler owe at least two qualities back to Kahn's museums: precision concrete work, and an unprecedented attunement to the civic potential of institutions that once only deflected the public. Explaining an earlier design for Mecklenburg, Kessler noted that ganged bands of 2'x2' square windows, rather than 5" wide slivers, made for less carceral elevations, which in turn led to street fairs and concerts being held in the recessed courts of the jail (a public embrace of correctional space not seen since floggings were celebrated within the walls at Newgate).

RICHMOND JUSTICE CENTER, HOK, Richmond, Virginia (opening 2014); Plan and Cell Module

Kessler professes a disquietingly earnest optimism about justice architecture in general, but projects a far more specific, and to me contagious, fascination with what artists such as Tony Smith and Carl Andre might have called the "systems logic" of interlocking concrete forms. In its malleability, serial configurability, and potential for progressive refinement, concrete seems for Kessler almost a metaphor for rehabilitation itself. To my surprise, he is less sanguine about "borrowed light," this decade's major correctional breakthrough. "Borrowed light" now factors into most inner-city proposals precisely because it allows jails to be completely walled off, usually behind fancy stone veneers, and keeps inmates from seeing, and often signaling, out to the street. According to Kessler, the jury is still out on whether inmates suffer from the deprivation of windows, or are instead pulled into a commons of directly supervised interaction. The more pressing issue, from his point of view, is that corrections, or indeed justice, be acknowledged as a civic necessity, not erased by architecture.

Opening almost exactly thirty years after CCCDF pioneered Podular Direct Supervision, the Richmond Justice Center restates the basic tenets of that earlier Contra Costa County building with greater architectural authority, but without a sea change in penal philosophy. The community of Richmond is no doubt fortunate to have HOK's Kessler designing its jail, but I wonder whether his ingenuity with concrete systems results in an architecture of greater optimism, or simply one of more evident rigor. A more hopeful architecture, in this context, would likely require a repurposing: the Justice Center is stately enough for a college, and Kessler's panoptic pods, with a reversal in their scopic orientation, might make fine auditoriums-in-the-round. Perhaps accommodations for such a conversion could be factored into future formwork.

POST-INDUSTRY

The site is on the Mall between the museums and monuments, and this museum is a fusion of the two.[228]

DAVID ADJAYE, ON HIS WINNING PROPOSAL FOR THE NATIONAL MUSEUM OF AFRICAN AMERICAN HISTORY AND CULTURE

THE SURGE in US museum and prison construction in the 1980s and 1990s reflected a new but provisional social contract. As deindustrialization set in, many Americans subscribed to a pair of complementary beliefs: first, in the wisdom of consolidating our history and cultural largess in public institutions, and, second, in the efficacy of concentrating our oversupply of undereducated, urban men through mass incarceration. This postindustrial pact held for twenty years, but has frayed in the last decades as "the information society" and globalization sweep away the last vestiges of American analog manufacturing.

Without blue-collar prospects, prisoners have little hope of rehabilitation, and the country has little use for their liberty. LWOP — Life Without Parole — sentences have spiked in part because there is so little pressure, except from inmates and their

260

families, to ever release felons, and so much — from guards' unions, victims' rights advocates, law-and-order politicians — to keep them inside. This temporal aphasia carries over to our extra-territorial policies as well: why should a terrorist at Guantanamo see a finish line when so many American convicts do not?

Similarly, we seem to have enshrined most of the history and all the art worth venerating in the last quarter of the 20th century. We built enormous new museums to commemorate all the major wars, accomplishments, and traumas of that century and most that preceded it. According to Paul Williams, we now build "performative museums," displacing the "interpreting museum" of the last century as well as the "legislating museum" of the 19th century, in hopes of producing drama and theatrical effects that can reach an increasingly benumbed audience.[229]

Perhaps two highly anticipated post-millennial museums will cast new — and less borrowed — light on this historical moment. As in many of the subterranean examples above, though for far more freighted reasons, the National September 11 Memorial Museum at Ground Zero delves below grade, while the National Museum of African American History and Culture, on the Mall in Washington, DC, hovers in a few distinct, though hardly standardized, volumes. As Thomas Krens did speaking of the Guggenheim Abu Dhabi, the newly awarded NMAAHC architect, David Adjaye, uses the term "Pharaonic" to explain the symbolism and monumentality of his undertaking. Lest museum designers presume their neo-Egyptian efforts will alone define the present, HOK's Kessler also spoke of "faces in the pyramid." Posterity will likely count them all in a single archeology, vastly ambitious but oddly mordant, undergirding the new millennium.

09. AFTERLIVES

On a May morning in 2006, I learned of an untimely death, one that made the completion of this book a personal obligation. Below the front-page fold and with the blunt diction of James Ellroy, that day's *Los Angeles Times* announced "A Death in Lockup." According to the *Times*, a forty-two-year-old Compton auto mechanic named Ramón Gavira had died in the Los Angeles County Men's Central Jail under suspicious circumstances almost four years earlier. He had been picked up for drunk driving in 2002, fallen off medication for depression and diabetes, run afoul of at least one guard (a boxer in her off time) and some fellow inmates, and was found dead in his cell, an apparent, but by no means certain, suicide by hanging.

I suspect I'm one of very few people outside the criminal justice system who could locate Mr. Gavira's cell in the vast complex of the 18,000-inmate jail based on the plumbing fixtures and the detail that the cell was windowless. It sits deep under the northerly wing of the old jail, to the left as one enters that building through a courtyard punctuated by a long, red LED ticker tape reeling off guidelines for visitors. Gavira's five-day fall from repairing his son's Chevy Blazer to strangulation in the dark depths of LAMCJ must have surpassed Dante's horrific plunge through the rings of the netherworld. Gavira died on the night of July 11, 2002 — precisely the same balmy Thursday evening my daughter was born, premature but healthy, a few miles away.

PRISON/MUSEUM RELIEF MODELS, Track 16 Gallery, Exhibition View; ddd llc, Santa Monica, California (2010)

DEAD SPACE

Right in we went, with soul intent
On Death and Dread and Doom
The hangman with his little bag
Went shuffling through the gloom
And I trembled as I groped my way
Into my numbered tomb.[230]

OSCAR WILDE, THE BALLAD OF READING GAOL

They got me rottin' in the time that I'm servin'
Tellin' you what happened the same time they're throwin'
4 of us packed in a cage like slaves, oh well
The same mother fucker's got us livin' in his hell.[231]

PUBLIC ENEMY, BLACK STEEL IN THE HOUR OF CHAOS

I OPENED A THESIS ON PRISONS almost twenty-five years ago,
"The Afterlives of Incarceration," with the two quotes above. They
still reverberate for me, although the work that followed — a con-
fidently rendered tale of penal architectural development, and
proposal for a "Liberty Deprivation Center" suspended over a
freeway cloverleaf — now looks pat.[232] Though I didn't know it at
the time, a dominant strain in the discussion of museums strikes
a similarly funereal note. In his essay "Some Void Thoughts on
the Museum," Robert Smithson wrote:

> Museums are tombs, and it looks like everything is turning
> into a museum. Painting, sculpture and architecture are
> finished, but the art habit continues.... Things flatten and
> fade.[244]

Since then, I have toured over two dozen prisons, and
perhaps ten times as many museums, but still grope for ways
to explain the odd, expectant stillness that often pervades both
institutions. Both the timelessness of museums and the time
served in prisons are temporal zones outside quotidian experi-

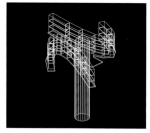

LIBERTY DEPRIVATION CENTER (LDC 10/405), Joe Day, Undergraduate Thesis, Yale College, advisor: Patrick Pinnell (1990)

ence, and, in certain respects, outside of life itself. This concluding chapter includes some conjectural projects — early projects
of mine, and by students I've taught — that explore these themes.

Utopian or dystopian, museums and prisons are follies of
a specific arrogance, the mistaken assumption that qualities of
the afterlife, any afterlife, can be delivered here and now. Penitentiaries arose to offer an earthly purgatory, a transitional state
between heaven and hell in Christian doctrine, and one devoted
to exacting penance and awaiting grace. Much of my undergraduate thesis went to keying the shifting logic of reform prisons to
evolving theological models of the afterlife spanning the Reformation. Though less explicitly celestial, the notion of museums
as secular cathedrals connects that building type to the claim
that a church is a terrestrial House of God. Our sense of transcendence in great art, and especially in the immersive domains
of contemporary art, has no more obvious analog than the ecsta-
sies offered by faith.

I no longer believe, however, that either prisons or museums
are best understood as projections of a hereafter. By virtue of
their scale and proliferation, they now play charged roles in the
daily lives of millions apart from whatever notions of sanctity and
redemption may have driven their invention. For all their hyper-
fortification and unlikely forms, today's prisons and museums
seem designed for a collective philosophical pause, perhaps an
earthly limbo, in which the developed world might mull its options
as the projects of modernity and industrialization draw to a close

KUNSTHAUS GRAZ, Peter Cook, Graz, Austria (2003)

or leave its shores. In important respects, both buildings are also "free trade zones" of neoliberal experimentation. As they do for the Asian superpowers, prisons in the United States function to modulate our labor force, especially the younger, undereducated male portion of it that might once have found ample work in our cities. Unlike our factories, however, US prisons have been free to "float" their pay scale, which they quickly pegged to a global minimum wage of twenty or thirty cents an hour. Museums also make their collections affordable in ways they are not otherwise, both by making art accessible to the public and by easing the tax burdens of those that offer it to be seen. The freeholds and black sites of the last chapter are extreme examples, but all prisons and museums stand in actual and idealized isolation from their context. Museums and prisons are utopia and dystopia writ small.

Many of both institutions are cities in miniature, governed by urban plans condensed to the microcosmic scale of discreet buildings. As such, many of the projects of the last fifty years

266

could be seen as variable manifestations of singular, visionary ideas: Archigram's *Walking City* (1964), for example, saw its partial realization in Peter Cook's Kunsthaus Graz (2003), and another more distant, but perhaps even more poetic, iteration in François Roche's proposal for B_mu, a museum of contemporary art in Bangkok (2002), a creature-like building designed to attract a thick coat of dust as its final exterior finish. A similar case could be built for Steven Holl's early "paper cities" and the proof of those ideas in his recent work, museums and otherwise. Though few contemporary designers of prisons have had to wait as long as Bentham to see their idea put into practice, correctional facilities spring from a hypothesis (*if* inmates are held thus, *then* they will behave thus…) and often "correct" one another and the diagrams that spawned them. Museums and prisons are conceptual structures, even when they try to be otherwise.

FUNNEL VISION

Structural linguistic studies developed in the 1960s in France and Italy conveniently suggested a possible answer: analogies with language appeared everywhere, some useful, some particularly misleading…. Whether through literal or phenomenal transgression, architecture is seen here as the momentary and sacrilegious convergence of real space and ideal space.[234]
BERNARD TSCHUMI

MY OUTLOOK IS FRAMED by my schooling in architecture and political theory in the late '80s and early '90s, a period of paranoid misapprehension regarding technology's impending, explosive potential. Within academia, Deconstruction still held sway, lingeringly as a mode of literary inquiry, but by then mostly as a generalized template for attacking traditional disciplines and scientific positivism. My undergraduate years were a litany of the *soixante-huitards* — French leftist intellectuals collectively known

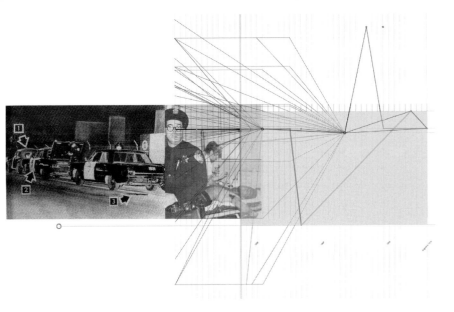

CRIME ANALYSIS AND TIMELINE. PRI/MUS Studio, SCI-Arc, Liliana Dirks-Goodman (2004)

as the Generation of '68 after the student protests many of them fomented that year. More specifically, I studied *their* studies of the French Revolution and proto-modern tendencies in the Enlightenment. It was a pretentious time.

I am reminded of my '68-inflected entry into design discourse almost daily by colleagues only a year or two younger but untouched by the Orwellian angst of the late '80s recession and urban decline. Though our early prospects were equally shaped by our command of software, I was burdened with doubts that were consistently proven unnecessary, if not exactly unfounded, through the boom years of the '90s and early 2000s.

Despite much seductively hermetic theory and design to the contrary, I believe architectural discourse remains an exercise in triangulation, a bastard child of more independently coherent, but also more limited, discussions related to urbanism, art, and technology. Though the "digital turn" has profoundly reconfigured the priorities and horizons of our discipline, the terms defining contemporary architecture remain "extroverted" and amalgamated from these three conceptual vectors. The rendering of urban conditions and response to those possibilities form one line of inquiry or "spoke" in this model; the (often late and mis-construed) application of theory and practices related to other creative disciplines such as literature, art, and cinema, a second; and the incorporation of technological advances in digital visu-alization, materials, and methods of design or construction, the third. Venturi favored the first vector, Eisenman the second, and Greg Lynn the third, but all three had to defend their preoccu-pations in the face of demands from the other two. All, further-more, became more salient within architecture as they became less defensively unipolar.

Under the umbrellas of prison and museum design, one finds an overlapping and timely range of attempts to reconcile or span among these three spokes. Urban conditions have inflected and, in turn, responded to the siting and configuration of prisons and museums since medieval times. Technological advances in security, surveillance, information management, lighting, cost-effective enclosure and new construction techniques — as well as vanguard geometric and performative research — have all been quickly showcased in museums and prisons, if not developed for them specifically. And no two structures play more charged roles in mediating between the individual and collective, setting the limits of expression and subjectivity in a manner that some feel imperils the role of contemporary art.

Hal Foster's *Art-Architecture Complex* wrestles mightily with this last disciplinary inequity, but his defense of transdisciplinary artists such as Anthony McCall against threats from architecture feels anachronistic. Today's artists, architects, filmmakers — cul-tural producers, all — work at common scales, in shared soft-ware platforms, and with similar audience attunement. Though disciplinary strengths and disputes inform the ambitions and reception of work differently, we are all, rather suddenly, mod-ulating the same variables in environmental innovation. The most advanced speculation on this predicament and its promise across the arts is Sylvia Lavin's in *Kissing Architecture*, extended

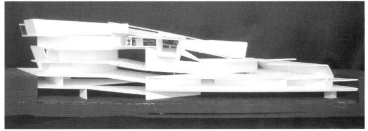

in her more recent reviews of work by Preston Scott Cohen and
Pipilotti Rist. Lavin sums up the convergence thus:

> "As installations grew more and more immersive and as
> conceptual architecture practices came to rely less and
> less on the withholding of the architectural object, the two
> types of production predicated on entirely different points
> of departure, came to be more and more isomorphic with
> one another." [235]

I like to note that the prison and the museum are two of three
six-letter typologies that corral sightlines and concretize visual
relationships as points of architectonic departure. *Cinema* is the
third, and has proven a frequent, welcome antidote to mulling
over corrections and collections as this project has taken shape.

All three situate viewers and viewed with extreme care and prejudice, and each allocates authority and creative agency in unique ways. Perspective, projection, and the many scopic properties codified by Robin Evans, Martin Jay, Anthony Vidler, Jonathan Crary, and others under the rubric of Visual Studies still fascinate me, and in many respects this work is an extrapolation of their investigations into specific ways of seeing and then reimagining spatial and cultural formations.

FROM COMPLEXITY AND CONGESTION TO CORRECTIONS AND COLLECTIONS

Very few grasp even the possibility that (architecture) aspires to a cultural performance distinct from identity, spectacle, and its obligations to a building type: the house, museum, or school. Want a great photograph of a really blank look? Get your camera ready, and then ask someone how architects use a roof to affect art, language, the family, democracy, the difference between democracy and freedom, or, for that matter, to improve orgasms.[236]

JEFF KIPNIS

ROBERT VENTURI'S *Learning From Las Vegas* and *Delirious New York* by Rem Koolhaas are the only post-WWII manifestos by architects to enjoy a broad readership outside the discipline. Though *Learning From Las Vegas* has an almost sociological tone and *Delirious New York* purports to be an architectural "novel," both have seduced and inspired students of art, literature, film, and urbanism for decades. Oddly, neither has much to say about how to design, draw, or even think about specific buildings. Both books follow in the tradition of Le Corbusier's *Towards a New Architecture* in structure, if not in polemic, seizing on an aspect of US urban expansion, extrapolating radically from singular examples, and arguing for new architectural paradigms based on the "realities" of current building outside the purview of high design.

Like Corbusier, Venturi and Koolhaas presume a *retardater* audience within the architectural community, willfully blind to — and therefore increasingly excluded from — the implications and possibilities of commercial expansion.

Learning From Las Vegas and *Delirious New York* sing the praises of developers who gambled on revolutionary building types — casinos and towers — that embody the transformations of urban space that each author wants to present as new, relevant parameters for design. It's fair, however, to ask how prescient either was in predicting the evolution of the US urban/suburban landscape. Neither Venturi nor Koolhaas was spot-on. Even before 9/11, tall buildings had faltered typologically since *Delirious*, first due to postmodern planning and New Urbanism, then recession, and finally from "new economy" business models that favor single expansive floor plates over stacked divisions. Venturi has recently agreed that Vegas has reversed course, becoming a boulevard of "ducks" rather than decorated sheds, with casinos buried under theme hotels cast in the mold of Disney rides. He at least has the solace of being exactly reversed, and in his own terms, while Koolhaas has seen his metropolitan vision undermined randomly by mediocrity and fickle civic economies.

Urban space is now more the result of bait-and-switch plays between developers and politicians, a chess game of familiar pieces played to consolidate tax bases and transit access. Within this new game, museums and prisons are the rooks that bookend either extreme of the market economy. Though in theory neither operates for profit, both ensure that the fictions of priceless objects and wageless time persist. These and other "outstanding" buildings may be pawns, knights, bishops, even royalty in city planning, but their roles are at most nodal rather than transformational. Any could alter the flow of urban transactions; none are allowed to actually redefine the parameters of the grid. It's tempting to decouple Venturi's diagram for the Decorated Shed and equate the new, architect-designed museums with spectacular but misleading signage, and the new jails, drawn by corporate

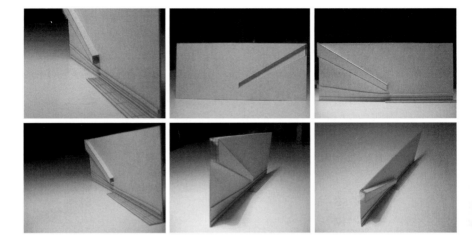

firms or the police departments themselves, with their corresponding sheds: civic soufflé rising not to signify, but to distract from a bleak co-reality at the city's edge.[237]

These center-to-periphery urban dynamics have been amplified to national scale. The most politically inflected trends in American institutional architecture in the last decade are landmark museums rising in Midwestern states, such as Missouri and especially Ohio (crucial swing states, both), and massive detention facilities, often just high-tech holding pens, erected at our border with Mexico in Texas and Arizona, as well as in Florida (all crucial Republican "hold" states). In the case of both typologies, political patronage has reached absurd extremes, as congressional leaders vie to support outlandish museums in the heartland (as *The New York Times* had it, "Pork Under Glass") and gain the endorsement of immigrant-hostile governors and sheriffs in the Sun Belt.[238] Like a vast medieval town, the United States now holds its most interesting new museums in the castle-keep of the Midwest and its most extreme new prisons at the outer ramparts of its frontier.

ANAMORPHIC CIRCULATION STUDY, PRI/MUS Studio, SCI-Arc, Shir Gale (2004)

SHALLOW AND DEEP TIME

Those who plotted the attack used the code word 'architecture' to refer to the World Trade Center and called the Pentagon 'arts.' No one reading their emails or listening in on their international phone conversations was supposed to make the connection between 'architecture' and 'international business,' 'art' and 'military affairs.'[239]

CHRISTINE SYLVESTER

THE DESIGN of prisons and museums has evolved more rapidly over the last fifty years than in the previous two centuries. As we've seen from examining both between 1960 and 2010, their accelerations can be correlated with one another, and those advances came in surges, more like a succession of upward gear-shifts than a single quickening push forward. These phases of the contemporary or postmodern period are split between broadly Minimal and then Millennial cycles.

Minimal and post-Minimal institutions share certain ambitions, as do Millennial and post-Millennial designs. If Minimalism isolated objects in space (bringing a carceral logic to bear on museums), and post-Minimalism relocated the viewer in relationship to objects, then a Millennial sensibility is characterized first by the premise that space could simply *become* the object, before the post-Millennial decade threw that optimism into question in as many ways as possible. In each pairing, I see a two-stroke

MUSEUM OF TERRORISM+TERRORIST ORGANIZATIONS (MOTTO), PRI/MUS Studio, SCI-Arc, Lauren Rosenbloom (2004)

Opposite: **SPRING STREET COMPLEX**, BROADacre Studio, SCI-Arc, Lionel Lambourn (2006)

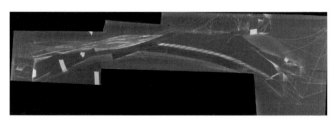

274

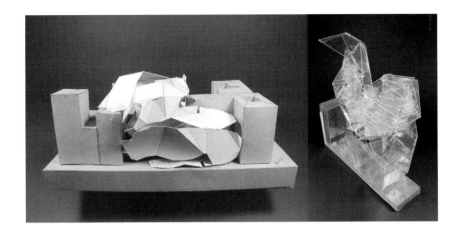

dynamic, in which a new sensibility emerges and is codified over ten to fifteen years, then reassessed and challenged in a "post-" period of about equal length.

If Minimalism circumscribed architectural expression in doctrinaire ways and then enforced new rules for multiplying those forms, post-Minimalism turned on those pieties and offered more elliptical, open-ended, and subject-centered alternatives. Though far less quantified at this point, Millennial and post-Millennial sensibilities reveal a similar pattern. The immersive, ambient, "formless" preoccupations of the newly digital 1990s brought us to the close of an epoch, but were then quickly eclipsed by events in the first decade of the next. Sept. 11 and subsequent wars and financial crises shook the developed world out of its *fin de siècle* revelry; in art and design, more contingent, collaborative, and technologically matter-of-fact strategies for producing work came to the fore.[240] Relational Aesthetics, in particular, seems committed to the ethic that a digital swarm may never substitute for an actual crowd.

The nature of crowds matters a great deal in prisons and museums, as shifting notions of "otherness" key to a longer time frame in the evolution of these institutions. Since their inception

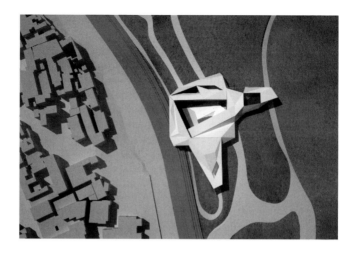

MEW TAIWAN CITY MUSEUM OF ART, Competition Proposal. Aerial View, ddd llc (2011)

in the Enlightenment, museums and prisons have not only seg-regated races and genres, periods and types of criminal, as well as the "fine" from the "applied" arts, they have also taught those distinctions to the "masses." The major and common historical theme in both institutions over the full course of their develop-ment is the West's digestion and exploitation of colonial popu-lations and their cultural dowry.[241] However, the recent temporal subtleties I've outlined above reveal some shifting notions of "otherness" that highlight a new Orientalism or postcolonial worldview in unexpected ways. It turns out we alternate in our demonizing of the poor and the strange in much the way aesthetic fashions oscillate between the found and the fantastic. Just as shifting notions of what constitutes contemporary art altered the shape and scale of museums, different specters of criminality reorganized buildings for detention as well.

Through WWII, and into the Minimalist phase I begin with here, the ascendant criminal stereotype in the United States ran to Bonnie and Clyde's desperate Okies and Prohibition's ethnic/ Catholic spectrum; the artists were Pollock and Judd, or trying to be — plain, if not poor, white, and male. Post-Minimalism features difference: more women, minorities, and orientations in both registers. The Millennial reverts to sameness, turf wars, uniform sentencing, and universal art; in the post-Millennial years, strangers are ever more foreign again, with terrorists (and artists, and immigrants) born in one country, to parents from two more nations, "attacking" yet another and held in perpetuity in a few others. Prisons and museums morphed quickly to sort out these fast-evolving differences in what we value, what we denounce, what we deem American. Although other countries came to terms with otherness in their midst, the United States carried this process of examination, embrace, and exclusion to far more diversified ends.

ENDGAME

It becomes people's world, and you can't trifle with that.[242]
JAMES KESSLER

Do you even like museums?[243]
BENNETT SIMPSON, MOCA

YES. I DO like museums, and, to a point, the more the merrier. Museums — and longer life spans — are perhaps the happiest accidents of advanced capitalism, and to oppose them is to deny the monumentalization of creativity in general and the advancement of "capital-A" architecture in particular. However, we should distinguish between buildings and situations that simply preserve things for posterity (not a minor task, but often not an interesting one), and those that ask — or force — us to see them anew. Many lament how often museum design devolves into architecture-for-its-own-sake, but the field has benefited exponentially from that license, as have many cities. As long as there's some decent light, and often even without it, artists will capitalize on any new building for art. Too few contemporary museums are willing to risk the gravitas of their holdings to resituate their con-

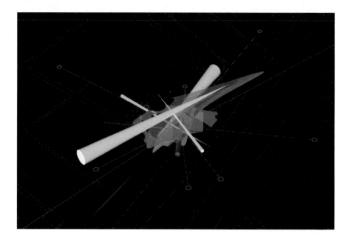

MUSEUM OF POLSIH HISTORY, Competition Proposal, ddd llc (2010)

Opposite: VECTOR DIAGRAM showing invasions of Poland by direction and magnitude

tents or reanimate their context. Not enough museums rise to the intensity of the art they contain, nor to the challenges of today's actual and virtual landscapes.

The fiscal landscape also poses its hurdles. The downturn since 2008 has left many US museums facing bankruptcy, closure, or, at least like LA's MoCA, a major leadership restructuring. Money is trumping design as an issue in the public perception of museums. After years of debating the character of the museum and other elements in the Ground Zero memorial, recent press focuses more on its $60 million projected annual operating cost, which includes $15 million for security and $5 million for two fountains to mark the absence of the twin towers. Do terrorists win when we pay that much, in perpetuity, to remember their atrocities?

More generally, the leveraged expansions of many museums over the last decades will weigh on their directors and boards for many years to come, and likely dim the prospects for daring new architecture. The last museum to launch within the scope of this study is a modest one, devoted to explaining the banking industry to an angry public: the Savings Museum in Turin (located, perhaps aptly, in the same city that sponsored the *YouPrison* exhibition in 2008). The five-room museum occupies a former bank

branch office of Intesa Sanpaolo, and claims sister museums of finance in Manhattan and Beijing, also opening in October 2012.[244]

But all proclamations of "the death of the museum" prove premature, as almost all critiques of the institution fall not on deaf ears, but on those of curators now eager to test the elasticity of their venues to any extreme. In what might prove the logical culmination of Institutional Critique, Michael Asher responded to the Santa Monica Museum of Art's invitation to mount a retrospective of his work by rebuilding the framing for all forty-four gallery installations since the museum's opening in 1989. Like most interrogations of the "White Cube," Asher's move suggests not a refusal of the museum, but a profound attunement to its history and potential. Far more areas of human endeavor should be as closely — and lovingly — assessed, argued over, and challenged as museums have been in the last fifty years.

Prisons could head that long list. Though my doubts outweigh my faith, I don't dispute the necessity of incarceration. There are people who pose a threat to themselves and others, and those who deserve the weight of society's approbation. We have,

STAN BRACKAGE ANALYSIS. BROADacre Studio, SCI-Arc, Benjamin Smith (2006)

however, built too many jails, penitentiaries, correctional and justice centers, and learned too little from those we've completed.

And by "learn," I don't mean, principally, how to build them better, faster, or more cheaply. Forty years ago, in the wake of rioting in US cities, Attica, and other prisons, some progressive architects argued that we should fight the inhumanity of incarceration by improving the spaces of those held. They argued that what was needed wasn't abstention, but more active participation in correctional planning and design. John Kibre, one of the principal architects of Contra Costa's innovative housing units, was of this view, as is James Kessler of HOK. The kindest assessment of this position I can offer is that some of those new, well-meaning facilities *might* still prove effective, if they are allowed to function at capacity rather than beyond it. Until that perhaps utopian condition is guaranteed, the more normalized, directly supervised, less coercive designs will likely be repurposed, as they have been throughout the Podular era, to more draconian ends. Each "New Generation Justice Facility" spawns another generation to right the wrongs of the last, but until overcrowding is accounted for, new jails and prisons will be no less miserable than their precursors — and that is *not* an argument for building more of them, but for revisiting how many people we lock up.[245]

For architects, as for anyone else concerned about mass incarceration, the basic mathematics of prison reform needs to be cast not in terms of spending, staffing, or construction, but strictly in terms of reducing the number of our fellow citizens we consign to a system proven to make them worse. In California, in particular, both our costs per inmate and rates of recidivism are among the highest in the world, so one can safely conclude that convicts aren't leaving the system better adjusted than they entered it, and not for lack of spending. One can ask only whether they should have been imprisoned in the first place. Mandatory minimum drug sentencing guidelines, petty probation-violation statutes, and three-strikes laws have flooded our jails and prisons with hapless charges. While acknowledging that a minority of prisoners are violent offenders who most of us would agree need to be kept at bay, our collective attention and political will must turn to the massive price we are paying in dollars and lost lives to contain the remainder of our inmates, who are more often poor or addicted than malevolent — at least on arrival.

By "learn," I mean something closer to what Aldous Huxley found by looking at Jeremy Bentham's Panopticon and then at Piranesi's *Carceri* in 1943, in the wake of WWII. Huxley wondered first at Bentham's tragically naive passion for order, a passion so clearly and horrifically misapplied by Germany in the war. He then turned to Piranesi's boundless, impossible subterranean realms (though Huxley doesn't extend the parallel, the interiors of the *Carceri* were perhaps less foreign then for his fellow countrymen, who took shelter from air raids in the Underground). Huxley notes the prescient abstraction of the *Carceri*, and their formative romanticism, but isolates their distinct timelessness in a pervasive tone of *acedia*, a Greek term without easy modern translation but meaning, roughly, a restless, worldly, solitary boredom. This condition colors both the ambiguous architectures and the minute, sketchy occupants of the *Carceri*, and suggests a disposition for coming to terms with massive — often sublime, but also incoherent — institutional expansion. Huxley's existential disconsolation seeps through the manifold spaces of the *Carceri,* and into our increasingly ambient and atomized times.

Today, the best arguments for more efficient, and even more humane, prisons have been tested, and none produces model citizens. All, in fact, yield graduates with a stigma of incarceration so profound in its consequences that neither the convicts nor their families will be free of its effects for generations. Piranesi has captured not their confinement, but their future.

As the *Carceri* allude to a fantastic version of ancient Rome, today's prisons and museums are echo-utopias, fragments and distillations of more extensive alternative worlds, many of them imagined in the 1960s. Both the ground control of Peter Eisenman's museums and Coop Himmelb(l)au's hover-craft — as well as the looming Federal towers and bermed mazes of contemporary correctional space — evacuate the quotidian middle landscape of conventional building. Whether floating above or delving below grade, the new monuments of constraint and display showcase our aspirations to defy not just gravity, but also the mundane limitations of contemporary urban space and streetlife.

One can debate the value of all these new architectures of detention and exhibition, but none can avoid the societal and cultural dynamics that have driven their growth, nor the reflections and shadows they cast through our cities. Architects should weigh whether to participate in the prison industry, but should also note the limits of protest. Architects/Designers/Planners for Social Responsibility (ADPSR) was founded in 1981 and in 2004 called for a Prison Design Boycott in which all cosigners pledged to refuse design work on correctional facilities. While noble, the boycott has sadly done little to slow the prison boom.

Though a plethora of museums and prisons was built in the last fifty years, we will only build more in the decades to come. Some architects will follow the lead of Rem Koolhaas and discover ways to make these buildings explain themselves, as he did at Arnhem, or listen to Jeff Kipnis and, grasping them as the instruments they are, try to locate their virtuosity. Next to the sym-

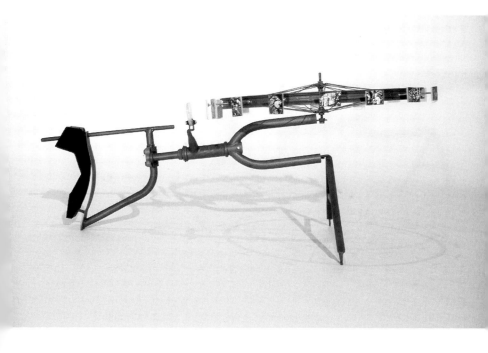

PIRANESI VEIWING MACHINE, Bike Parts, Magnifying Glass, 16 Carceri @ 1/10th Scale, SCI-Arc Thesis, SCI-Arc, Joe Day (1994)

phonic violins or the burning guitars that some hear in museums, prisons resound with a constant percussive bass line. Both are now defining tracks on the mixing board of US cities.

I will end, though, with a more concrete parallel. If museums are today's cathedrals, prisons are our pyramids. Future archeologists revisiting the late 20th century will marvel at these rival architectures of light and opacity, and struggle to imagine a belief system that could have led us to so many vexed designs for looking at objects, and at each other. Both are *circumspect* architectures, literally so in the case of the "all-seeing" Panopticon and like structures, but also, more broadly speaking, in the musings that lead to and from museums. All these holding spaces are uneasy monuments to an era defined more by its transgressions than its aspirations. The contrasts and parallels between these architectures cast their surroundings and our priorities in sharp relief.

NOTES

1　These acronyms are culled from US federal and state prison systems: AD-SEG and D-SEG, Administrative and Disciplinary Segregation, are housing classifications for dangerous or endangered inmates; SHU stands for Secure Housing Unit, for AD- and D-SEG inmates; LWOP — Life Without Parole; 270s — housing units with 270 degrees of internal visibility; and J-CAT — "J" Category inmates are sex offenders.

2　For museum numbers in the US, see Joseph Lewis Ettle, "Irrational Exuberance: Calculating the Total Number of Museums in the United States" (doctoral thesis, Baylor University, 2006), https://beardocs.baylor.edu/xmlui/bitstream/handle/2104/4196/joseph_ettle_masters. pdf. For prisons, see Fox Butterfield, "Study Tracks Boom in Prisons and Notes Impact on Counties," *New York Times*, April 30, 2004, A15: "The number of federal and state prisons grew from 592 in 1974 to 1,023 in 2000."

3　Though China may soon also compete for gallery space: "A Museum Boom," *Economist*, June 16, 2007, 49: China had roughly 300 museums in 1977; 3,000 are projected by 2015.

4　See Michelle Alexander, *The New Jim Crow: Mass Incarceration in the Age of Colorblindness* (London/New York: New Press, 2010, revised edition 2012), 6.

5　See "Steady Climb: State Corrections Spending in California" prepared by the California Budget Project, September 11, 2011, 5: "State spending on corrections rose from $604.2 million in 1980–81 to $9.6 billion in 2010–11, a nearly 1,500 percent increase that significantly outpaced the growth of total state General Fund spending during the same period. As a result, state spending on corrections has more than tripled as a share of General Fund expenditures, rising from 2.9 percent in 1980–81 to 10.5 percent in 2010–11." www.cbp.org/pdfs/2011/110914_Corrections_ Spending_BB.pdf.

6　In 1995, these were the top national incarceration totals: US — 1.59 million inmates at a rate of 600 per 100,000; China — 1.24 million at 103 per 100,000; Russia — 1.02 million at 690 per 100,000, according to Marc Mauer, director, Sentencing Project. *Race to Incarcerate* (New York: New Press, 1999), 21–2. For current figures, see International Centre for Prison Studies: www.prisonstudies.org/info/worldbrief/wpb_stats. php?area=all&category=wb_poptotal. Per *Jurist*, University of Pittsburgh School of Law, November 20, 2007, the US inmate total is up eightfold since 1970: www.jurist. org/paperchase/2007/11/us-prison-population-up-eight-fold.php. Also www.prisonstudies.org/info/worldbrief/wpb_stats. php?area=all&category=wb_poptotal.

7　Also BBC: news.bbc.co.uk/2/shared/ spl/hi/uk/06/prisons/html/nn2page1.stm.

8　For overall US museum figures, see www.aam-us.org. Also the European Group on Museum Statistics: www.egmus.eu/index. php?id=10.

9　And MoMA doesn't top the list: The nearby Metropolitan Museum of Art greeted 5.24 million visitors, more than the White House and Graceland combined. See www.artmarketmonitor.com/2010/07/01/ moma-attendance-soars/.

10　Mauer, *Race to Incarcerate*, 23.

11　Joseph Rykwert, *The Judicious Eye: Architecture Against the Other Arts* (Chicago/ London: University of Chicago Press, 2008), 366–7.

12   Douglas Crimp, *On the Museum's Ruins* (Cambridge, MA/London: MIT Press, 1993), 287. First published as "The Postmodern Museum," *Parachute* No. 46, Spring 1987.

13   Crimp, *On the Museum's Ruins*, 282.

14   Sylvia Lavin, "Surface Activation," *ArtForum*, January 2012, www.artforum.com

15   Peter Halley, "Notes on the Paintings," in *The Art Life: On Creativity and Career*, ed. Stuart Horodner (Atlanta: Atlanta Contemporary Art Center, 2012), 99–100.

16   For histories of prison design, see the exemplary Norman Johnson, *Forms of Constraint: A History of Prison Architecture* (Chicago/Urbana: University of Chicago Press, 2000); United Nations Social Defence Research, *Prison Architecture* (London: UNSDRI, 1975); Norval Morris and David Rothman, *The Oxford History of the Prison* (Oxford: Oxford University Press, 1990); and Leslie Fairweather, *The Architecture of Incarceration* (London: Academy Editions, 1994). The literature on museum design is exponentially more extensive and contested. For some contemporary perspectives, see *Museum Culture: Histories, Discourses, Spectacles*, eds. Daniel Sherman and Irit Rogoff (Minneapolis: University of Minnesota Press, 1994) and *Grasping the World: The Idea of the Museum*, eds. Donald Preziosi and Clair Farago (Burlington: Ashgate, 2000). Anthony Vidler's *The Writing of the Walls* (Princeton: Princeton Architectural Press, 1987) was the first discussion of prisons and museums I encountered, and remains the most elegant. Vidler's later scholarship, especially *The Architectural Uncanny: Essays in the Modern Unhomely*, expands and updates his perspective through the 20th century.

17   Michel Foucault, *Discipline and Punish: The Birth of the Prison*, trans. Alan Sheridan (New York: Vintage, 1979), especially part 3, chapter 3, "Panopticism," 195–230. Foucault elevates Jeremy Bentham's Panopticon as a paradigmatic modern structure, an "all-seeing eye" that stands as a metaphor for the hyper-empowerment of the propertied classes. At the time of his writing, Foucault posited an anachronistic, failed prototype as a basis of his theory, and the philosophical model he derived from the Panopticon leads to what many see as a gross oversimplification of human relations, in that in fact people rarely relate to one another strictly as keeper and kept. But time has been on Foucault's side. Though the Panopticon had been for eighty years out of correctional fashion when he wrote, prisons have returned to a panoptic parti since. New Generation Justice Facilities, the new urban tower jails, require the triangulation of cellblock layouts into miniature panoptic fields.

18   To brutally oversimplify the major scholarship after Michel Foucault on museums, Douglas Crimp seeks an instrumental politics in Foucault, which leads to a call for the end of the museum and similarly coercive institutional structures, and celebration of protest art based on photography/new media that dispense with the idea/value of the original. In her important essay "The Museum as a Way of Seeing," in *Exhibiting Culture*, ed. Steven Lavine (Washington, DC: Smithsonian, 1991), Svetlana Alpers moves from Foucault to assess all art as essentially anthropological artifacts and calls for much more multiculturally sensitized museums of culture — or more criticism of existing hamfisted exhibitions of other cultures. With, to me, the most promising perspective among these, Tony Bennett looks at both museums and expositions as exercises in an "exhibitionary complex" complementing Foucault's disciplinary complex — both mold people to the will of authority, but with different ends and dexterities. See both Bennett's *The Exhibitionary Complex* (London: Routledge, 1995) and more recent *Past Beyond Memory: Evolutions, Museums, Colonialism* (London: Routledge, 2004). Eilean Hooper-Greenhill reads Foucault and renaissance museums beautifully in *Museums and the Shaping of Knowledge* (London: Routledge, 1992), but favors more literalist exhibitions of working life — life-size dioramas of fish mongers, for example. Thomas Markus fits a discussion of prisons and museums into *Buildings and Power: Freedom and Control in the Origins of Modern Building Types* (London: Routledge, 1993), a wide, valuable catalog that runs the risk of leveling many of the distinctions between the buildings included. See also Foucault's main text on art vis-à-vis surrealism and language: *This Is Not a Pipe* (Berkeley: University of California Press, 1968).

19 Rosalind Krauss, "The Cultural Logic of the Late Capitalist Museum," in *October: The Second Decade, 1986–96* (Cambridge, MA: MIT Press, 1997), 427–41. And Hal Foster, *Design and Crime (and other Diatribes)* (London: Verso, 2002). Foster and others are dismissive about the belle-lettrist tendencies of recent West Coast cultural criticism and art theory, but my work shares proudly in a local vernacular I would term "mal-lettrism" exemplified by Mike Davis' neo-noir reading of LA's civic priorities in *Ecology of Fear* and *Dead Cities* (London: Verso, 1999 and 2002, respectively); the abject coupling of art and forensics cataloged by Ralph Rugoff, Peter Wollen, and Anthony Vidler for Rugoff's 1997 exhibition, *Scene of the Crime* (catalog published by UCLA/Hammer/MIT, 1997); and the macabre aspect of celebrity museums evoked in many essays by Dave Hickey.

20 Robert Smithson, "Some Void Thoughts on Museums," in *The Writings of Robert Smithson: Essays with Illustrations*, ed. Nancy Holt (New York: New York University Press, 1979) and Brian O'Doherty, *Inside the White Cube: The Ideology of the Gallery Space* (Santa Monica: Lapis Press, 1976).

21 Andrea Fraser, *Museum Highlights: The Writings of Andrea Fraser*, ed. Alexander Alberro (Cambridge: MIT Press, 2005), 240–49. See also Loic Wacquant, *Prisons of Poverty* (Minneapolis/London: University of Minnesota Press, 2009).

22 John Lobell, *Between Silence and Light* (Boston: Shambhala Publications, 1979), 8.

23 Lobell, *Between Silence and Light*, 10. Kahn continues, "It is a first response to the intuitive, the intuitive being the odyssey, or the record of the odyssey, of our making through the untold billion years of making."

24 Manfredo Tafuri, "The Ashes of Jefferson," in *The Sphere and the Labyrinth, Avant-Gardes and Architecture From Piranesi to the 1070s* (Cambridge, MA: MIT Press, 1986), 291–303. See in particular pp. 293–94: "What Europeans have almost always undervalued in the work of Kahn is the profound 'Americanness' of his desperate attempt to recuperate the dimension of myth….To the promise of Kahn — communication is possible by giving voice to institutions — Robert Venturi has responded with the following objection: the only institution is the real, and only the real speaks….If Kahn could have produced a school of mystics without religions to defend, Venturi has in fact created a school of the disenchanted without any values to transgress."

25 Thomas Leslie, *Louis I. Kahn: Building Art, Building Science* (New York: George Braziller, 2005), 60–61. Anne Tyng's role in Kahn's buildings for art cannot be overstated.

26 The donor, Paul Mellon, is partly to credit for this innovation: the block of Chapel Street to be occupied by the BAC included his favorite pub as an undergraduate, and he required that the bar be leased space in the new design. Mellon also insisted that his name not be featured in the museum's signage. See www.yaledailynews.com/news/2009/oct/28/british-art-center-seeks-more-undergraduate/.

27 Leslie, *Louis I. Kahn*, 51. The Yale University Art Gallery's budget was approved by the Yale Corporation on December 9, 1950.

28 On Documenta 5, 1972, see *Art in Theory 1900–2000: An Anthology of Changing Ideas*, eds. Charles Harrison and Paul J. Wood (New York/London: Wiley, 2002), 970.

29 Ada Louise Huxtable, *Kicked a Building Lately?* (New York: Quadrangle/New York Times Books,1976), 10. The original New York Times byline appeared October 6, 1974.

30 *Thomas Jefferson: Writings* (Washington: Library of America, 1984), 41–42.

31 Alexis de Tocqueville and Gustave

de Beaumont, *On the Penitentiary System in the United States and Its Application in France*, intro. Thorsten Sellin (Carbondale: Southern Illinois University Press, 1964), originally published in France, 1833. A seven page excerpt can be found at www.correctionhistory.org/tocqueville/html/B&T_report1.html. For an updated perspective on Tocqueville and American prisons, see Bernard-Henri Levy, *America Vertigo: Traveling America in the Footsteps of Tocqueville* (New York: Random House, 2006).

32   Shelley Bookspan, *A Germ of Goodness: The California State Prison System, 1851–1944* (Lincoln: University of Nebraska Press, 1991), vii-xv and footnote 3.

33   On the discovery of Jefferson's design for the Nelson County Jail, see www.readthehook.com/files/old/stories/2006/01/26/onarchjail.html.

34   Confusingly, at least three prisons called Newgate are prominent in Anglo-American penal architecture, with the other two, in London, discussed later here.

35   See Katrina Koerting, "Letters Trace History of Jefferson Jail Building," *Nelson County Times*, January 11, 2012, updated January 13, 2012, www2.newsadvance.com/news/2012/jan/11/4/letters-trace-history-jefferson-jail-building-ar-1603015/.

36   Joan Didion, "Rock of Ages," in *Slouching Towards Bethlehem* (New York: Dell, 1967), 207.

37   Perhaps the closest example to the Yale Art Galley in the 1950s, in terms of both its material and managerial economies and its post-WWII optimism toward its wards, is the Men's Colony in San Luis Obispo, CA.

38   Federal Bureau of Prisons, *A Brief History of the Bureau of Prisons*: "By 1940, the Bureau had grown to 24 facilities with 24,360 inmates. Except for a few fluctuations, the number of inmates did not change significantly between 1940 and 1980." See www.bop.gov/about/history.jsp.

39   Adolf Loos, "Ornament and Crime," in *Spoken into the Void* (Cambridge, MA: MIT Press, 1987). See also Benedetto

Gravagnuolo, "Sick Ears and the Desire for Empty Space," in *Adolf Loos* (New York: Rizzoli, 1982), 78–88.

40   Brian O'Doherty, *Inside the White Cube: The Ideology of the Gallery Space* (Santa Monica: Lapis Press, 1976), 27. Also in that essay, pp.13–14: "From a certain height people are generally good....Those paradoxical achievements huddle down there, awaiting the revisions that will add the avant-garde era to tradition, or, as we sometimes fear, end it. Indeed, tradition itself, as the spaceship withdraws, looks like another piece of bric-a-brac on the coffee table — no more than a kinetic assemblage glued together with reproductions, powered by little mythic motors, and sporting tiny models of museums. And in its midst, one notices an evenly lighted 'cell' that appears crucial to making the thing work: the gallery space."

41   Ibid., 15.

42   Quoted in *The End(s) of the Museum* (Madrid: Fundacio Antoni Tapies, 1995), 79.

43   Bernard Stiegler, "Philosophizing by Accident," *Public 33: Errata* (Toronto: York University Press, 2006), 104 (italics in original).

44   The degree to which architects, artists, and their historians still differ in their use of these terms, as reflected in Huxtable's misreading of the Hirshhorn, expanded rather than diminished in the 1980s. In researching this project, one surprise has been the wealth of positive contemporary reviews Philip Johnson's work elicited from unlikely quarters: Donald Judd praised the Glass House, Robert Smithson liked his subterranean sculpture pavilion, and Ada Louise Huxtable adored the MoMA garden. Coming of age when revisionism was orthodoxy, I knew Johnson for his kitsch '80s towers, early Nazi sympathies, and the career-ending elisions he made in The International Style exhibition.

45   Joseph Masheck, *Building-Art: Modern Architecture Under Cultural Construction* (Cambridge: Cambridge University Press, 1993), 128.

46   Mark Linder, *Nothing Less Than*

Literal: Architecture After Minimalism (Cambridge, MA: MIT Press, 2004), 4–7. In particular, Linder describes a bifurcation in the major theoretical perspectives driving each discipline — in fine art and especially painting, the pictorial formalism of Clement Greenberg, and in architecture, what Linder terms the pictorial impropriety of Colin Rowe — that explains much of the critical disconnect between late-modern architectural commentary and its subject. Greenberg famously refused any discussion of content and composition beyond questions of frame, color, and optical presence. By contrast, Rowe's influential and persistent interest in Cubist collage and in modes of translating those pictorial strategies into buildings and spaces left architectural discourse out of step with advances in painting, sculpture, and art criticism that had renounced those compositional strategies in favor of Greenberg's "medium-specific" investigations.

47   Ibid., 7: "One of the lingering legacies of architectural formalism is a rejection of sculptural tendencies and a persistent assimilation and application of techniques that regard architectural representations and the buildings they produce as though they were a kind of painting, or at least a picture. At the same moment architects intensified their interest in pictorialist practices, the literalist artist-critics advanced a 'confused' relationship between architecture and sculpture to escape the dominance of pictorial formalism. In this way, the literalists initiated critical practices that can be understood as selective usurpations of the architectural discipline."

48   Christian Bonnefoi, "Louis Kahn and Minimalism," *Oppositions 24*, trans. Dan Cooper (Cambridge, MA: MIT Press, Spring 1981).

49   Ibid., 2.

50   Ibid., 4 (italics in Bonnefoi's original).

51   Stan Allen and others have extended Linder's scholarship, drawing out the reciprocities between neo-avant-garde architecture and post-Minimalist art practices. See Allen's "Minimalism: Architecture and Sculpture," *Art & Design 12*, nos. 7–8 (July-August 1997): 22–29 and *Points + Lines: Diagrams and Projects for the City* (Princeton: Princeton Architectural Press, 1999).

52   Beatriz Colomina, "The Endless Museum: Le Corbusier and Mies van der Rohe," *Log 15* (Winter 2009): 55–68, quote on 67. Unpublished drafts of this chapter long proceeded my encounter with Professor Colomina's excellent 2009 essay, as I had been fascinated with Le Corbusier's and Wright's competing visions for spiral museums for many years, and convinced that Mies was the hinge to the next generation, but I feel obliged to cede almost all credit for the analysis of those two buildings here to Colomina, save for whatever errors I may have failed to correct after reading her more convincingly detailed and nuanced history. To her theory that Mies' and Corbusier's museums were fundamentally indebted to earlier houses — a thesis that supports her broader work on how the private becomes public — I'd add that the carceral turn of the next generation of Johnson, Kahn, and Breuer could be read as a reversion to more generic architectures of the "Big House," a common epithet for prisons at mid-century.

53   The three art museums completed by Le Corbusier are the Main Building of the National Museum of Western Art, Sanskar Kendra (Museum at Ahmedabad) (India,1957), and the Government Museum and Art Gallery, Chandigarh (India, 1965), all of which are based on the Musée à croissance illimitée concept. See http://whc.unesco.org/en/tentativelists/5164/.

54   Corbusier's Museum of Western Art in Tokyo was built to house a large collection of Impressionist paintings belonging to a Japanese expatriate living in Paris between WWI and WWII. The construction of the museum, and presumably Corbusier's commission, were part of the deal brokered for those canvases to leave France. *Le Corbusier: Oeuvre Complete* (Birkhauser edition, 1990).

55 For a more complete discussion of Le Corbusier, Mies, and early global museum networks, see Colomina, *Log 15*, 66–68.

56 Kazys Varnelis, ed., *The Philip Johnson Tapes: Interviews by Robert A.M.Stern* (New York: Monacelli Press, 2008), 130, 171.

57 Francesco Dal Co, "House of Dreams and Memories," *Lotus International 35* (Venice: Electa, 1982), 122–28.

58 Robert Smithson, "What Is a Museum/A Dialogue With Allan Kaprow," in *The Writings of Robert Smithson*, 61. We will see a similar shift from the 1980s Post-Minimalist watershed projects of Peter Eisenman (Wexner), Frank Gehry (Bilbao), and Rem Koolhaas (Rotterdam Kunsthal) to a more generalized, Millennial sensibility in Libeskind's Jewish Museum, Zaha Hadid and UNStudio's museums in Cincinnati and Stuttgart, and Diller+Scofidio's Boston Museum of Contemporary Art.

59 Cynthia Davidson, "Observations on the End of an Era," *Log 9* Winter/Spring 2007 (New York: Anyone Corp., 2007), 86.

60 For a compelling recent survey of Roche's work, see the entirety of *Perspecta 40: Monster*, ed. Mark Foster Gage (Cambridge, MA: MIT Press, 2008).

61 Donald Judd, in "Art and Architecture," *Donald Judd: Architecture Architektur* (Ostfildern: Hatje Cantz, 1991), 28.

62 Joseph E. Persico, *The Imperial Rockefeller: A Biography of Nelson A. Rockefeller* (New York: Simon & Schuster, 1982), 141.

63 Persico, *The Imperial Rockefeller*, 177.

64 Michael Kramer and Sam Roberts, *"I Never Wanted to Be Vice-President of Anything!" An Investigative Biography of Nelson Rockefeller* (New York: Basic Books, 1976), 352–54.

65 Persico, *The Imperial Rockefeller*, 143–44.

66 In the late 1960s, John D. Rockefeller was responsible for the creation of the Commission on Foundations and Private Philanthropy (usually known as the Peterson Commission, headed by Peter G. Peterson) and the Commission on Private Philanthropy and Public Needs (usually known as the Filer Commission) from http://en.wikipedia.org/wiki/John_D_Rockefeller_III.

In 1969, President Richard Nixon received the Legion of Honor in Paris in recognition of his help in securing Rockefeller funding for the rebuilding of Versailles. Specifically, the Tax Reform Act of 1969, which Nixon signed into law, allowed "operating foundations" such as museums to forgo the distribution of income, and deduct contributions in the manner of charitable organizations (see www.irs.gov/pub/irs-tege/eotopicn84.pdf). However, the 1969 act also limited the valuations of deductions to the "donor's cost basis" rather than the previous standard, fair market value, of a work of art — thus, for artists donating original work, deductions were limited to material costs. See www.aamd.org/advocacy/tax_rec.php.

67 David Rockefeller, *Memoirs* (New York: Random House, 2003), 457. See also Suzanne Loebl, *America's Medicis: The Rockefellers and Their Astonishing Cultural Legacy* (New York: HarperCollins, 2010), 287–306.

68 Rockefeller, *Memoirs*, 458.

69 For prison growth, see H. Bruce Franklin, "From Plantation to Penitentiary to the Prison-Industrial Complex: Literature of the American Prison." Paper delivered at the Modern Language Association Convention, December 2000. For estimates of museum numbers, see Ettle, "Irrational Exuberance: Calculating the Total Number of Museums in the United States."

70 For Texas/California prison populations, Bureau of Justice Statistics Data Brief: "Prisoners at Yearend 2009 — Advance Counts" (June 2010), 6. For Texas increase, see www-958.ibm.com/software/data/cognos/manyeyes/visualizations/us-prison-population-by-state-5. The totals were 166,719 in Texas to 163,001 in California in 2009 — though to be "fair" to California, its leaders have labored under a 2008 federal consent decree to lower its number.

71 Barbara Rose in *Vogue*, October

1972, as quoted by Donald Judd in *Donald Judd, Complete Writings 1959–1975* (New York/ Nova Scotia: NSCAD, 2005), 208.

72   Renzo Piano, in his Logbook, quoted in the notice for his Pritzker Architecture Prize, www.pritzkerprize.com/98piano.htm. Also "Four Museums in Detail: Renzo Piano," PRAXIS 7 (2005): 32–39.

73   Donald Judd, "Specific Objects," *Arts Yearbook 8* (1965), reprinted in *Donald Judd, Complete Writings 1959–1975*, 184.

74   Douglas Davis, *The Museum Transformed: Design and Culture in the Post-Pompidou Age* (New York: Cross River Press, 1990), 38, 59.

75   "Warning Over Giant Prisons Plan," BBC News, March 18, 2008.

76   Jean Baudrillard, "The Beaubourg-Effect: Implosion and Deterrence," *October 20* (1982): 3–13, quotes on 7, 9.

77   Aldous Huxley, "Variations on the Prisons," in *Themes and Variations* (New York: Harper and Brothers, 1943), 203.

78   Herbert Muschamp, *Man About Town: Frank Lloyd Wright in New York City* (Cambridge, MA: MIT Press, 1983), 118.

79   *Frank Lloyd Wright: The Guggenheim Correspondence*, ed. Bruce Brooks Pfeiffer (Carbondale: Southern Illinois University Press, 1987), 2, 30. Wright and his wife had their teeth extracted at curator/client Hilla Rebay's insistence that dentures were far superior.

80   Robin Evans, *The Fabrication of Virtue: English Prison Architecture, 1750–1840* (Cambridge: Cambridge University Press, 1982), 196.

81   See Evans, *The Fabrication of Virtue*, chapter 6, "A Way of Obtaining Power," 195–235. Bentham's final 1791 design was in collaboration with draughtsman Willey Reveley.

82   A startling number of later "Panoptic" prisons by others would repeat this failing, enlarging in circumference to house more inmates, filling the intermediate void with other needs, and obscuring most of the view from the center. Early versions, such as those at Stateville and Arnheim, were catastrophically overscaled. Vast radial spans proved exorbitant to build, impossible to manage and, beyond a 50' focal length, no longer panoptic. See Johnson, *Forms of Constraint*, "Panoptic Experiments," 82–84.

83   See Bentham's critique of prisoner transport to Australia or "New South Wales" in *The Oxford History of the Prison*, 245–47.

84   Three cylindrical Panopticons were built in the Netherlands between 1880 and 1900, one in Cuba, and a last at Stateville, IL, in the mid-20th century. For a critique of the last of these, see James Jacobs, *Stateville: The Penitentiary in Mass Society* (Chicago: University of Chicago Press, 1977).

85   *Frank Lloyd Wright: The Guggenheim Correspondence*, 4.

86   Matthew Drutt, "The Frank Lloyd Wright Building" from www.guggenheim.org/ new-york/about/frank-lloyd-wright-building. The Solomon R. Guggenheim Foundation.

87   Tony Bennett, *The Birth of the Museum: History, Theory, Politics* (London/ New York: Routledge, 1995), 168ck

88   It is this openly epicurean disposition that marks Wright, for Philip Johnson, as a holdover from the century that Wright was in fact born into. For Johnson's clarification, see Blair Kamin, "Breaking All the Rules: Philip Johnson Breathed Life Into a Once Stodgy Profession," *Chicago Tribune*, January 30, 2005, articles.chicagotribune.com/2005-01-30/news/0501300453_1_pennzoil-place-philip-johnson-celebrity-architects.

89   Jack Leonard, "Helping Vets in Jail Get a Fresh Start," *Los Angeles Times*, January 30, 2005, B1. For more on inmate sorting at LA County Jail, see Russell K. Robinson, "Masculinity as Prison: Sexual Identity, Race and Incarceration," *California Law Review 99* (2011): 1309, www.californialawreview.org/ assets/pdfs/99-5/03-Robinson.pdf.

90   Shumon Basar, "All That Is Solid Floats in the Air," *Modern Painters* (Winter 2003), 62-64, writing on the Lois and Richard Rosenthal Center for Contemporary Art.

91   "What Is a Museum? A Dialogue Between Allan Kaprow and Robert

Smithson," in *The Writings of Robert Smithson*, 66.

92   Diana Crane, *The Transformation of the Avant-Garde: The New York Art World 1940–1985* (Chicago: University of Chicago Press, 1987), 125.

93   Leonard, "Helping Vets in Jail Get a Fresh Start," B16.

94   Novey quoted by John Roemer, "Taking Three Strikes Outside the Walls," *California Lawyer*, October 1996, 86.

95   Deborah Solomon, "Is the Go-Go Guggenheim Going, Going…," *New York Times Magazine*, June 30, 2002, 38.

96   Ruth Wilson Gilmore, *Golden Gulag: Prisons, Surplus, Crisis and Opposition in Globalizing California* (Berkeley: UC Press, 2007), 104.

97   Thomas Krens, interviewed by Kim Bradley in *Art in America*, July 1997, 53. See also in same issue, "Deal of the Century," cover story on the Guggenheim Bilbao.

98   Gilmore, *Golden Gulag: Prisons, Surplus, Crisis and Opposition in Globalizing California*, 91.

99   Joshua Page, *The Toughest Beat: Politics, Punishment and the Prison Officers Union in California* (Oxford: Oxford University Press, 2011), 32. Also Johnny Cash, "Folsom Prison Blues," Sun Records, 1959.

100   Rosalind Krauss, "Cultural Logic of the Late Capitalist Museum," *October 54* (1990): 7.

101   See http://en.wikipedia.org/wiki/Thomas_Krens.

102   Tony Bennett, *The Birth of the Museum: History, Theory, Politics* (London/New York: Routledge, 1995), 168.

103   Paul Werner, *Museum, Inc.: Inside the Global Art World* (Chicago: Prickly Paradigm, 2005), 75: "At the tail end of modernism Krens' vision of the museum was something like a DNA strand: two parallel systems, one based on the belief that art would improve us, the other based on the belief that money would; built, actually, on a slipshod model of capital, symbolic capital and their relation."

104   "Guggenheim Abu Dhabi Will Be 'Pharaonic,' " *Spiegel Online*, March 27, 2008, www.spiegel.de/international/world/0,1518,543601,00.html. The interview continues:

Der Spiegel: And Las Vegas? You wanted to connect casino culture with art there, which included flying in works from the Hermitage in St. Petersburg. But it didn't really work. Your museum was ultimately derided as a McGuggenheim — an allusion to the omnipresent fast-food chain McDonald's.

Krens: Those who call us that have no idea. Do we have the same facade, the same emblem, the same contents everywhere? No. We have established a local accent everywhere — with exhibitions and with acquisitions for the respective collections — with Italian art in Italy and with Basque art in Bilbao. It will work the same way in Abu Dhabi.

Der Spiegel: You established the Guggenheim brand, but also the Krens brand. Have you become too self-confident for the board of directors?

Krens: I'm sure that this played a role when I was the topic of discussion. But my top priority is the Guggenheim.

105   Solomon, "Is the Go-Go Guggenheim Going, Going…," 39.

106   See Werner, *Museum, Inc.*, introduction: "Krens, should this book wash up on future shores, was Director of the Guggenheim Museum throughout the nineties. He found a new way of thinking about museums without thinking about art, but he thought about museums so thoughtfully that by the beginning of the twenty-first century there were Guggenheim branches all over the world (Venice, Berlin, New York, Bilbao) with unfinished or failed projects in New York, Las Vegas, Salzburg, Rio, Taiwan — or was it Guadalajara? Krens was widely hailed or hated as the 'CEO of Culture, Inc.': the man who was doing for the Art World what the new monster corporations were doing to the Global Economy."

107   Peter Reina, Janice Tuchman, Rob McManamy, and Paul Rosta, "Museum's

Modular Steel Grid Sets Free-Form Surfaces Straight," *Engineering News-Record* 239, no. 15 (October 13, 1997): 60. And a following editorial, "Behind Bilbao's Miracle," *ENR* 239, no. 17 (October 27, 1997): 78.

108 Denny Lee, "Bilbao Ten Years Later," *New York Times*, September 23, 2007, Travel 1, 8–9. "The so-called Bilbao Effect was studied in universities throughout the world as a textbook example of how to repackage cities with 'wow-factor' architecture. And as cities from Denver to Dubai followed in Bilbao's footsteps, Mr. Gehry and his fellow starchitects were elevated to the role of urban messiahs." "A world-class museum swimming in third-world biohazard."

109 The development is currently imperiled, Keith Bradsher writes in *The New York Times*, February 22, 2006, B1: "The Hong Kong Government retreated from plans to build one of the world's largest cultural centers after real estate developers refused to participate, complaining that the financial terms had become too onerous." They were asked to ante up $3.87 billion US for a trust fund to operate the complex after construction.

110 "In Place of God: Culture Replaces Religion," *Economist*, May 5, 2007, 14–15. "One museum does not make a cultural complex, and the more skillful exponents of the art of dazzle-and-regenerate go for a succession of buildings. Abu Dhabi is to open branches of both the Louvre and the Guggenheim." And Carol Vogel, "Guggenheim's Provocative Director Steps Down: Krens Will Play an Advisory Role on Satellite in Abu Dhabi," *New York Times*, February 28, 2008, B1, 10.

111 Sharon Oster and William N. Goetzmann, "Does Governance Matter? The Case of Art Museums," in *The Governance of Not-for-Profit Organizations*, ed. Edward L. Glaeser (University of Chicago Press, 2003), 81. Conference, January 17–19, 2002. See www.nber.org/books/glae03-1 and www.nber.org/chapters/c9966.

112 Las Vegas average January high temperature is 57 degrees Fahrenheit; Abu Dhabi is 66°F, with a 56°F minimum average: www.meoweather.com/history/United%20Arab%20Emirates/na/24.4666667/54.3666667/Abu%20Dhabi.html.

113 Ruth Wilson Gilmore, *Golden Gulag: Prisons, Surplus, Crisis and Opposition in Globalizing California*, 116.

114 "Court Sides With CCPOA, Rejects Don Novey Bankruptcy Plan," The State Worker column, *Sacramento Bee*, February 22, 2012, http://blogs.sacbee.com/the_state_worker/2012/02/court-rejects-don-novey-bankruptcy-plan.html.

115 Vince Beiser, "The Cruelest Prison/A Necessary Evil?," *Los Angeles Times Magazine*, October 19, 2003, cover story, 12–17, 33.

116 Joelle Fraser, "An American Seduction: Portrait of a Prison Town," in Tara Herivel and Paul Wright, *Prison Nation: The Warehousing of America's Poor* (London: Routledge, 2003): 75

117 Rose Braz, in conversation with Trevor Paglen, for *Recording Carceral Landscapes*: www.paglen.com.

118 Joelle Fraser, "An American Seduction: Portrait of a Prison Town," 74, regarding Susanville: The first civic compensatory payment — $2 million from the state to compensate for the impacts on schools, courts and roads. "Welcome prison employees and inmates." And pp. 74–75 "The police department faces rising domestic violence, a 50% jump in juvenile delinquency and trade in hard-core drugs like heroin from gang members associated with the prison."

119 "California Uber Alles" covered/altered by Disposable Heroes of Hiphoprisy, *Hypocrisy Is the Greatest Luxury*, 1992. Original song lyrics by Dead Kennedys, Jello Biafra, and John Greenway.

120 See www.latimes.com

121 Jill Stewart, "Prison Union Thinks It Runs the Capitol, And Why Not, Since Legislators Quake and Turn Tail?," syndicated column, *Capitol Punishment* (April 8, 2004):
     "The prison guards have extraordinary power over politicians in California," says Speier. "Why do you think district

attorneys in California won't take cases with videos showing prison guards hitting inmates 40 and 50 times?... D.A.s won't prosecute because in Kings County, a D.A. who took on a correctional guard was targeted, and he was driven out of office." See http://jillstewart.net. See also her follow-up column: www.newsreview.com/sacramento/correctional-action-plan/content?oid=28637. See http://republican.sen.ca.gov.

122   "Sheriff Lee Baca Listens to Inmate Complaints at Town Hall Meeting," *Los Angeles Times*, October 1, 2011, http://articles.latimes.com/2011/oct/01/local/la-me-1002-baca-jail-tour-20111002.

123   Mike Davis, *Ecology of Fear*, 411

124   See www.clinicalpsychiatrynews.com/news/adult-psychiatry/single-article/quetiapine-abuse-common-in-prison-populations/9364749eec83846ed3ad02cebc222ccb.html:

"Major Finding: An estimated 30% of inmates in the Los Angeles County Jail malingered to obtain quetiapine; many of the malingerers were substance abusers who would snort the crushed tablets."

125   Kanye West, see lyrics credits

126   Roland Barthes, "From The Neutral," trans. Rosalind Krauss, *October 122* (Spring 2005): 168.

127   For more on a Millennial disposition, see Neil Leach, "The Year 2000 Will Not Happen," in *Millennium Culture* (London: Ellipsis, 1999).

128   Roland Barthes, "From The Neutral," 3, 22.

129   Jonathan Mahler, www.nytimes.com/2012/08/05/magazine/oakland-occupy-movement.html?pagewanted=all&_moc.semityn.

130   For more on camouflage as architecture, see Neil Leach, *Camouflage* (Cambridge: MIT Press, 2006) and also his "Tony Blair/Camouflage London," *Domus 877* (January 2005): 88–93.

131   From a letter to Dan Forrester, dated April 2, 1975, cited by Sandra Zalman in "The Non-u-ment: Gordon Matta-Clark and the Contingency of Space," *Octopus 1* (Fall 2005), http://yoda.hnet.uci.edu/fvc/vsgsa/octopus/octo_archive/vol-01-f2005/pdfs/zalman.pdf.

132   Matt Crawford, www.chicagomodern.wordpress.com/2012/03/19/metropolitan-correctional-center/.

133   Christopher Hawthorne, "Museum Lays Tracks All Across the City," *Los Angeles Times*, January 20, 2007, E24.

134   Paul Goldberger, "Sanctum on the Coast: Rafael Moneo's New Cathedral Looms Large," Skyline column, *New Yorker*, September 23, 2002, 97.

135   Robert Hughes refered to MoMA as the "Kremlin of Modernism" in *The Guardian*, February 2005, though its coinage may be earlier: www.guardian.co.uk/arts/features/story/0,,1337482,00.html.

136   For a great review of MoMA's evolution before its most recent expansion, see Alan Wallach, *Exhibiting Contradiction: Essays on the Art Museum in the United States* (Boston: University of Massachusetts Press, 1998), ch. 5, "The Museum of Modern Art: The Past's Future," 73–87. See also Sybil Gordon Kantor, *Alfred Barr, Jr. and the Intellectual Origins of the Museum of Modern Art* (Cambridge, MA: MIT Press, 2001).

137   On Leoben, see https://411webmagazine.wordpress.com/. On SFMOMA, see David A. Greene, "A Museum by the Numbers," *Los Angeles Reader*, August 11, 1995, 14.

138   Edward Rothstein, "In Berlin, Teaching Germany's Jewish History," *New York Times*, May 2, 2009, C7.

139   See "In Remembrance," *Architecture*, July 1993, 54–65.

140   See Rothstein, "In Berlin, Teaching Germany's Jewish History," C1, 7.

141   J.G. Ballard, *High Rise* (New York: Popular Library, 1978, US edition).

142   Colin Joyce, "On Top of Tokyo, Views of Modern Art," *Los Angeles Times*, October 18, 2003, E1. Also the Mori's website: www.mori.art.museum/html/eng/architecture.html.

143   www.mori.art.museum/html/eng/mission.html: The Mori's mission is pointedly agnostic between the East and West, and stipulates no permanent collection at least for a period after opening:

"15. DECIDE WHAT KIND OF COL-LECTION WOULD BE MOST APPROPRI-ATE ONCE IT HAS BEEN OPERATING FOR TWO YEARS."

144   Joan Didion, "The Getty," in *The White Album* (New York: Simon & Schuster, 1979), 78.

145   For a quantitative approach to comparing the major New York museums, see Crane, *The Transformation of the Avant-Garde*.

146   See Hugh Eakin, "Museums Under Fire on Ancient Artifacts," *New York Times*, November 17, 2005, B1, 8. Also Jason Felch, "Munitz Steps Down as Head of Getty," *Los Angeles Times*, February 10, 2006.

147   Hooper-Greenhill, *Museums and the Shaping of Knowledge*, 120–22.

148   Markus, *Buildings and Power*, 190–91.

149   Hooper-Greenhill, *Museums and the Shaping of Knowledge*, 69–71.

150   See www.recentpast.org: "Designed by Edward Durell Stone and completed in 1964, Huntington Hartford's Gallery of Modern Art at 2 Columbus Circle has been loved, loathed, and continues to be at the center of heated debate concerning modern architecture and its preservation."

151   Ford quote, Steven Conn, *Museums and American Intellectual Life, 1876–1926* (Chicago: University of Chicago Press, 1998), 187.

152   The Peale has been the object of much recent scholarship. Among the most thorough is Susan Stewart, "Death and Life, in That Order, in the Works of Charles Willson Peale," in *Visual Display: Culture Beyond Appearances*, eds. Lynne Cook and Peter Wollen (Seattle: Bay Press, 1995), 30–53.

153   For the Mutter's history, see www.collphyphil.org .

154   Jonathan Franzen introduced me to the Mercer Museum in his collection of essays, *How to Be Alone* (New York: Farrar, Straus and Giroux, 2002). Conn offers a more thoroughgoing assessment of the Mercer and Ford museums in *Museums and American*

Intellectual Life. Basic facts available at: www.mercermuseum.org .

155   See John Steele Gordon, *An Empire of Wealth: The Epic History of American Economic Power* (New York: HarperCollins, 2004), 245–55.

156   www.frick.org/collection/history.htm.

157   Cost calculated as .7% of the 2006 US budget of $2.3 trillion. The Getty was completed in 1997 for $1.3 billion.

158   For more on the Barnes Collection, see Roberta Smith, "Does It Matter Where This Painting Hangs?," *New York Times*, December 15, 2004, B1, 7. Also Ralph Blumenthal, "Release of Audit Roils Trust Fight at the Barnes," *New York Times*, May 5, 2003, B1, 8 and Lee Rosenbaum, "Destroying the Museum to Save It," *New York Times*, January 10, 2004, A31. Eric Wills, "The Burden of History," cover story, *Architect*, April 2012, 80–87.

159   In Bourdieu's *The Field of Cultural Production* (New York: Columbia University Press, 1993), 257.

160   Museums for historical figures outside the fine arts are common as well, e.g., museums for presidents, writers, sports figures, war heroes, and local personalities. Arguably, the discussion of museums for specific artists should be viewed in this same light. They have been included in this discussion because of their recent effect on single-patron institutions.

161   For a sense of scale, see www.gagosian.com and www.saatchi-gallery.co.uk.

162   Don DeLillo, *Underworld* (New York: Scribner, 1997), 86.

163   Including the de Menil and Warhol museums mentioned above, and the Liberace Museum in Las Vegas and the Wolfsonian Museum of Decorative and Propaganda Art in Miami. The Wolfsonian Museum is actually a museum dedicated to studying the Cold War. See Paula Harper, "Wolfsonian Redux — Miami, Florida, Museum Makes an Alliance With the State University System," *Art in America*, January 1997.

In part because major individual

collectors were long spurned by LACMA and other established museums, Los Angeles has lost a lot of great art, most painfully, in hindsight, the Arensberg and Annenberg collections. See Suzanne Muchnic, "Corralling the Collectors," *Los Angeles Times*, November 27, 2005. She writes, "L.A. galleries are filled with masterworks. Then there are the great ones that got away."

164 Though not a personal museum, Kahn's British Art Center offered a template for mixing retail and exhibition space in a single structure that the architects of the Hammer really should have stolen.

165 For the evolution of the Norton Simon, see www.nortonsimon.org

166 See www.lannan.org/lf/about/history/.

167 Lawrence Weschler, *Mr. Wilson's Cabinet of Wonder: Pronged Ants, Horned Humans, Mice on Toast, and Other Marvels of Jurassic Technology* (New York: Vintage, 1995).

168 Dominique de Menil (1908–1997), art collector, born in Paris. An heir to the Schlumberger fortune, Menil immigrated to the United States in 1941 and began collecting art. Together with her husband, she established the Menil Foundation in Houston. Her daughter Philippa founded Dia in the mid-1970s with Heiner Friedrich and Helen Winkler. See www.diacenter.org.

169 The Chinati Foundation, a related nonprofit with shared board members, maintains Judd's Marfa campus since his death in 1994. If one were to look for more parallel institutions from generation to generation, the Dahesh Museum, founded to exhibit an extensive collection of decorative and symbolist art and housed on an anonymous floor of a midtown tower, runs the Mannerist risk of reprising the kitsch Gallery of Modern Art at 2 Columbus Circle.

170 Benefactors Solomon Guggenheim and Nelson Rockefeller were both rumored to have died in the throes of passion, though it's likely only Rockefeller did. See www.hedyobeil.com/hilla_rebay.html and home.earthlink.net/~zkkatz/page67.html.

171 See Koolhaas, *Content* (New York: Taschen, 2004).

172 Kevin Pratt, "Player Piano," *ArtForum*, September 2004, 77: "… a recent readjustment of architectural priorities within the tightly knit world of museum trustees and directors had had one obvious consequence: Rem Koolhaas is out; Renzo Piano is in."

173 Werner, *Museum, Inc.*, 14

174 Paul Allen's Experience Music Project in Seattle, originally titled the Jimi Hendrix Museum, may be naiveté writ large, and Paul Lewis' $70 million bailout of the Guggenheim now looks rash in the wake of his leaving the board, but Broad found ways to leverage his collection, gifts, and directorships on an alphabet soup of institutions (MoCA, LACMA, MoMA) into an unprecedented sphere of influence over the reception of contemporary art — and the value of his own collection.

175 Crystal Bridges opened on November 11, 2011.

176 For an in-depth and inspired appreciation of the Soane Museum in this vein, see Helene Furjan, *Glorious Visions: John Soane's Spectacular Theater* (London/New York: Routledge, 2011).

177 Dan Morain, "Private Prison Has Everything but Prisoners," *Los Angeles Times*, July 13, 1999, A1, 17.

178 Karin Miller, Associated Press, "Doctor Crants Is No Doctor — He's America's Private Prison Warden," *SouthCoastTODAY*, January 4, 1998, www.southcoasttoday.com/apps/pbcs.dll/article?AID=/19980104/NEWS/301049932.

179 See www.geogroup.com/documents/2011-report.pdf: "GEO's U.S. Corrections and Detention division oversees the operation and management of approximately 66,000 beds in 65 correctional and detention facilities, which represents the sixth largest correctional system in the United States." See also www.businessofdetention.com/?p=7: The share price of CCA has risen from a public offering in 1986 of $9 a share to a current value of $30.

180 Karin Miller, Associated Press, "Doctor Crants Is No Doctor — He's America's Private Prison Warden," *South-CoastTODAY*, January 4, 1998, www.southcoasttoday.com/apps/pbcs.dll/article?AID=/19980104/NEWS/301049932.

181 See "Go Directly to Jail," *Businessweek*, December 15, 1997, 139; Anthony Ramirez, "Privatizing America's Prisons, Slowly," *New York Times*, August 14, 1994, B1, 7; and ir.correctionscorp.com/phoenix.zhtml?c=117983&p=irol-faq.

182 See bjs.ojp.usdoj.gov/index.cfm?ty=tp&tid=141.

183 See www.detentionwatchnetwork.org/privateprisons.

184 Leslie Berestein, Copley News Service, May 11, 2008, www.infowars.com/private-prison-industry-experiences-boom/: In 2000, the Federal Bureau of Prisons entered into an agreement with CCA to house foreign-born convicts in a California City prison, initially built on spec in the late 1990s for state prisoners that didn't arrive.

185 Vicky Pelaez, "The Prison Industry in the United States: Big Business or a New Form of Slavery?," *Global Research*, March 10, 2008, El Diario-La Prensa, New York, www.globalresearch.ca/index.php?context=va&aid=8289. See also www.aclu.org/prisoners-rights/private-prisons.

186 Richard Oppel Jr., "Private Prisons Found to Offer Little in Savings," *New York Times*, May 18, 2011, www.nytimes.com/2011/05/19/us/19prisons.html?pagewanted=all and Charles Blow, "Plantations, Prisons and Profits," May 26, 2012, www.nytimes.com/2012/05/26/opinion/blow-plantations-prisons-and-profits.html.

187 Jenifer Warren, "Inmates Are Moved After Riot Kills 2," *Los Angeles Times*, October 29, 2003, C1.

188 Abby Goodnough and Monica Davey, "A Record of Failure at a Center for Sex Offenders," *New York Times*, March 5, 2007, A1.

189 See http://bjs.ojp.usdoj.gov/content/pub/pdf/p10.pdf; for 1970, indyreader.org/content/women-prison.

190 Angela Davis in *AULA: Architecture and Urbanism in Las Americas*, inaugural issue (Berkeley, 1998).

191 California Department of Corrections, "CDC Facts" sheet, dated March 1, 1995.

192 John Hurst, "State Denies Health Care to Women Inmates, Suit Says," *Los Angeles Times*, April 5, 1995, and Keith Fahey, "Trial and Error: Was Maria Suarez Falsely Convicted of Murder?," *Los Angeles Reader*, April 14, 1995.

193 See Barry Yeoman, "Steel Town Lockdown," *Mother Jones*, May/June 2000, 38–47.

194 See Sam Dolnick, "Inside New Jersey Halfway Houses: As Escapees Stream Out, a Penal Business Thrives," *New York Times*, June 17, 2012, www.nytimes.com/2012/06/17/nyregion/in-new-jersey-halfway-houses-escapees-stream-out-as-a-penal-business-thrives.html?_r=3.

Also: www.nytimes.com/2012/06/22/opinion/krugman-prisons-privatization-patronage.html

www.nytimes.com/2012/06/21/opinion/collins-political-private-practice.html

http://www.nytimes.com/2011/05/19/us/19prisons.html?pagewanted=all.

195 Hilton Kramer, *The Age of the Avant-Garde*, original New York Times byline July 9, 1972 (New York: Farrar, Straus and Giroux, 1972), 546.

196 Caroline Winter, "With a Hammer, Finding Ghosts in the Glass," *New York Times*, August 5, 2007. Seth Wulsin selectively broke windowpanes in the abandoned Cárcel de Caseros in Buenos Aires, creating pixilated portraits of forty-eight faces. Lightless tower prison — vitamin D deficiency turned inmates green. For more on crime-as-art, see: Edwin Heathcote, "Shibboleth," *Financial Times*, October 13, 14, 2007, 9. Doris Salcedo cracks the foundation of the Tate Turbine Hall. Randy Kennedy, "Accusations, Deposition: Just More Fodder for Art," *New York Times*,

March 2, 2008, Arts 1, 31. "Hung along the walls of a room and stacked in boxes, the documents give the impression of something assembled by the prosecution in a windowless tribunal roon in Guantanamo Bay. But they are exhibits, of a sort, of a different kind of trial. ... Swiss artist Christoph Buchel and Mass MOCA went to war with each other." Peter Schjeldahl, "Performance: Chris Burden and the Limits of Art," *New Yorker*, May 14, 2007, 152–53. "Artists of the Duchampian sort delighted in effacing the boundaries which, with increasingly avid complicity on the authorities' part, kept being redrawn to corral the effacements." Tomaz Toporisic, "The Politics of Performing Arts and Its Strategies: From Pocha Nostra to Refugee Camps for First World Citizens" (ARTMargins, Ivory Tower Media.com, 2005). "In Baudrillard's transpolitical, transhistorical, and transeconomic post-millennial world, art returns to the tactics and strategies of the political and politicized with less certainty of its impact and with a strong consciousness of the utopian and marginalized nature of its own being. ...Whom can artists shock anymore? Is it their new role just to reflect on the very impossibility of transgression?" Suzanne Muchnic, "A Perfect Lack of Plan: Santa Monica Museum of Art Stumbles Into an Ideal Way to Honor Its First 20 Years," *Los Angeles Times*, January 20, 2008, Calendar, E1.

197   Paul Williams, *Memorial Museums: The Global Rush to Commemorate Atrocities* (New York/Oxford: Berg, 2007), 88. See also Robert R. Janes, *Museums in a Troubled World: Renewal, Irrelevance or Collapse?* (London/New York: Routledge, 2009).

198   For more on prison to museum conversions, see Williams, *Memorial Museums*. Also "Back From the Dead," *Economist*, February 24, 2007, 52, on the Tuol Sleng Genocide Museum and Maura J. Casey, "In the Big House... Just Visiting," *New York Times*, May 11, 2007, D1, 6. In 1971, Eastern Penitentiary closed and Alcatraz opened to tourists and now hosts one million visitors per year. There are thirty-six prisons-turned-museums in the US, among them the Hale Paahao Prison in Maui and the Crime and Punishment Museum in Ashburn, GA.

199   Monique Parsons, "Art That Evil Men Do Has Eerie Attraction," *Chicago Tribune*, May 15, 1992, http://articles.chicagotribune.com/1992-05-15/news/9202130307_1_galleries-art-institute-stateville-correctional-center.

200   http://digitallibrary.usc.edu/asset-server/controller/item/etd-Zylka-3511.pdf.

201   For more on crimes against art, see Michael Kimmelman, "A Symbol of Freedom and a Target for Terrorists," *New York Times*, October 13, 2007, A1, 21. Monet punctured at the Musée d'Orsay, Serrano photographs destroyed in Sweden, broadcast on You-Tube to a death metal soundtrack. Also Elizabeth Olson, "Embattled Smithsonian Official Resigns," *New York Times*, March 27, 2007, A12. Lawrence Small, secretary of the Smithsonian, made $915,698 in 2006. Geraldine Baum, "Thieves Take Art Worth $163 Million," *Los Angeles Times*, February 12, 2008, A3. A Zurich Museum, the E.G. Bührle Collection, is robbed of Monet, Cezanne, Van Gogh, and Degas at gunpoint, after two Picassos, two weeks earlier. A 1990 heist at the Isabella Stewart Gardner Museum in Boston set a record of $200 million. See also, Anne-Marie O'Connor, "Guns Guard BCAM's Lamb," *Los Angeles Times*, May 31, 2008, E1, 15.

202   Paul von Zielbauer, "Art and Temptation at Rikers: Theft of Dalí Drawing Leaves 4 Guards Facing Bars," *New York Times*, October 4, 2003, A13.

203   "Comedy Is Tragedy, Plus Time," *Crimes and Misdemeanors* (1989), written and directed by Woody Allen.

204   Judith H. Dobrzynski, "Glory Days for the Art Museum," *New York Times*, October 5, 1997, 1, 44. There were 100 million visitors to art museums estimated in 1996.

205   Christopher Goffard, "Rampant Abuse Seen at O.C. Jail," *Los Angeles Times*, April 8, 2008, A1, 12. Ranking guard sent text messages and watched Cops as a 41-year-old computer technician was stomped to death. Christine Hanley, Stuart Pfeifer, and

Christian Berthelsen, "O.C. Deputies Lied, Record Shows," *Los Angeles Times*, April 13, 2008, B1, 10. "They lied, they changed their stories and they compared notes even after being ordered not to by a special Orange County grand jury investigating a deadly beating at Theo Lacy Jail."

206 See www.movieweb.com/movies/ film/37/5237/boxoffice/.

207 For more on incarceration and celebrity culture, see Jennifer Steinhauer, "For $82 a Day, Booking a Cell in a 5-Star Jail," *New York Times*, April 29, 2007, A1, 24. "The California prison system, severely overcrowded, teeming with violence and infectious disease and so dysfunctional that much of it is under court supervision, is one that anyone with the slightest means would most likely pay to avoid." Our sales pitch was, "Bad things happen to Good People." Also Andrew Blankstein, "Paris Hilton Will Be Living the Simple Life When She's in Jail," *Los Angeles Times*, May 8, 2007, B7. He notes the threat of 130-thread count poly-cotton sheets. And Michael Mechanic, "Voluntary Confinement," *Mother Jones*, March/April 2008, 50–51, 96. "Contestants on the Fox Reality show Solitary forgo sleep and food and submit to debasements some would call torture — all for a crack at $50,000."

208 Foucault, *Discipline and Punish*, chap 1. Grand Theft Auto partakes of a long tradition of seeing through the eyes of an outlaw, but the most remarkable aspect of Prison Break, the video game, is its rote assumption that the gamer/convict's escape needs neither backstory nor justification.

209 "MSNBC's 'Lockup' a Controversial Ratings Magnet," *Huffington Post*, July 9, 2011, www.huffingtonpost.com/2011/07/09/ msnbcs-lockup-a-controver_n_893789.html.

210 Seen on JetBlue, New York City to Los Angeles flight, August 29, 2012.

211 "San Diego Zoo, Prison Merge," *The Onion*, May 15, 2008, 1.

212 Mimi Zeiger, *New Museums: Contemporary Museum Architecture Around the World* (New York: Rizzoli/Universe, 2005), 14.

213 Raul Barreneche, *New Museums* (London/New York: Phaidon, 2005). Barreneche and I overlapped at *Architecture* magazine in 1993, and he wrote a feature for *Dwell* magazine in 2004 on a house I designed. Zeiger included a book review of mine in *Loud Paper* in 2001.

214 John Updike, "Museums and Women" in *Museums and Women and Other Stories* (Greenwich, CT: Fawcett, 1973) 17.

215 Kevin Pratt, "Player Piano," *ArtForum*, September 2004, 77.

216 For more on the boom in museums and its impact, see "The Global Museum? A profile of Neil MacGregor," interview by Peter Aspden, *Financial Times, Art of Our Time*, March 17, 2008, 8-15 and "Architecture as Art: The Spectacular Growth of the Cultural City," Zaha Hadid interview, *Financial Times, Art of Our Time*, March 17, 2008, 6.

For more general background, see Edwin Heathcote, "Conspicuous Construction: Branding Cities Through Trophy Cultural Buildings," *Financial Times, Art of Our Time*, March 17, 2008, 16–21; Michael Kimmelman, "Twombly in the Land of Michelangelo," *New York Times*, March 16, 2008, 1, 26; Andrew Ferren, "Welcome to the Land of 'Wow-Factor' Museums," *New York Times*, September 23, 2007, Travel 8; Edward Wyatt, "The Art's Here. Where's the Crowd? Los Angeles Has the Museums and Artists, Now It Wants the Attention," *New York Times*, March 25, 2007, Arts 1, 28; and, finally, Nicolai Ouroussoff, "Architectural Shifts, Global and Local," *New York Times*, September 9, 2007, 98: "Overwhelmed by the globetrotting needed to keep up with the new museums opening every year? Well, put on your track shoes...."

217 Jan Dalley, "Warming to the Frieze Effect," *Financial Times*, October 13–14, 2007, 9.

218 For post-9/11 exhibition and incarceration, see "Gitmo: A National Disgrace" and "Jail Time for Scooter Libby," editorial, *New York Times*, June 6, 2007, A22; "The Vanishing Arts at Ground Zero," editorial, *New York Times*, March 29, 2007, A18; Molly

Hennessy-Fiske and Said Rifai, "Iraqi Jails in 'Appalling' State," *Los Angeles Times*, July 21, 2007, A1, 8; and Alissa J. Rubin, "U.S. Remakes Jails in Iraq, but Gains Are at Risk," *New York Times*, June 2, 2008, A1, 8.

219 Andrew K. Woods, "Hard Man, Soft Sell," *Financial Times*, June 28, 2008, Arts 1–2.

220 http://mssi.us: "Through a unique joint venture agreement, MSSI, Inc. and Colorado Correction Industries have combined resources.... We are very excited about the opportunity to work with one of the country's most progressive correction industries."

221 David Segal, "Swiss Freeports Are Home for a Growing Treasury of Art," *New York Times*, July 21, 2012, www.nytimes.com/2012/07/22/business/swiss-freeports-are-home-for-a-growing-treasury-of-art.html.

222 From the Schaulager website: www.schaulager.org/en/index.php?pfad=schaulager/gebaeude.

223 Richard Massey, email to the author, July 3, 2008: "Schaulager comes off as much bigger — perhaps two to three times bigger — than The Fortress. Some of that's perhaps ascribable to the design of the Schaulager facade, which is pretty overwhelming — it really dwarfs you."

224 James Kessler, AIA, LEED BD+C, senior principal/director, Justice HOK, Washington, DC, email to the author, sent August 14, 2012, 9:50 a.m.

225 Richard Rapaport, "The Marin County Civic Center Part 1: The Jail: Wright or Wrong," *San Rafael Patch*, December 24, 2010, http://sanrafael.patch.com/articles/the-rap-report-the-marin-county-civic-center-part-i-the-jail-wright-or-wrong.

226 See www.clrsearch.com/Richmond_Demographics/VA/Population-by-Race-and-Ethnicity http://richmondvirginiamayor.blogspot.com/2012/01/mayor-jones-and-city-officials-break.html and www.richmondgov.com/content/PressSecretaryMayor/documents/RichmondJusticeCenterMayor IntroductiontoCityCouncil06092011.pdf.

227 See Craig A. Shutt, "Corrections Evolution: HOK's James Kessler Has Seen Designs for Correctional and Justice Facilities Evolve Due to New Philosophies, Design-Build Formats and Precast Concrete Techniques," *Ascent*, Summer 2012, 22–24, http://pci.org/view_file.cfm?file=AS-12SU-5.pdf.

228 David Adjaye interviewed by Edwin Heathcote, "Showman to Statesman," Lunch With the FT, *Financial Times*, September 15, Life & Arts 3.

229 Williams, *Memorial Museums*, 96.

230 *The Indispensable Oscar Wilde*, ed. Richard Aldington (New York: Book Society, 1950), 588.

231 Public Enemy, *Takes a Nation of Millions to Hold Us Back*, Def Jam Recordings, 1988.

232 Joseph Deegan-Day, "The Afterlives of Incarceration: A Critical Evaluation of Imprisonment From Newgate to New Generation," advisor Patrick Pinnell (unpublished thesis, Yale College, 1990).

233 Robert Smithson, "Some Void Thoughts on Museums," in *The Writings of Robert Smithson*, 58.

Full quote: "Visiting a museum is a matter of going from void to void. Hallways lead viewers to things once called 'pictures' and 'statues.' Anachronisms hang and protrude from every angle. Themes without meaning press on the eye.... Museums are tombs, and it looks like everything is turning into a museum. Painting, sculpture and architecture are finished, but the art habit continues. Art settles into a stupendous inertia. Silence supplies the dominant chord. Bright colors conceal the abyss that holds the museum together. Every solid is a bit of clogged air or space. Things flatten and fade. The museum spreads its surfaces everywhere, and becomes an untitled collection of generalizations that immobilize the eye."

234 Bernard Tschumi, "Architecture and Transgression," in *Architecture and Disjunction* (Cambridge: MIT Press, 1996), 68, 78.

235 Sylvia Lavin, "Tenderness," *Log 24*, Winter/Spring 2012, 96.

236 Jeff Kipnis, "Dear Paula…" letter, *Log 20*, Fall 2010, 94.

237 Steven Litt, "The New Serenity," *ARTnews*, March 2005, 88–93. For more on neo-Minimalist museums, see Thomas Crow, "The Museum as Muse: Artists Reflect," MoMA show review, in *ArtForum*, Summer 1999, 145–46: "Like an old-line company absorbing a young upstart for its innovative capacities and ability to scout the peripheries, MoMA may in a stroke have shored up one of its most conspicuous weak spots.…" Nicolai Ouroussoff, "So Where's the Art?" and "Museums: Is Art Losing Out to Architecture?," *Los Angeles Times*, March 31, 2002, Calendar E4–5, 74–75: "A more extreme case of art as sideshow can be found in the Milwaukee Museum of Art… throughout, art is an afterthought." Glenn D. Lowry, "The State of the Art Museum, Ever Changing," *New York Times*, January 10, 1999, 1, 40.

238 Bill Marsh, "Pork Under Glass? Small Museums and Their Patrons on Capitol Hill," *New York Times*, April 30, 2006, E13. Includes the Sparta Teapot Museum, Sparta, NC; Ohio Glass Museum; and others related to early industries or immigrants. Citizens Against Government Waste identifies 1,030 museum-related projects since 1995, worth $527.4 million, and seventy-nine more, for $27.3 million, in 2006.

239 Christine Sylvester, *Art/Museums: International Relations Where We Least Expect It* (Boulder: Paradigm, 2009), 146.

240 That isn't to say that these phases immediately displace one another. The rivalry between Millennial and post-Millennial sensibilities is easiest to read in cinema: the grandiose but vague abstraction of *The Matrix* gives way to the sprawling post-Millennial collage of *Inception,* and the sense-over-cyber, topical engagement of *The Hurt Locker.*

241 See *Exhibiting Culture: The Poetics and Politics of Museum Display*, eds.

Ivan Karp and Steven D. Lavine (Washington, DC: Smithsonian, 1990) especially the editors' introduction and chapter 2 and Michael Baxandall, "Exhibiting Intention: Some Preconditions of the Visual Display of Cultural Purposeful Objects," 33–41.

242 Kessler, in phone conversation with the author, August 7, 2012.

243 Bennett Simpson, Associate Curator, MoCA, in conversation with the author, April 17, 2008.

244 Eric Sylvers, "Art of Money Management," *Financial Times*, September 28, 2012, 12.

245 Most facilities are designed either by national A&E firms or in-house by construction companies working from templates provided by state agencies, which guarantees their easy permitting and largely excludes the involvement of architects.

REPRINTS

Portions of chapter 04 appear in "Carceral California" © 1997 by Kim Colin and Margi Reeve. *From the Center: Design Process at SCI-Arc* © 1997 by Monacelli Press, pp.206–08. Reprinted by permission of Monacelli Press/Joe Day.

Portions of chapters 07 and 08 appear as "Holding Patterns" in PROJECT 2 (2013), © Joe Day, reprinted with permission of the editors.

Portions of chapter 06 are excerpted from *Evil Paradises: Dreamworlds of Neoliberalism* © 2007 by Mike Davis and Daniel Bertrand Monk. *Hubrispace: Personal Museums and the Architectures of Self-Deification* © 2007 by Joe Day. Reprinted by permission of The New Press. www.the-newpress.com

CREDITS

Joe Day/deegan-day design llc: pages 4, 51, 52, 57, 61, 64, 68, 74, 78, 85, 97, 104, 110, 114-15, 135, 136, 172, 192, 196, 214, 224-25, 242-43, 247, 262, 276, 278-79, 282

Taiyo Watanabe, photography: 55, 59, 108, 113, 154, 156-157, 159, 163, 167, 169, 202, 237, 241, 249

Public Domain: 22, 37, 62, 72-73, 77, 190, 228

Google Maps © 2012 Google: 82, 135, 212, 232, 257

00.

p. 1 © 2013 The LeWitt Estate/Artists Rights Society (ARS), New York

p. 4 Chart: *Prison Pop. vs. Museum Visitors* Recorded Museum Attendance (US): Sharon Oster and William N. Goetzmann, "Does Governance Matter? The Case of Art Museums," pp.92, 93, Table 2.9, www.nber.org/chapters/c9966.pdf. Prison Population [US]: Correctional Population in the United States, 2010. U.S. Department of Justice, Bureau of Justice Statistics http://www.bjs.ojp.usdoj.gov/content/pub/pdf/cpus10.pdf

p. 6 © 2006 SASI Group (University of Sheffield) and Mark Newman (University of Michigan)

p. 8 Courtesy the artist & Galerie Micheline Szwajcer

p. 9 © Nico Bick

p.12 © Tadao Ando

p.13 © Shawn Toner, Explosive Illusions, Inc.

p.14 © Korab Photo/Balthazar Korab

p.15 Courtesy HOK Architects/Photographer Steve Swalwell

p. 20 Collection The Rubell Family, Miami, FL/ Image courtesy of the artist.

p. 21 Courtesy of Andrea Fraser

p. 24-25 © 2013 The LeWitt Estate/Artists

Rights Society (ARS), New York; Photograph by Ellen Labenski, courtesy Pace Gallery

01.

p. 27 Louis Isadore Kahn collection, 1951-1978 (inclusive), 1962-1977 (bulk). Manuscripts & Archives, Yale University

p. 28 © Hagen Stier

p. 31 Louis Isadore Kahn collection, 1951-1978 (inclusive), 1962-1977 (bulk). Manuscripts & Archives, Yale University

p. 31 Photographer Deidi Von Schaewen

p. 37 Photo courtesy Hirshhorn Museum and Sculpture Garden, Smithsonian Institution, Washington DC

p. 40 Courtesy of the Massachusetts Historical Society

p. 43 © Grant Mudford

p. 45 © Rudivan Cattani/http://enbusquedadelaformamoderna.blogspot.com/

p. 46 © BPK, Berlin/(Neue Nationalgalerie)/ (Reinhard Friedrich)/Art Resource, NY

p. 47 © 2013 Artists Rights Society (ARS), New York/ADAGP, Paris/F.L.C.

p. 58 Courtesy of Kevin Roche John Dinkeloo and Associates

02.

p. 67 Image © The Museum of Modern Art/ Lisensed by SCALA/Art Resource, NY

p. 68 Chart: *US Prisons/Museums 1960 – 2010* Prisons (US): Correctional Population in the United States, 2010: U.S. Department of Justice, Bureau of Justice Statistics, http://www.bjs.ojp.usdoj.gov/content/pub/pdf/cpus10.pdf. Museums (US): American Alliance of Museums, www.aam-us.org

p. 70 Piano & Fitzgerald, architects , ph. Paul Hester, courtesy Renzo Piano Building Workshop

p. 72-73: 1 © 2013 Artists Rights Society (ARS), New York/ADAGP, Paris/F.L.C.; 3 Creative Commons (CC) Flickr@graba-donut; 4 CC Flickr@joevare; 5 CC, Brad-ley Huchteman; 6 CC, Antonio Campoy; 7 CC@ChicagoGeek; 8-10 CC@Leon L; 12 CC@dsa66503; 13, 14 CC@Dyanna Hyde; 15 CC, Lian Chang; 16 © José Lorenzo Torres; 18, 19 CC, Naquib Hossain; 20, 21 CC, Daniel Rubio; 24 CC, Steven Coutts; 25 CC, Rob Zand; 26 CC, Pablo Twose; 28 CC, Jonathan Assink; 29 CC, Daniel Julià Lundgren

p. 80 © Sir John Soane's Museum

p. 83 © Jean-Pierre Dalbéra

p. 85 © UNSDRI, Prison Architecture. London: 1975.

p. 86-87 © Shawn Toner, Explosive Illusions

03.

p. 89 © Magnum Photos/Doug DuBois and Jim Goldberg

p. 92 Photograph by David Heald. ©The Solomon R. Guggenheim Foundation, NY

p. 93 Wikimedia Commons

p. 93 Photograph by William Short ©The Solomon R. Guggenheim Foudation, NY

p. 98 © 2013 Artists Rights Society (ARS), NY/ADAGP, Paris/Succession Marcel Duchamp

p. 112 © Brad Feinknopf

p. 118 Amy DeDonato

04.

p. 121 © Nicholas Whitman nwphoto.com

p. 122 © Sacramento Bee/ZUMApress.com

p. 123 Thomas Krens. Photograph by David Heald ©The Solomon R. Guggenheim Foundation, NY

p. 124 © San Francisco History Center, San Francisco Public Library.

p. 130 Bing TM screen shot reprinted with permission from Microsoft Corporation.

p. 132 1-7, 12, 15 Public Domain. 8, 14 Reprinted with permission from FOGA. 9, 11, 13 Courtesy Zaha Hadid Architects. 10, Courtesy Foster + Partners.

p. 141 © Courtesy Koplin Del Rio Gallery, Culver City, CA

p. 144-145 Public domain via California Department of Rehabilitation and Corrections

p. 147 Courtesy SCI-Arc, 1995.

p. 149 © Martin Schall

p. 150 Public domain via California Department of Rehabilitation and Corrections

05.

p. 164 Photograph by Enrico Cano, Courtesy Studio arch. Mario Botta

p. 168 Photograph courtesy of An Te Liu

p. 171 © Andrew Burkholder

p. 172 Courtesy USS Midway Museum

p. 174 Courtesy Little/HOK JV Architects

p. 174 Image ©The Museum of Modern Art/ Licensed by SCALA/Art Resource, NY

p. 178 © VIEW Pictures Ltd.

p. 179 Photograph courtesy Mark Lyons

p. 181 © Paul Ott

p. 183 © Bitter Bret/Courtesy Studio Daniel Liebeskind

06.

p. 185 Photograph courtesy Mark Lyons

p. 195 © Woodhaven Historic/Mercer Museum, Doylestown PA

p. 203 © DIA Art Foundation/Karsten Schubert Gallery

p. 206 © OMA

p. 207 Ezra Stoller © Esto

p. 209 Bing TM screen shot reprinted with permission from Microsoft Corporation.

p. 214 Chart: *Comparative Prison Pops.* Correctional Population in the United States, 2010, U.S. Department of Justice, Bureau of Justice Statistics, http:// www.bjs.ojp.usdoj.gov/content/pub/pdf/ cpus10.pdf. Prison Pop. [California]: CDCR Annual Report 1990-2011, California Department of Corrections and Rehabilitations, http://www.cdcr.ca.gov/ Reports/CDCR-Annual-Reports.html. Private Prison Pop. [US]Private Adult Correctional Facility Census, 1995 and 2001 Editions, U.S. Department of Justice /

Office of Justice Programs / Bureau of
Justice Statistics, http://bjs.ojp.usdoj.
gov/content/pub/pdf/csfcf05.pdf. Female
Prison Pop. [US]: Correctional Population
in the United States, 2010, U.S. Department of Justice, Bureau of Justice Statistics, http://www.bjs.ojp.usdoj.gov/content/
pub/pdf/cpus10.pdf. Prison Pop. [UK]:
Table A1.2 Offender Management Case-
load Statistics, 2010. UK Ministry of Justice, http://www.justice.gov.uk/statistics/
prisons-and-probation/

p. 217 Photograph by Kirsten Luce/www.kirst-
enluce.com

p. 218-219 Courtesy Santa Monica Museum of
Art, Photograph by Grant Mudford

07.

p. 221 © 2013 Artists Rights Society (ARS),
New York/ADAGP, Paris/Succession
Marcel Duchamp

p. 222 Courtesy of the artist Seth Wulsin

p. 224 © OMA photographs by Phillipe Rualt

p. 227 Courtesy Studio Langlands and Bell

p. 233 © 2013 Artists Rights Society (ARS),
NY/VG Bild-Kunst, Bonn/Courtesy Matthew Marks Gallery

p. 239 © OMA

08.

p. 244 Photo: Iwan Baan

p. 248 © Richard Ross Photography

p. 250 Creative Commons Flickr

p. 255 © Margherita Spiluttini/Herzog de
Meuron

p. 258 Courtesy HOK Architects

p. 259 Courtesy HOK Architects/Photogra-
pher James Kessler

09.

p. 265 Courtesy Joe Day and Yale University

p. 266 © Zepp-Cam. 2004/Graz, Austria

p. 268 Courtesy SCI-Arc/Lili Dirks-Goodman

p. 270 Courtesy SCI-Arc/Yo Oshima

p. 273 Courtesy SCI-Arc/Shir Gale

p. 274 Courtesy SCI-Arc/Lauren Rosenbloom

p. 275 Courtesy SCI-Arc/Lionel Lambourn

p. 280 Courtesy SCI-Arc/Benjamin Smith

LYRICS

p. 127 Excerpt from *Folsom Prison Blues.*
Words and Music by John R. Cash.
Copyright © 1956 (Renewed 1984) House
of Cash, Inc (BMI) / All Rights Admin-
istered by BUG MUSIC, INC., A BMG
Chrysalis Company. All Rights Reserved.
Used By Permission. *Reprinted by Per-
mission of Alfred Publishing Co., Inc.
Reprinted by Permission of Hal Leonard
Corporation.*

p. 144 Excerpt from *Hipocracy is the Greatest
Luxury* by Michael Franti. *Reprinted by
Permission of Guerilla Management.*

p. 155 Excerpt from *Flashing Lights.* Words
and Music by Eric Hudson and Kanye West
© 2007 EMI BLACKWOOD MUSIC INC.,
PLEASE GIMME MY PUBLISHING, INC.,
E. HUDSON MUSIC LLC and WARNER
-TAMERLANE PUBLISHING CORP. All
Rights for PLEASE GIMME MY PUBLISH-
ING, INC. Controlled and Administered
by EMI BLACKWOOD MUSIC INC. All
Rights for E. HUDSON MUSIC LLC Con-
trolled and Administered by WARNER-
TAMERLANE PUBLISHING CORP. All
Rights Reserved. International Copyright
Secured. *Reprinted By Permission of Alfred
Publishing Co., Inc. Reprinted by Permis-
sion of Hal Leonard Corporation.*

p. 266 Excerpt from *Black Steel in the Hour
of Chaos.* Words and Music by
Carlton Ridenhour, William Drayton,
James Boxley III and Eric Sadler. Copy-
right © 1988 SONGS OF UNIVERSAL,
INC., TERRORDOME MUSIC PUBLISH-
ING LLC, REACH GLOBAL SONGS,
SHOCKLEE MUSIC and YOUR MOTH-
ER'S MUSIC, INC. All Rights Reseved.
Used by Pemission. *Reprinted by Permis-
sion of Reach Music. Reprinted by permis-
sion of Hal Leonard Corporation.*

ACKNOWLEDGEMENTS

CORRECTIONS & COLLECTIONS has taken many years and many forms. I'm very grateful to Routledge for finding the promise in this curious comparison and seeing it through from there. Both the financial assistance and the imprimatur of a grant from the Graham Foundation in 2011 were crucial to the book's completion.

My editors Wendy Fuller, Laura Williamson, and Siobhán Greaney at Routledge sustained and supported the publication invaluably, both in their initial enthusiasm and understanding through its final gestation. Sheri Gordon's copyediting sharpened the text in innumerable ways. Paul Wysocan put together a beautiful early précis of *Corrections and Collections*, and graphic designer Ninotchka Regets has taken the project beyond my hopes and expectations, fleshing out and transforming the material into its current — and for me, intensely gratifying — form.

Most of the research and thematic development has taken place in the context of seminars and studios taught at the Southern California Institute of Architecture, but some of the foundational ideas date back to undergraduate and graduate and theses projects at Yale and SCI-Arc, respectively. The current work spans three directorships at SCI-Arc — Directors Michael Rotondi, Neil Denari, and Eric Owen Moss, along with program heads Robert Mangurian, Margaret Crawford, Michael Speaks, Ming Fung, Dora Epstein Jones, and Todd Gannon have all been very generous in their support. I probably would not have embarked on this project without the mentorship, example, and introduction to teaching that Mike Davis gave me when we taught a few seminars on the California prison system together in the mid-1990s.

I've been the incredibly fortunate beneficiary of advice and comments from many astute readers. Rachel Allen, Aaron Betsky, Andrea Fraser, Bennett Simpson, Peter Zellner, and Marcelo Spina have all offered much sage counsel and truly vital encouragement. Mentors and colleagues contributed crucial ideas, among them Patrick Pinnell, Frank Israel, Christian Hubert, Gary Paige, Roger Sherman, Kazys Varnelis, Benjamin Bratton, Jennifer Dunlop, Coy Howard, Hernan Diaz Alonso, Florencia Pita, Jane

McFadden, Patrick Lakey, Jeffrey Inaba, and Andrew Zago. A few recent conversations at Yale helped me finish, especially those with Dean Robert A.M. Stern, Nina Rappaport, Deborah Berke, Victor Agran, Stanislaus von Moos, and Peggy Deamer. Some quick observations from Sylvia Lavin, Jeff Kipnis and Peter Eisenman reoriented the project considerably.

Many people in my studio, deegan-day design, especially Mark Lyons, Bonnie Carlson, and Felicia Martin, have added both their vision, in the form of many images included here, and their perspective in critical ways. Current designers Yo Oshima and Taiyo Watanabe have devoted much of 2012 to the final diagrams and photography here, and their judgement, care and precision improve almost every page. I owe Shir Gale, Anne Wysocan, and many students in seminars *California Gulag*, *Corrections+Collections*, *PRI|MUS*, and *Minimally Invasive* an enormous debt of gratitude for all their intrepid and in-depth research into the many institutions included here. In every class, students have taken the basic comparison in new and completely unforeseen directions. Avani Sheth, Tanja Werner, Sasha Monge, Evan Robertson, and Amy de Donato drafted the many plans and analyses included here. All of the contributions above, as well as most of the images included throughout were consolidated and enhanced by research coordinator Michelle Paul, without whom this final publication could not have taken shape.

Many friends have sustained my momentum through this long, if cyclical, effort: Tony Optican, Ante Liu, Arden Yang, Richard Massey, Leigh Crawford, Anabel and Eric Avery, Yael Malemed, Adam Topol, Noelle Miller, Peter Wolson, Rhoni Epstein and Cristina Pestana. Lindsie Bear at UC Press and Jill Marsal at the Dijkstra Agency were wonderful, early advocates, and Alex Smithline has given me much good advice toward publication.

My family, including many Days, Hachigians, Forstmanns and Deegans, have been endlessly interested and supportive, especially my parents.

My brilliant and well-focused wife Nina showed me how writing a book could be done, then gave me the time, room, and generous reinforcement for this one. This is for our children, Sosi and Avo, and for my nephews Taj and Ziggy — toward their better future.

I'd like to dedicate *Corrections and Collections* to Margarete Hachigian, Nina's mother, and my most avid reader.

INDEX